CHANGING MEDIA, HOMES AND HOUSEHOLDS

Media technologies have played a central role in shaping ideas about home life over the last two centuries. *Changing Media, Homes and Households* explores the complex relationship between homes, householders, families and media technologies by charting the evolution of the media-rich home, from the early twentieth century to the present.

Moving beyond a narrow focus on media texts, production and audiences, Deborah Chambers investigates the physical presence of media objects in the home and their symbolic importance for home life. The book identifies the role of home-based media in altering relationships between home, leisure, work and the outside world in the context of entertainment, communication and work. It assesses whether domestic media are transforming or reinforcing traditional identities and relations of gender, generation, class and migrancy.

Mediatisation theory is employed to assess the domestication of media and media saturation of home life in the context of wider global changes. The author also develops the concept of media imaginaries to explain the role of public discourses in shaping changing meanings, values and uses of domestic media. Framed within these approaches, four chapters also provide in-depth case studies of the processes involved in media's home adoption: early television design, family-centred video gaming, the domestication of tablet computers and the shift from 'smart homes' to today's 'connected' homes.

This is an ideal text for students and researchers interested in media and cultural studies, communication and sociology.

Deborah Chambers is Professor of Media and Cultural Studies at Newcastle University. Her previous publications include *Social Media and Personal Relationships* (2013); *A Sociology of Family Life* (2012); *New Social Ties* (2006); *Women and Journalism* (2004) with Linda Steiner and Carol Fleming; and *Representing the Family* (2001).

CHANGING MEDIA, HOMES AND HOUSEHOLDS

Cultures, technologies and meanings

Deborah Chambers

Routledge
Taylor & Francis Group

LONDON AND NEW YORK

First published 2016
by Routledge
2 Park Square, Milton Park, Abingdon, Oxon OX14 4RN

and by Routledge
711 Third Avenue, New York, NY 10017

Routledge is an imprint of the Taylor & Francis Group, an informa business

British Library Cataloguing-in-Publication Data
A catalogue record for this book is available from the British Library

Library of Congress Cataloging-in-Publication Data
Names: Chambers, Deborah, 1954- author.
Title: Changing media, homes and households : cultures, technologies
    and meanings / Deborah Chambers.
Description: London and New York : Routledge, 2016. | Includes
    bibliographical references and index.
Identifiers: LCCN 2015044515| ISBN 9780415706353 (hbk) |
    ISBN 9781138791602 (pbk) | ISBN 9781315630397 (ebk)
Subjects: LCSH: Families and mass media. | Households—
    Technological innovations. | Technology—Sociological aspects. |
    Technological innovations—Social aspects.
Classification: LCC P94.5.F34 C47 2016 | DDC 306.85—dc23
LC record available at http://lccn.loc.gov/2015044515

ISBN: 978-0-415-70635-3 (hbk)
ISBN: 978-1-138-79160-2 (pbk)
ISBN: 978-1-315-63039-7 (ebk)

Coventry University Colleg

Typeset in Bembo Std
by Swales & Willis Ltd, Exeter, Devon, UK
Printed in Great Britain by Ashford Colour Press Ltd

MIX
Paper from
responsible sources
FSC
www.fsc.org   FSC® C011748

CONTENTS

ACKNOWLEDGEMENTS

Some of the research that underpins this book has been undertaken over a number of years. I thank my colleagues and PhD students in Media, Cultural and Heritage at Newcastle University who have generated an exciting environment in which to teach and research. I'm also grateful to our Master's students in media programmes on the module, Media Analysis, who took part in fascinating debates about aspects of the central themes in this book. I would also like to express my gratitude to a number of people for their advice, support, intellectual inspiration and valuable discussions. In particular, I'd like to mention James Ash, Norah Altuwayjiri, David Baines, Chris Falzon, Areti Galani, Peter Golding, Darren Kelsey, Chris Haywood, Vesela Harizanova, Majid Khoravinik, Gareth Longstaff, Rhiannon Mason, Yuzuh Peng, Liviu Popoviciu, Karen Ross and Steve Walls. I am also grateful to the Faculty of Humanities and Social Sciences at Newcastle University for the research leave I received for a semester which enabled me to complete the research and writing of the book.

I am thankful for having the opportunity to take part in events which have either directly or indirectly helped develop or improve the ideas in the book. This includes the seminar series at the Department of Sociology at Essex University and the Media and Communication and Cultural Studies Association conference at Northumbria University. I gratefully acknowledge and thank the editors and anonymous reviewers of *Media History* and *Leisure Studies* for publication of articles that relate to the subject matter of some of the chapters. I am grateful to Natalie Foster, Editor at Routledge, for her excellent advice and encouragement during the early stages of preparing this book. I also thank the anonymous reviewers of my book proposal who provided thoughtful and positive comments. Finally, I thank Lis Joyce for her terrific patience and support throughout.

1

INTRODUCTION

Over the last two centuries, media technologies have played a central role in shaping ideas about the nature of living in a modern home. Written during a period of far-reaching social and technological changes, this book explores the complex relationship between home, householders and media technologies by charting key developments in domestic media technologies from the early twentieth century to the present. It traces the key socio-cultural trends involved, from the entrance of early radio and television (TV) in the living room to today's digitally networked homes. The diverse processes of adoption and integration of digital media technologies into the domestic sphere are examined, including the ways in which mobile technologies are changing household dynamics. From analogue TV to video gaming, and from tablet computers to futuristic imaginaries of 'smart homes' and home automation systems comprising 'connected homes', the following chapters address the various ways in which domestic technologies are publicly imagined, designed and promoted, and then privately perceived, adopted and integrated into everyday home lives. The book assesses the ways that today's digital technologies undermine, complicate or reinforce relations of gender, generation and social class; how media technologies contribute to changing relationships between home and the outside world; and how the domestic uses of personalised mobile media devices, such as tablet computers, contribute to today's networked household.

The acceleration of globalised networks has prompted a primary focus in media studies on global flows, digital connectivity and media mobility. However, this book confirms the importance of home, households and domestic space for an understanding of the changing uses and meanings of media within today's global context. Although internet access is branching out from the home via handheld mobile devices, mediated interactions continue to be conducted mainly from home. The acceleration in global and digitalised mobile media coincides with dramatic transformations in the cultural significance and experiences of 'home'.

The home has transformed into a complex media environment with mobile gadgets such as laptops, smartphones and tablet computers now common features of home life. Today's households are, then, organising domestic settings as 'home' and managing their mediated relationships between home and the outside world through local and global processes of mediatisation. Technological convergence is enabling communication between digital devices including internet TV, online interactive media and streaming media, with far-reaching consequences which affect the micro-social dynamics of home life. The book addresses some of the key ways in which media uses in the home correspond with broader changes in the organisation of intimate and work relationships beyond the home, which in turn alter the relationship between work, leisure and home.

The media facility of continuous connectivity has prompted several changes in our ideas and experiences of the relationship between home and the 'outside world'. The ability to bring work-related activities into the home and to extend personal communications beyond the home through information and communication technologies (ICTs) generates perceptions of a public sphere encroaching on the home life and of 'domestic' values and practices moving beyond the confines of the household (Hollows 2008). As Roger Silverstone states, 'Home, then, is no longer singular, no longer static, no longer, in an increasingly mobile and disrupted world, capable of being taken for granted' (Silverstone 2006: 242). Mobile media technologies make a central contribution to these new experiences, imaginings and configurations of home, families and personal life. Operating within shifting local and global media networks, these new mediated processes involve changing discourses of nation, family and belonging (Morley 2002; Hollows 2008).

As well as its tendency to focus on global networks, media studies has been characterised by an emphasis on media content. Until the 1990s, mainstream media studies focused on the production, interpretation and effects of media texts as well as features of the media system. The physical manifestation and material form of the media that carried the content – from TV sets to personal computers (PCs) – tended to be of secondary interest. This resulted in a neglect of the 'material presence' of media equipment in the home in terms of the processes of its incorporation into the everyday routines of family and household lives and how, in turn, those domestic routines are adapted to the technology's affordances. As Matthew Geller (1990: 7) says of TV, too often we simply 'look through' the object of TV to the images it provides while the set itself remains, as it were, 'invisible' to us and we ignore its role as a totemic object of enormous symbolic importance in the household. Similarly, David Morley (1995) reminds us of the importance of analysing the 'physics of TV as a material and symbolic object in the home'.

This book provides a particular focus on the physical materiality of media and their symbolic importance for home life. The following chapters approach the home as a site of media technology to understand the roles played by media and communication technologies in reproducing and transforming cultural values associated with that space. The aim is to explain how personal, domestic and household relations are shaped and facilitated by the materiality of media equipment and by mediated social interactions that comprise home, households and families. The multiple forms and technological affordances of home-based media equipment and the shifting dynamics of domestic life have led to dramatic changes in the very nature and meanings of 'home'. With digital media technologies now firmly embedded in personal, family and home life, important questions arise about how households communicate with the outside world, manage the shifting boundaries between work and home-based leisure, use digital media to foster household and family cohesion, and connect families across geographical distances.

Media households

Media technologies are adapted to and transform the home in differing ways, depending on the types of households. The *household* is therefore a central concept in media studies in relation to the role of domestic media. The term 'household' is used in the following chapters to indicate the significance of differing living arrangements in relation to media's use in the home. Treated as a social, economic and political unit, the household is not only a unit of socialisation of the next generation, which facilitates the production, transmission and sustaining of family values (Chapman 2004). In terms of its material reality, and at the institutional level of the state, the household is also defined in wider societies as the source of taxes and receipt of social welfare benefits. However, the dominant nuclear family household, idealised in the early twentieth century, has been overtaken by today's increasingly diverse living arrangements (Chambers 2012).

A significant rise in family households with adult children aged 20 to 34 results from the extension of the life phase of youth dependence, known as 'extended youth' (Livingstone and Das 2010; and see Mortimer 2012). This trend is likely to have occurred in response to economic austerity measures in western countries relating to a decline in job prospects for young people, high housing costs and a rise in the cost of funding tertiary education. Economic austerity has also triggered a return of young people to the family home, known as the 'boomerang generation' (Berngruber 2015; Kaplan 2009; Mitchell 2006; Stone et al. 2014). For example, in the UK, households with adult children have increased by 25 per cent in between 1996 and 2013 (ONS 2014). These are likely to be media-rich households with adult children's bedrooms packed with media gadgets. While unable to afford to set up homes of their own, these young adults tend to have bedrooms filled with media equipment as a way of managing personal space and media-related home entertainment. Single person and gay and lesbian households have also increased as a feature of more flexible living arrangements and the weakening of traditional nuclear family values (Chambers 2012).

Single-parent families with dependent children now form a significant category of households. In the UK, this household type comprises 25 per cent of all families with dependent children, with 91 per cent headed by women (ONS 2014). Single-parent households tend to suffer from limited financial resources and are therefore likely to struggle to furnish their children's media wishes (Russo Lemor 2005). Moreover, children whose parents are divorced or separated tend to move regularly between the households of both parents. They are therefore likely to experience different types of media homes and distinctive, sometimes contradictory, forms of parental restrictions on their access to media equipment. These differences in parental media monitoring can lead to tensions between ex-partners. Busy dual-career family households with concomitant demands of work and family often operate in a world of 'virtual parenting' and childcare. Dual-career families tend to experience challenges concerning connectivity with other family members, which are often resolved through varying levels of dependence on communication technologies such as mobile phones (Clark 2013). These issues are addressed in Chapter 4 on mediatised childhoods and the rise of a new kind of media parenting. Shifting patterns of migration involve transnational family ties and the negotiation of intimate modes of communication across great distances, generating new ideas about home. The uses of ICTs among migrants and diasporic communities highlight the issues of mediated family connectivity over distance. Digital communication such as Skyping and social media are increasingly employed to facilitate transnational family ties by supporting intimate connections between family members across distances among those separated by migration (Madianou and Miller 2012).

The following chapters indicate, then, that differing household and family arrangements affect the ways in which media and communication technologies are used in the home whether in terms of modes of adoption, integration and routines of use; communicating with household members while away from home; or keeping in touch with families 'back home' in other parts of the world. However, it is difficult to separate the idea of 'family' from that of home privatisation and domesticity, as Morley (2002) observes. Despite the existence of diverse household types, governments of western countries have actively promoted the conflation of house, home and family as part of a broader ideological agenda relating to the decline of the welfare state. These state agendas correspond with powerful public and popular discourses that advance and idealise a particular nuclear version of the 'family', and a particular vision of domesticity for which media technologies are to be designed to sustain. The nuclear family ideal underpins national ideas about a stable and reproducing society. In turn, this ideal family type places particular symbolic significance on ideas of 'home' (Blunt and Dowling 2006).

Ideologies that influence notions of 'normal' or appropriate family and household types also have a bearing on the fluid, inclusive – or hegemonic – manner in which 'family' tends to be used to refer to non-nuclear and non-heteronormative types of intimacy (Roseneil and Budgeon 2004; Chambers 2012). Within contemporary sociological debates, the term 'family' is now used to include single-parent, blended and reconstituted families, 'friends as family' (Spencer and Pahl 2006) and same-sex households (Cook 2014; Gorman-Murray 2006, 2008) in recognition of fluctuating and diverse intimacies and meanings of home. The concept of 'domestic media imaginaries' is addressed in the final chapter to identify some of the complex cultural processes, including processes of regulation, through which media technologies are promoted for home use by drawing on, reinforcing and contesting dominant ideas about households, families and home. This concept enables an interrogation of the various ways that media engagement and discourses can both undermine and validate traditional ideas of 'home' and 'family' at particular junctures of media-related social changes throughout the twentieth and twenty-first centuries.

Types of media engagement in the home

With media technology now at the heart of home-making and the privatisation process, many homes have evolved into highly complex communication hubs by facilitating personal and shared engagement in a wide range of media-based activities. For all household types, the share of household budgets spent on media appliances, media services and leisure media is rising (Livingstone and Das 2010; Johnsson-Smaragdi 2002). However, the dynamics and arrangements of households and family composition have a major influence on the appropriation of media technologies in the home. For example, research confirms that the presence of children in a household is a key indicator of whether or not it is likely to have internet connection and broadband service compared to households in general (US Department of Commerce 2002; Gora 2009; Clark 2013).

The domestic environment continues to be the most likely setting for internet use, particularly among children and adolescents, with 87 per cent accessing social digital media from home (Livingstone et al. 2011). A key motive for creating a media-rich home is the parental purchase of digital devices for children to improve their educational and social skills (Buckingham 2007; Livingstone 2009). Households comprising families with children are, then, major drivers of social change by shaping the ways we relate to media and communication technologies. These families usually regard a media-rich home as one that is bountiful, one 'well-provided' for (Livingstone and Das 2010: 19). Given these trends, the increasing deregulation and commercialisation of media access becomes a major issue, exemplified by the acceleration of pay TV for accessing films, sport and other specialist leisure programmes.

With its capacity to contest ideological boundaries around the home, media's entrance into the private spaces of the home is often regarded with deep suspicion. Negative and positive public commentaries have been triggered about its impact on everyday home and family life, in news, government and academic reports. Domestic media has been blamed for accelerating the trend of individualisation at the expense of communal practices and identities by undermining traditional norms and values associated with family reciprocity. The miniaturisation and digitalisation of media and communication devices leading to portable media and multi-screen homes gave rise to public concerns about the scattering of family members into separate rooms and an erosion of family unity. By the 1980s, research drew attention to family conflicts over the TV tuner and then the remote control, generating arguments that it was splitting up families (see, for example, Morley 1986).

More recently, global and personal networks are said to be dismantling the boundaries around the home through an erosion of privacy and seeping of paid work into the home. Mobile media such as the iPad and computer tablet has sparked public concerns about anti-social families, with householders pursuing individualised media entertainment. Today's digital media generate pessimistic claims that excessive use of home-based media undermine family communication and face-to-face interaction, isolate children from parents, and fracture traditional boundaries between home and the outside world through the encroachment of work on home life and the infringement of privacy (Kayany and Yelsma 2000; Nie et al. 2002; Vandewater et al. 2005). In an era of global media, these concerns have been exacerbated by the potential for children to be digitally connected to the rest of the world in the privacy of their own bedrooms and at younger and younger ages, including 6- to 11-year-olds (Livingstone 2009; Livingstone and Das 2010). Media-rich children's bedrooms generate parental uncertainties about how to monitor children's use of social media, such as protecting children against the growing risks associated with cyberbullying and internet stranger danger. Parental concerns are framed within new kinds of negotiations between parents and children resulting from parental attempts to curb children's media use at home.

However, while new media technologies can intensify individualisation and personalisation of use through media convergence and the introduction of mobile devices, their domestic functions are complex, diverse and often unpredictable. Media in the home can bring together families and household members by organising household schedules and domestic space as planned or spontaneous, shared or separate, distant or close. For example, TV is used variously as a companion, a time organiser, a babysitter and a form of relaxation (Livingstone and Das 2010). Media provide opportunities for shared leisure activities by drawing together the whole household to strengthen social and familial networks. While media can displace family dialogue and act as a barrier to interaction, research also shows that watching TV and films together can offer an amicable shared activity and act as a facilitator of communication by providing common topics of conversation.

Research on domestic media in the 1980s and 1990s confirmed media's capacity to bring the family together, as well as separate it. TV supported family subgroups and subsystems, strengthening bonds between mothers and daughters, fathers and sons or between grandparents and grandchildren (Livingstone and Das 2010; Gillespie 1995; Livingstone 2002). James Lull (1990) advanced debates about the management of this familial separation and togetherness by establishing conceptual reference points to identify routine behaviours of the household and the role of TV in everyday life. Within relational uses, TV can act as a mode of 'affiliation or avoidance'. While it may be a 'communication facilitator' by bringing the family together and opening up conversation, TV viewing can also create conflict (Lull 1990: 36). In response, householders usually develop finely tuned knowledge of each others' domestic habits and related uses of media technologies, ranging from computer gaming to radio listening. This intimate domestic knowledge helps householders coordinate the daily routines of family life within a moral economy of the household to avoid tensions by, for example, using different media content in separate rooms (see O'Brien and Rodden 1997; see Chapters 2 and 3).

Similarly, Elaine Lally (2002: 136) explains that households organise a sense of collective identity through the separation and individualisation of media-related activities by referring to the 'techniques of managing their living together'. Tensions arise between householders when, for example, a child monopolises the gaming system or an adult spends too long on the landline. The following chapters explore these issues in relation to the following: new parent–child dynamics in households that support children's media-rich bedrooms; changing features of family togetherness relating to the rise of home-based video gaming; and the role of mobile multi-screen technologies such as computer tablets in the home. One of the key aims is to consider whether these new digital technologies are used for affiliation or avoidance of company in shared spaces.

Online interactions are said to enhance family and other modes of intimate connectivity by coordinating activities and developing information networks (Livingstone 2003; Sook-Jung and Young-Gil 2007; Subrahmanyam and Greenfield 2008; Van Rompaey and Roe 2001). A US study of networked families and the effects of technology on their lives indicates that new media is generating 'networked households' and 'networked families'. In a US study, Barry Wellman and colleagues (2008) found that media and communication technology facilitates new forms of connectedness between householders, particularly between parents and children. American families are using a broad variety of communication media to keep in touch with one another, evolving around mobile phone interactions and communal internet engagement. While critics have conveyed anxieties about technology pulling families apart, Wellman and colleagues found that couples use their mobile phones to connect and coordinate their lives, particularly if they have children. Spouses go off in different directions to work during the day yet remain closely connected through mobile phone and, to a lesser extent, via the internet. Wellman et al. (2008) refer to a new kind of connectivity, via phone and screen-sharing which corresponds with certain benefits for family life. Family households with the most media access are more likely to share experiences and events with their family members while they are online, and to interact about some forms of family communications such as coordinating events. However, the research by Wellman et al. (2008) suggest that these busy, 'tech-using' families are less likely to share meals and have lower levels of satisfaction with their leisure time. Those with the most media and communication technologies are likely to comprise busy, dual-income households, and work longer hours, partly through the presence and use of the internet. Those who have access to multiple communication devices are slightly less likely than those with lower levels of ownership to eat dinner together with other members of the household and to convey high levels of satisfaction with their family and leisure time.

The following chapters confirm that new communication technologies are extending the time some people spend working from home or at the office. While people confirm that new communication tools enable them to stay in touch with friends and family, findings suggest that the use of these technologies has blurred traditional boundaries between 'work' and 'home'. With more time spent working, including from home, householders tend to have less time for relaxing, or taking part in hobbies or other activities. Overall, then, this enhanced mediated connectivity seems to have come at a price. The following chapters explore these trends, indicating that while mobile media allow household members to manage relations and the connections between the home and outside activities, these media gadgets are prompting changing social interactions in the living room and the character of home living.

The mediatisation of the home

The embedded quality and diverse roles of today's media and communication technologies ensure that media has become much more than just an aspect of private life and entertainment. Once thought of as a refuge from the disruptiveness of technological transformations, the home has become a specialised setting for technological change (Morley 2002). The 'domestication' debate, addressed in Chapter 3, entails the micro-social level of media as a process involving the appropriation and integration of technology within households and personal life. However, media domestication is also situated within a larger, macro-social level of global networks, trends and patterns of mediatisation. These processes involve transformations in the relationship between public and private spheres of life that include changing local and global discourses and experiences of nation, family and domesticity.

Until the mid 2000s, three approaches to media research dominated media and communications studies: textual analysis, political economy of the media and reception studies. Yet, as Couldry and Hepp (2013) point out, major questions about 'why media mattered so much' were not satisfactorily addressed through these methods.

> Put simply, something is going on with media in our lives, and it is deep enough not to be reached simply by accumulating more and more specific studies that analyze this newspaper, describe how that programme was produced, or trace how particular audiences make sense of that film on a particular occasion.
>
> *(Couldry and Hepp 2013: 191)*

Efforts to move beyond production–text–audience approaches were initiated in the late twentieth century, exemplified by the work of Roger Silverstone (1999) who, among others, searched for a more multidimensional, non-linear approach to the study of media. In *Consuming Technologies* (1992), Silverstone and colleagues explained that media technologies in the home are shaped to adapt to the domestic environment and yet also transform that environment. They developed the concept of 'domestication' in the 1980s and 1990s to address the relationship between the phenomenology of the home and the political economy of the household (Silverstone 2006: 242). As addressed in Chapter 3, the aim of the domestication approach was to capture the ubiquitous quality and multi-contextual nature of media's role in everyday life, even before the arrival of today's omnipresent digital media (Couldry 2000, 2014).

By developing the concept of the 'moral economy' of the household, the domestication approach conceives the household as the setting in which vital relations of trust and ontological security are generated (Berker et al. 2006). An emphasis on the moral exchanges of the household highlights the importance of the moral judgements and expectations involved in the household construction of domestic media spaces, routine uses of media and the micro-social decisions made by householders about the domestic uses of media (Silverstone et al. 1992). Media is used by households to demarcate activities according to the suitability of the timing or space in which they are used. Moral decisions are involved in the type of media and communication technologies selected to sustain intimate relationships between individuals, and between home and beyond home, such as among transnational families, to sustain connections with relatives overseas (Madianou and Miller 2012). These moral decisions relate to several factors such as parental monitoring of children's media uses, how media are used to foster and enhance family and household connectivity, or, alternatively, how media are used to support individual media-related pursuits in the home. Thus, the introduction of media technology and its 'domestication' in the home can be considered as a moral force, as Silverstone (2006: 45) emphasises (see Chapter 3).

From the late 1980s, Roger Silverstone (1994), David Morley (1992) and Morley and Charlotte Brunsdon (1999) were among scholars who drew attention to the role of TV in the regulation of the 'family' as a point of intersection within a range of key regulatory institutions such as the state, education and leisure. Silverstone (1999) identified the need to study the concurrent, interconnecting multiple sites that relate to media. Later, he developed the concept of 'mediation' to address the dialectical nature of media as a set of processes shaped by and shaping wider social and cultural realms (Silverstone 2005). After Silverstone's death in 2006, the concept of 'mediatisation' was advanced to overcome the provisional sites of media production, texts and reception by addressing the traversing nature and wider consequences of mediated communications. The term 'mediatisation' emerged, then, as an integrative conceptual frame in the late 2000s to address the macro-social and omnipresent quality of today's media and allow consideration of an entire range of practices interconnected with or oriented to media. Accordingly, mediatisation allows an analysis of the connections between transformations in media and communications and wider global changes in culture and society (Couldry 2012; Couldry and Hepp 2013; Hjarvard 2008; Krotz and Hepp 2012; Lundby 2013). Recognising that the media can no longer be considered as separate from other institutions in society, the term 'mediatisation' is identified as a social process within a society saturated and suffused by the media.

The earlier term 'mediation' remains relevant as a description of media transmission and distribution of communication in late modernity. However, 'mediatisation' denotes the role of media in broader evolving processes of social and cultural change to address its ubiquitous character and the ways it becomes embedded in everyday life. As Andre Jansson (2013: 281) states, 'Whereas mediation, in simplified terms, refers to the process of transmission, dissemination or circulation of something (typically information) between sources, mediatisation points to the extended social prevalence of certain regimes of media dependence.' One aspect of mediatisation involves a recent transformation of the public sphere, underpinned by the growing interdependent of politics and media. A second aspect, relating to the role of media in home and family life, is the recognition of a shift from direct communication to indirect mediated forms of communication involving changes in the significance of time, place and sense of communication processes. With widespread access to fast internet, the vast expansion of web search capacity and pervasive use of mobile phones, blogs, YouTube, social media and integrated digital systems, today's media are now ubiquitous, interactive and no longer inevitably situated in particular material realms such as 'home' or 'workplace' (Hartmann 2009: 227). Yet, at the same time, the living room remains a dominant site for shared TV and film viewing, particularly in the light of advances in TV technology including smart TVs, large wall-mounted TVs and 'wallpaper TV'. Concurrently, the distinctive and familiar cultural meanings associated with these material spaces are both vigorously defended and gradually transformed.

Comprising a general approach rather than a specific theory, mediatisation refers to a process involving the accelerated temporal, spatial and social proliferation in mediated communication and changes in types of media used for particular forms of communication (Couldry and Hepp 2013). The mediatisation approach informs the following chapters for an understanding of media's status and positioning within home life. Rather than treating the media as an external, separate institution that affects or makes an 'impact' on households, individuals, families and home life, the concept of mediatisation allows an exploration of the complex roles of media in everyday life, both socio-culturally and historically. Mediatisation emphasises the double articulation of media, as both technologies of transmission and representational content as advanced by the domestication approach outlined in Chapter 3. The term also signals the ways media are shaped by, influence and mobilise ideas of home life through mediatised rituals such as watching the news each evening on TV, regularly Skyping relatives on the other side of the world, or watching favourite films and TV programmes with family, flatmates or friends. Mediatisation also points to a wider media saturation of society and the often futuristic imaginings of a fully mediated society that underpins and propels this media diffusion. In the context of mediatisation, the home is considered a field of action which constitutes one of several overlapping 'mediatised worlds' (Krotz and Hepp 2012) comprising evolving communication cultures.

Henri Lefebvre's model of spatial production addresses the social and spatial significance of mediatisation, emphasising that space is socially produced in relation to social or economic conditions, rather than something natural. For Lefebvre (1974/1991), the production of space, such as 'home' can be viewed as three dialectically interconnected dimensions: 'perceived', 'conceived' and 'lived' spaces. The concept of 'perceived space' is the first dimension within the production of space to emphasise the idea of space as an inherently 'social' product. Perceptions of space are mediated through conceived and lived spaces. 'Conceived space' involves the representations used by dominant professional groups to define space, such as scientists, engineers, urban designers and architects. It addresses the mediation of diverse representations of space, drawing attention to the media's implication for configuring our understandings and anticipations about the social world. 'Lived space' is directly experienced space comprising the spatial representations that ordinary people develop to give meaning to their everyday lives, involving the mental constructs through which they view the physical world. In a mediatised world, these three types of spaces are interconnected. By crossing between domestic and public spaces, media have changed the material character of daily life by altering ideas about the spaces through which we engage with people. This is exemplified by terms such as 'virtual space' or 'cyberspace', often used to describe the context of these encounters. Likewise, face-to-face conversation over the internet such as FaceTime and Skype has changed the material meanings of home by opening it up, making it more porous through continuous connectivity.

Informed by Lefebvre's triadic model of social space, Jansson (2013) argues that certain social trends are transforming the conditions of communication and, at the same time, problematising the status of major spatial categories such as place, space, territory, borders, movement and mobility. Jansson proposes three socio-spatial regimes of mediatisation which can be applied to differing sectors of society and which are relevant for an understanding of the ways that the mediatised home is perceived, conceived and lived in as a space: 1) material indispensability and adaptation; 2) premediation of experience; and 3) normalisation of social practice. Relating to Lefebvre's perceived space, Jansson's concept of 'material indispensability and adaptation' refers to the tools and systems that have been constructed as requisite elements of normal daily life. It highlights the material presence of the media object – whether it be a radio, TV set or PC – as well as the uses to which the object is put. The process of mediatisation occurs at the stage when certain technologies attain the status of a 'cultural form', following Raymond Williams' (1974) approach in his discussion of TV. This status is achieved through ritual social practices such as watching TV each evening, using the PC daily or weekly to perform work tasks or accessing the internet to keep in touch with people by email, and so on. The sense of indispensability associated with digital media such as TV and computers denotes the widespread social acceptance of the media as essential modes of entertainment, information access and communication.

Jansson's concept of 'premediation of experience' relates to Lefebvre's notion of conceived space. 'Premediation' is a term initially introduced by Richard Grusin

(2010) to emphasise that the media generate specific types of action and interaction which are mediated in a particular representational register. Certain kinds of social practices are triggered mainly through representations. Jansson uses the example of tourism, which is a set of conventions based mainly on the circulation of appealing images of other places that cultivate desires to experience, share and archive those places as part of ones' life biography (Larsen 2005). Premediation mobilises affect through the use of numerous forms of mediation and remediation to create a mood or structure of feeling that motivates certain thoughts, actions or motives (Jansson 2013). As well as shaping our expectations about future experiences and events, media generate the staging of particular types of action and social interaction. Jansson's concept of premediation of spatial experience confirms the innate relationship between mediatisation and the contested production of social space. Jansson's premediation of experience coincides with the concept of media imaginaries that I deploy, which is outlined below.

Relating to Lefebvres' notion of lived space, Jansson's concept of the 'normalisation of social practice' explains how the social conventions, norms and expectations associated with media change are articulated through everyday practices. These normalisations relate to the timing and particular organisation of everyday activities. He uses the example of 'television culture' which involves the adaptation of social life to the scheduling of broadcasting and, conversely, the adaptation of broadcasting to social life. For example, as Chapter 2 explains, radio and TV programme content and schedules were designed to fit into and reflect the existing domestic routines of housewives in the first half of the twentieth century, thereby reinforcing nuclear family values and naturalising unequal gender relations. These institutionalised forms of regulation have shaped the routines of households, the informal topics of media-related conversations, forms of parental monitoring and control of children, and stratified prospects associated with cultural and media literacy. However, digital networked media are creating new modes of regulation in relation to multiple changes including video gaming in the home, the multi-screen and touchscreen home, changing dynamics of the living room, use of media among transnational families, and the digitally connected home. These issues indicate the significance of mediatisation from a socio-spatial standpoint for an understanding of media's changing roles in the context of home, family and domesticity.

Media imaginaries

Home, domestic relations and family are not just tangible physical contexts but are also symbolically constructed realms. This is emphasised by Blunt and Dowling (2006: 3) who approach 'home' as both a place and a spatial imaginary. They stress that 'home' invokes multiple ideas and emotions ranging from a sense of belonging to a sense of alienation. They examine the intersections between 'material and imaginative geographies of home' which are generated not only as lived experiences of home but also as imagined physical spaces and cultural meanings infused with feelings. Imaginaries of the ideal home inform our ideas about what home should be. Meanings of home are not only created by their residents but also by powerful local, regional, national and transnational ideas about home as an ideal domestic space with particular qualities and characteristics that inform social identities. As Silverstone (2006: 242) puts it, 'To be homeless is to be beyond reach, and to be without identity.' Importantly, the spatial reality of home is now mediated by culture and communications and can no longer be understood outside a mediatised environment (Sinclair 2002). The lived space of home is perceived and conceived through multiple competing and complementary media discourses.

The following chapters address the ways in which the promotion of media technologies by media corporations, government policies and through popular culture have been shaped by and reinforced powerful gendered and familial values that often evoke middle-class, nuclear family visions of home life. From an early stage, media technologies such as radio and TV have been feminised and domesticated through associations with home and family. Yet the more recent digitalisation and mobilisation of technology has often entailed an endorsement of mobile gadgetry within masculinised representations of domestic space through gendered discourses of action, adventure and agency (see, for example, Chapters 6 and 8). Lefebvre's socio-spatial regimes of mediatisation together with Jansson's (2013) emphasis on the premediation of experience underpin the ideological and mythological processes involved in the domestic appropriation of media. They highlight the central role of public discourses and popular culture within disputes and struggles over meanings about media and the spatial dimensions of home.

The concept of 'media imaginary' is employed in this book to address the popular discourses and public meanings associated with media technologies. The stage just before and during the widespread adoption of new technologies involves the process of 'media imaginary'. Comprising media fantasies and mythologies, this is when the technology's potential is debated, contested and agreed upon. This stage of public deliberation involves the emergent popularisation of the technology that forms part of public consciousness, sustaining the technology's social acceptance and widespread domestic adoption. Carolyn Marvin (1988) highlighted the significance of visions and fantasies about media technologies, explaining that they help societies establish and agree on the 'consciousness' that defines an era in terms of the ideas considered to be viable, to be suppressed or unable to be contemplated. Within media history, media fantasies and mythologies are now recognised as significant parts of the early phases of technological innovation (Natale and Balbi 2014). Fantasies invoked before the invention of a medium form 'media prophesies' (Nye 2004). Imaginaries can also be explored in terms of the roles played by the specific stages in the 'life cycle' of a medium (Natale and Balbi 2014). The emotional suggestions and imaginative association surrounding media are invoked at different points of the media technology's evolution.

The term 'imaginary' relates to the aims of Roland Barthes' (1972) concept of 'mythologies' and Benedict Anderson's (1983) influential idea of the modern nation-state as an 'imagined community'. Drawing on Anderson's conception,

Charles Taylor (2004) refers to a shared and collective 'social imaginary', a shared cognitive schema that represents the system of meanings that govern a given social structure. This imaginary can be inferred from popular media and public policy debates, involving shared discourses of family, community, neighbourhood and nation. Marvin (1988: 7) argued for the incorporation of the imaginary into the history of media, drawing on the history of communication technologies by James W. Carey and John J. Quirk (1970) who advanced the concept 'electric sublime'.

For the purposes of this book, the concept of 'media imaginary' is employed not only in relation to the vital, early stages of the adoption of media technologies but also during their phases of appropriation. I identify imaginaries involved in the stages immediately before, during and after the introduction of a medium. First, a stronger emphasis on the role of 'media imaginary' during the early phases of technology's public promotion and early adoption can help understand how the 'newness' and the potential of the technology is conceived within the wider public imagination. This emergent phase comprises the stage when the media technology is first promoted and is in the process of being adopted. Whether involving TVs, video games or tablet computers, this stage entails public contestations about the technology's potential. It involves attempts by vested interests, such as media corporations and governments, to endorse and assimilate it into the wider social imagination. The values and meanings of the technology are publicly and privately conceded and contested. Production, design and marketing attempt to 'pre-domesticate' technologies so that the meanings bestowed on them correspond with the values that people associate with domestic culture (Silverstone 1994). Media imaginaries facilitate the possibilities of opening up the home to global flows.

Second, media imaginaries are involved in inspiring the household adoption of new technologies. Comprising popular discourses that harness prevailing frameworks of knowledge, they advance ideas about appropriate ways to use media in the home. Broadly speaking, imaginaries about new kinds of media technologies generate their own agency and momentum rather than being governed by a specific external force such as the state. The concept therefore facilitates an enquiry into the ways that a range of discourses relate to and frame motives for consuming and experiencing domestic media equipment and how they embrace, reproduce or undermine particular moral values and lifestyles. 'Media imaginary' concerns the cultural work involved during the technology's assignment into society through a series of policies, design and marketing strategies, and popular cultural visions which attempt to alleviate the potential fears and anxieties about the new product, whether it be an analogue TV set, PC or smart TV. The concept is employed in this book to highlight and explain the role of media technologies within ideas about domesticity as an ongoing spatial and mobile cultural process.

Chapter 2 identifies the ways in which the home has traditionally been conceived as a feminine site through media imaginaries. Powerful ideas and values that inform 'domestic' media imaginaries involve dominant discourses about family, home and femininity. These mediated fantasies and aspirations are conveyed through a range of representational and material media channels that naturalise ideal versions of home and intimacy and also household routines relating to housework, home-making and heterosexual nuclear family relations. They are presented via public policy and popular discourses about domestic media to incorporate these technologies within discourses of nation, family, gender difference, domesticity, leisure, privacy and physical mobility (Blunt and Dowling 2006; Gorman-Murray 2008). In the final chapter, I develop the term 'domestic media imaginary' to identify four key categories of mediated domesticity that have shaped ideas of home relating to the meanings and uses of particular individual or groups of media technologies.

Organisation of the book and overview of chapters

While forming part of a media, communication and cultural studies tradition, the book addresses the changing roles of media in the home from a range of perspectives and is interdisciplinary in scope. It draws on and combines approaches and debates in sociology, feminism, cultural studies, cultural geography, cultural history and design history. The book provides a broad focus on past and present trends in the UK and US but also draws on key research findings from global and other national contexts for comparison and contextualisation. The chapters are sequenced both chronologically and thematically. Key stages in the social and cultural history of media are traced while critically engaging with relevant debates in the field through the study of particular media technologies. Beginning with the early twentieth-century introduction of TV into the home, the chapters trace the major phases of the mediatisation of the home from early TV to today's multiscreen, touchscreen homes and the automated home. The wider trends emerging from household patterns of media adoption and use are addressed by charting the macro-cultural media imaginaries and micro-social processes involved in the household adoption and appropriation of particular media technologies.

Four chapters address the major trends and academic debates through in-depth case studies of particular media technologies. These case studies are underpinned by research I have conducted on media technologies in relation to changing intimacies, families and households (Chambers 2001, 2011a, 2011b, 2012, 2013). In this respect, Chapter 2 comprises a historical study of the early years of TV with a focus on the role of design in the shaping of the technology for home use. Chapter 5 traces the history of video gaming's entrance into the home from the 1970s to the twenty-first century with a case study of the rise of family-centred gaming from 2006 via home video game consoles such as Nintendo Wii. Chapter 6 comprises a case study of the tablet computer by focusing on the meanings conferred on the object through advertising since its arrival on the market in 2010. Involving the domestication of mobile technologies, these meanings underpin and correspond with the rise of the multi-screen and touchscreen home. And in Chapter 8, the history of futuristic 'smart homes' is chronicled. It draws on significant earlier research on the smart home by Lynn

Spigel (2005) and Anne-Jorunn Berg (1985, 1992) to support a contemporary analysis of the social meanings, values, aspirations and identities associated with the contemporary digitally automated 'connected home'.

In terms of themes and issues, Chapters 2 and 3 chronicle the instatement of particular forms of media equipment in the home, from the TV to the computer. Chapter 2 explains that the history of TV's entrance into the home was preceded by media imaginaries of a new kind of media home, that promoted the TV set as a commodity to households from the late 1930s via design, advertising and popular media discourses publicised in lifestyle magazines. In this chapter, the design of the TV set provides a lens through which to address these themes. From furniture-styled cabinets to space-age portable styles, TV console design provides an understanding of the major popular discourses surrounding home life that motivated families to adopt TV in the home. Home was conceived as a feminine space in the early years of TV, through an explosion of discourses about the role of the housewife. Imaginaries of home and nation were recast through a mediatised domestic sphere. Yet the technology soon came to represent visions of a media future by conveying ideas of mobility, scientific progress and adventure beyond the home. Prompting concerns about individualisation and the loss of family togetherness, this history involves debates and contestations over changing family values related to ideas about TV's appropriate place in the home. Forming part of the media imaginaries about early TV, the themes addressed in Chapter 2 underpin issues raised about later stages of the household domestication of media technologies addressed in Chapter 3.

Chapter 3 outlines and critically engages with the domestication approach introduced in the UK in the 1980s and 1990s. The domestication perspective questions arguments that new media, particularly the internet, represent a globalised, placeless space of flows and standardised media experiences. Confirming that the presence of these technologies in the home affects the dynamics of the household, Chapter 3 considers the complex ways that technologies such as computers extended from the office to the home. The presence of these gadgets in the home throws up numerous challenges in terms of regulating and maintaining boundaries between home and the outside world. Addressing the concept of the moral economy of the home, the chapter explains the tensions generated around the encroachment of work in the home and ways in which media in the home both reinforce and challenge gendered social relations. For example, women played an active part in the domestic appropriation of the internet for work purposes. The chapter concludes by critically reviewing the pertinence of the approach in the context of mobilisation, personalisation and mediatisation.

Chapter 4 examines the rise of a youth-centred media and a screen-based 'bedroom culture'. Children's patterns of media engagement and changes in the relationship between children and parents relating to media devices in the home are identified. Differences in social class and in household types also have a major impact on children's access to media and the dynamics of parenting. Single-parent households can pose challenges for parental mediation through limited resources and the need to negotiate children's media habits with ex-partners' households. The chapter identifies a new form of media parenting and draws attention to the pressures placed on parental meditation in the context of children's use of media while on the move or in their privatised bedrooms.

Chapter 5 traces the history of home-based video gaming by chronicling the history behind the entrance of video gaming in the home. Video gaming began as a masculine toy played in amusement arcades and gradually moved into the home, to be presented as a wholesome form of family-centred leisure. The chapter illustrates the striking changes involved in the technology's migration from the arcade to the home. In the domestic arena, it was gradually transformed from a personalised masculine device to a family-centred leisure activity. The chapter highlights the gendered contestations over home as leisure and domestic space. It also identifies the motives behind and implications of the dramatic shift in meanings and uses of contemporary media-based home entertainment brought about by the release of Nintendo Wii, Microsoft Xbox and Sony Playstation. Nintendo Wii commercials are analysed in relation to recent survey findings on patterns of video gaming between parents and children to assess the implications of this new kind of gaming for family dynamics in the home.

Chapter 6 addresses debates about mobile interactivity and the shifting meanings of public space triggered by the accelerated use of mobile media gadgets such as tablet computers. A tendency to focus on geographical movement and global digital connectivity beyond the home has led to a neglect of the growing presence and uses of touchscreen mobile technology in the home. The continuing changes in the relationship between 'home' and the outside world are highlighted by the entrance of the tablet computer to the home. The chapter examines the role of advertising in the domestication process through the findings of a textual analysis of computer tablet advertisements. It explains emerging popular media discourses and meanings about the new 'touchscreen' multi-screen home. It addresses the ways in which advertisements of touchscreen technologies such as the computer tablet signify the 'mobile' as 'domestic'. Emerging research is assessed to consider changing family dynamics in 'touchscreen homes'. The chapter suggests that, through the use of the computer tablet in the shared setting of the living room, a form of 'ambient domestic connectivity' may be evolving.

Chapter 7 examines the role played by media and communication technologies within meanings of home for migrants and diasporic communities. Confirming that migrants are among the most advanced users of communications technology, the chapter addresses the ways in which transnational families engage with communication technologies to keep connected. For newly arrived migrants, the mobile phone is symptomatic of a process of 'mobile domestication', by playing a major part in nurturing a sense of normality and by easing feelings of loneliness and separation. The positive role of media content in creating and communicating powerful ideas of distant 'homelands' is confirmed by research on migrant transnationalism. Global technology enables individuals and families to be in 'two places at once'. Chapter 7 also examines the negative impact of media technologies for migrants in certain circumstances and addresses migrant children's media habits and how they influence parents' experiences of the new home. Drawing on research I have conducted on family photograph albums (Chambers 2006), I also outline debates on the uses of family photography by migrants within meanings of home and belonging and examine photography's role as migrant place-making (Aguirre and Davies 2014).

Chapter 8 examines the cultural values that shape visions of the future home by tracing the history behind the electronic 'smart home' agenda from the early twentieth century. The chapter shows how these 'homes of the future' underpin ideals associated with today's digitally 'connected home'. Confirming and celebrating transformations in the relationship between work and home, futuristic homes are manifestations of changing attitudes towards public and private spheres of life. Ironically, futuristic designs of a labour and energy-saving smart home failed to address the thorny issue of housework. They present a technical solution that preserves gendered power relations. The chapter explains that the technologised home forms a 'niche market' that grants access to an exclusive group as an endorsement of the domestication of electronic and then digital technology.

Chapter 9 draws together key aspects of the debates and findings in this book to address some major trends associated with the 'mediatised home'. The first section identifies the roles played by mobile, digital media and communication technologies in uncoupling domesticity from the spatial specificity of 'home'. The chapter addresses the implications of the roles played by mobile and digital media and communication technologies in uncoupling domesticity from the spatial specificity of 'home'. The concept of 'domestic media imaginaries' is developed to identify four sequential phases in the mediatisation of domesticity. These phases draw attention to the highly contested and conditional nature of the mediatised home. They involve competing visions of domesticity that correspond to contradictory domestic demands and affinities: the demand for intensified intimacy and privacy within the home on the one hand, and the desire for accelerated permeability on the other. In this section, I suggest that emergent mediated conceptions of domesticity associated with masculine identities simultaneously invoke and contest earlier traditional idealisations of domesticity associated with femininity. The final part of the concluding chapter highlights some of the implications of the accelerated commercialisation and privatisation of domestic media within globalised media markets. The example of smart TVs highlights the commercial monitoring of householders' viewing habits, which at the time of writing, is undertaken by multinational media corporations in order to pass the data on to advertisers. This trend reminds us that the mediatisation of the home not only entails optimistic scenarios of accelerated connectivity with the outside world but also negative consequences concerning increased commercial surveillance.

References

Aguirre, A.C. and Davies, S.G. (2014) 'Imperfect Strangers: Picturing Place, Family, and Migrant Identity on Facebook', *Discourse, Context and Media* 7, pp. 3–17, available at: *http://dx.doi.org/10.1016/j.dcm.2014.12.001*, accessed 5 December 2015.

Anderson, B. (1983) *Imagined Communities*, London: Verso.

Barthes, R. (1972) *Mythologies*, London: Jonathan Cape.

Berg, A.-J. (1985) 'A Gendered Socio-technical Construction: The Smart House', in Donald McKenzie and Judy Wajcman (eds) *The Social Shaping of Technology*, Buckingham: Open University Press, pp. 301–313.

Berg, A.-J. (1992) 'The Smart House as a Gendered Socio-technical Construction', *Working Paper 14/92*, Centre for Technology and Society, University of Trondheim, Norway, available at: *https://www.ntnu.no/c/document_library/get_file?uuid=b77e6da1-2511-4d43-a390-33d61b378e28&groupId=10265*, accessed 5 December 2015.

Berker, T., Hartmann, M., Punie, Y. and Ward, K.J. (2006) 'Introduction', in Thomas Berker, Maren Hartmann, Yves Punie and Katie Ward (eds) *Domestication of Media and Technology*, Maidenhead: Open University Press, pp. 1–18.

Berngruber, A. (2015) '"Generation boomerang" in Germany? Returning to the Parental Home in Young Adulthood', *Journal of Youth Studies* 18 (10), pp. 1274–1290, DOI: 10.1080/13676261.2015.1039969, http://dx.doi.org/10.1080/13676261.2015.1039969.

Blunt, A. and Dowling, R. (2006) *Home*, London: Routledge.

Buckingham, D. (2007) *Beyond Technology: Children's Learning in the Age of Digital Culture*, Cambridge: Polity Press.

Carey, J.W. and Quirk, J.J. (1970) 'The Mythos of the Electric Revolution', *The American Scholar* 9 (Spring and Summer), pp. 219–241.

Chambers, D. (2001) *Representing the Family*, London: Sage.

Chambers, D. (2006) 'Family as Place: Family Photograph Albums and the Domestication of Public and Private Space', in Joan M. Schwartz and James R. Ryan (eds) *Picturing Place: Photography and the Geographical Imagination*, New York: I.B. Tauris, pp. 96–114.

Chambers, D. (2011a) 'The Material Form of the Television Set: A Cultural History', *Media History* 17 (4), pp. 359–376.

Chambers, D. (2011b) '"Wii Play as Family": The Rise in Family-centred Video Gaming', *Leisure Studies* 31 (1), pp. 69–82.

Chambers, D. (2012) *A Sociology of Family Life: Change and Diversity in Intimate Relations*, Cambridge: Polity Press.

Chapman, T. (2004) *Gender and Domestic Life: Changing Practices in Families and Households*, London: Palgrave Macmillan.

Clark, L.S. (2013) *The Parent App: Understanding Families in the Digital Age*, Oxford: Oxford University Press.

Cook, M. (2014) *Queer Domesticities: Homosexuality and Home Life in Twentieth-Century London*, Basingstoke: Palgrave Macmillan.

Couldry, N. (2000) *The Place of Media Power: Pilgrims and Witnesses of the Media Age*, London: Routledge.

Couldry, N. (2012) *Media, Society, World: Social Theory and Digital Media Practice*, Cambridge: Polity.

Couldry, N. (2014) 'When Mediatisation Hits the Ground', in Andreas Hepp and Fredrich Krotz (eds) *Mediatised Worlds: Culture and Society in a Media Age*, Basingstoke: Palgrave Macmillan, pp. 54–71.

Couldry, N. and Hepp, A. (2013) 'Conceptualizing Mediatisation: Contexts, Traditions, Arguments', *Communication Theory* 23 (3), pp. 191–202.

Geller, M. (1990) 'Introduction', in Matthew Geller (ed.) *From Receiver to Remote Control: The Television Set*, New York: The New Museum of Contemporary Art, pp. 7–10.

Gillespie, M. (1995) *Television, Ethnicity and Cultural Change*, London: Routledge.

Gora, Y. (2009) 'Information and Communication Technologies (ICT) and Effects on 'Togetherness' Family Households', in Franco Papandrea and Mark Armstrong (eds) *Record of the Communications Policy and Research Forum 2009*, Sydney: Network Insight, pp. 88–105.

Gorman-Murray, A. (2006) 'Gay and Lesbian Couples at Home: Identity Work in Domestic Space', *Home Cultures* 3 (2), pp. 145–167.

Gorman-Murray. A. (2008) 'Masculinity and the Home: A Critical Review and Conceptual Framework', *Australian Geographer* 9 (3), pp. 367–379.

Grusin, R. (2010) *Premediation: Affect and Mediality after 9/11*, Basingstoke: Palgrave Macmillan.

Hartmann, M. (2009) 'Everyday: Domestication of Mediatisation or Mediatized Domestication?', in Knut Lundby (ed) *Mediatization: Concept, Changes, Consequences*, New York: Peter Lang Publishing, pp. 225–242.

Hjarvard, S. (2008) 'The Mediatisation of Society: A Theory of the Media as Agents of Social Change', *Nordicom Review* 29 (2), pp.105–134.

Hollows, J. (2008) *Domestic Cultures*, Maidenhead: Open University Press.

Jansson, A. (2013) 'Mediatisation and Social Space: Reconstructing Mediatisation for the Transmedia Age', *Communication Theory* 23 (3), pp. 279–296.

Johnsson-Smaragdi, U. (2002) 'A Swedish Perspective on Media Access and Use', *Special Issue of Nordicom Communication Review* 23 (1–2), pp. 37–46, available at: *http://nordicom.gu.se/sites/default/files/bilder/reykjavik_2001_nr_1-2_2002.pdf*, accessed 5 December 2015.

Kaplan, G. (2009) 'Boomerang Kids: Labor Market Dynamics and Moving Back Home. Federal Reserve Bank of Minneapolis, Research Department', *Working Paper No. 675.*

Kayany, J. and Yelsma, P. (2000) 'Displacement Effects of Online Media in the Socio-Technical Contexts of Households', *Journal of Broadcasting and Electronic Media* 44 (2), pp. 215–229.

Krotz, F. and Hepp, A. (2012) 'A Concretization of Mediatization: How "Mediatization Works" and Why Mediatized Worlds Are a Helpful Concept for Empirical Mediatization Research Empedocles', *European Journal for the Philosophy of Communication* 3 (2), pp. 137–152.

Lally, E. (2002) *At Home with Computers*, Berg: Oxford.

Larsen, J. (2005) 'Families Seen Sightseeing: Performativity of Tourist Photography', *Space and Culture* 8 (4), pp. 416–434.

Lefebvre, H. (1974/1991) *The Production of Space*, Oxford and New York: Blackwell.

Livingstone, S. (2002) *Young People and New Media: Childhood and the Changing Media Environment*, London: Sage Publications.

Livingstone, S. (2003) 'Children's Use of the Internet: Reflections on the Emerging Research Agenda', *New Media & Society* 5 (2), pp. 147–166.

Livingstone, S. (2009) *Children and the Internet*, Cambridge: Polity Press.

Livingstone, S. and Das, R. (with contributions from Georgiou, M., Haddon, L., Helsper, E. and Wang, Y.) (2010) 'Media, Communication and Information Technologies in the European Family', Working Report (April). Family Platform, Existential Field 8, available at: *http://eprints.lse.ac.uk/29788/1/EF8_LSE_MediaFamily_Education.pdf*, accessed 5 December 2015.

Livingstone, S., Haddon, L., Görzig, A. and Ólafsson, K. (2011) 'EU Kids Online II: Final Report'. LSE, London: EU Kids Online, available at: *http://eprints.lse.ac.uk/39351/1/EU_kids_online_final_report_%5BLSERO%5D.pdf*, accessed 5 December 2015.

Lull, J. (1990) *Inside Family Viewing: Ethnographic Research on Television's Audiences*, London: Routledge.

Lundby, K. (2013) *Mediatization of Communication: Handbooks of Communication Sciences* (Vol. 21), Berlin, Germany: De Gruyter Mouton.

Madianou, M. and Miller, D. (2012) *Migration and New Media: Transnational Families and Polymedia*, London: Routledge.

Marvin, C. (1988) *When Old Technologies Were New: Thinking About Electrical Communication in the Late Nineteenth Century*, Oxford: Oxford University Press.

Mitchell, B.A. (2006) 'The Boomerang Age from Childhood to Adulthood: Emergent Trends and Issues for Aging Families', *Canadian Studies in Population* 33 (22), pp. 155–178.

Morley, D. (1986) *Family Television: Cultural Power and Domestic Leisure*, London: Comedia.

Morley, D. (2002) *Home Territories: Media, Mobility and Identity*, London: Routledge.

Morley, D. and Brunsdon, C. (1999) *The Nationwide Television Studies*, London: Routledge.

Mortimer, J. (2012) 'The Evolution, Contributions, and Prospects of the Youth Development Study: An Investigation in Life Course Social Psychology', *Social Psychology Quarterly* 75 (1), pp. 5–27.

Natale, S. and Balbi, G. (2014) 'Media and the Imaginary in History', *Media History* 20 (2), pp. 203–218.

Nie, N., Hillygus, D. and Erbring, L. (2002) 'Internet Use, Interpersonal Relations and Sociability: A Time Diary Study', in Barry Wellman and Carolyne Haythorntwaite (eds) *The Internet in Everyday Life*, Oxford: Blackwell, pp. 215–243.

Nye, D.E. (2004) 'Technological Prediction: A Promethean Problem', in Marita Sturken, Douglas Thomas and Sandra Ball-Rokeach (eds) *Technological Visions: The Hopes and Fears That Shape New Technologies*, Philadelphia, PA: Temple University Press, pp. 159–176.

O'Brien, J. and Rodden, T. (1997) 'Interactive Systems in Domestic Environments', Proceedings of the 2nd Conference on Designing Interactive Systems: Processes, Practices, Methods, and Techniques, Association for Computing Machinery, pp. 247–259.

Office for National Statistics (ONS) (2014) 'Statistical Bulletin, Families and Households', available at: *http://www.ons.gov.uk/ons/dcp171778_393133.pdf*, accessed 8 August 2015.

Roseneil, S. and Budgeon, S. (2004) 'Cultures of Intimacy and Care Beyond "the Family": Personal Life and Social Change in the Early 21st Century', *Current Sociology* 52 (2), pp. 135–159.

Russo Lemor, A.-M. (2005) 'Making a "Home": The Domestication of Information and Communication Technologies in Single Parents' Households', in Thomas Berker, Maran Hartmann, Yves Punie and Katie Ward (eds) *Domestication of Media and Technologies*, Maidenhead: Open University Press, pp. 165–184.

Silverstone, R. (1994) *Television and Everyday Life*, London: Routledge.

Silverstone, R. (1999) *Why Study the Media?* London: Sage.

Silverstone, R. (ed.) (2005) *Media, Technology and Everyday Life in Europe: From Information to Communication*, Aldershot: Ashgate.

Silverstone, R. (2006) 'Domesticating Domestication: Reflections on the Life of a Concept', in Thomas Berker, Maran Hartmann, Yves Punie and Katie Ward (eds) *Domestication of Media and Technologies*, Maidenhead: Open University Press, pp. 229–247.

Silverstone, R., and Hirsch, E. (eds) (1992) *Consuming Technologies: Media and Information in Domestic Spaces*, London: Routledge.

Sinclair, J. (2002) 'Review of David Morley's Home Territories', *International Journal of Cultural Studies* 5(1), pp. 111–113.

Sook-Jung, L. and Young-Gil, C. (2007) 'Children's Internet Use in a Family Context: Influence on Family Relationships and Parental Mediation', *CyberPsychology and Behavior* 10 (5), pp. 640–644.

Spencer, L. and Pahl, R. (2006) *Rethinking Friendship: Hidden Solidarities Today*, Princeton, NJ: Princeton University Press.

Spigel, L. (2005) 'Designing the Smart House: Posthuman Domesticity and Conspicuous Production', *European Journal of Cultural Studies* 8 (4), pp. 403–426.

Stone, J., Berrington, A. and Falkingham, J. (2014) 'Gender, Turning Points, and Boomerangs: Returning Home in Young Adulthood in Great Britain', *Demography* 51 (1), pp. 257–276.

Subrahmanyam, K. and Greenfield, P. (2008) 'Online Communication and Adolescent Relationships', *Project Muse* 18 (1), pp. 119–146.

Taylor, C. (2004) *Modern Social Imaginaries*, Durham, NC: Duke University Press.

US Department of Commerce (2002) 'A Nation Online: How Americans Are Expanding Their Use of the Internet', Economics and Statistics Administration, National Telecommunications and Information Administration, US Department of Commerce, February 2002, available at: https://www.ntia.doc.gov/legacy/ntiahome/dn/anationonline2.pdf, accessed 5 December 2015.

Van Rompaey, V. and Roe, K. (2001) 'The Home as a Multimedia Environment: Families' Conception of Space and the Introduction of Information and Communication Technologies in the Home', *Communications* 26 (4), pp. 351–369.

Vandewater, E.A., Bickham, D.S., Lee, J.H., Cummings, H.M., Wartella, E.A. and Rideout, V.J. (2005) 'When the Television Is Always On: Heavy Television Exposure and Young Children's Development', *American Behavioral Scientist* 48 (5), pp. 562–577.

Wellman, B., Smith, A., Wells, A. and Kennedy, T. (2008) 'Networked Families', Pew Research Centre, available at: http://www.pewinternet.org/2008/10/19/networked-families/ (accessed 3 August 2015).

Williams, R. (1974) *Television: Technology and Cultural Form*, London: Fontana.

2

EARLY TELEVISION

Introduction

From the beginning of broadcasting's history, media have been a platform for public concerns and debates about the meanings and values associated with home, domesticity and family life. Powerful discourses about home, family and domestic culture accompanied the launch of broadcasting in the US and Europe during the early twenty-first century. Public and popular debates surrounding the emergence of broadcasting for home use were underscored by severe wartime disruption. Television's (TV) development from the 1930s was interrupted across Europe by the Second World War and resumed thereafter, to become a routine part of domestic life by the 1950s. Early ideas about TV broadcasting were, then, marked by severe social and physical upheavals. This period of social turbulence brought into sharp focus changing meanings and values associated with family life, private and public spheres of society, the roles of women, and the nature of community and nation. Post-war initiatives to recover a sense of national and domestic stability shaped social responses to radio and TV, provoking public concerns about home, family and nation.

These social concerns about the effects of media on families and domestic life were articulated through and corresponded with utopian and dystopian media imaginaries about TV as a technology and cultural form. Traditional ideals of home and family projected an intrinsically white, middle-class nuclear unit structured by hierarchal gendered and generational relations. Home and households were conceived as domestic spaces and cultures through a web of economic and popular cultural discursive processes involved in the imagining and promotion of media technologies for the home. Utopian media imaginaries envisaged TV as a medium capable of fostering traditional, domestic ideals of family togetherness while dystopian visions of the technology stressed the medium's power to fragment family relations and breach the boundaries between public and private spheres of life. As the following chapters indicate, these contradictory imaginaries have, to this day, remained central to debates about the roles and meanings of media technologies in the home.

This chapter explores how these public concerns and wider popular discourses about 'home' and 'family' values influenced the TV's arrival into and colonisation of the home. Media technologies go through a process of enculturation or domestic 'appropriation' after entering the home, comprising micro-social processes which are focused on in Chapter 3. The cultural acceptance of early TV depended initially on its desirability to ensure its household adoption. Attempts to generate widespread consumer demand for this new, expensive and unfamiliar technology immediately after the war at a time of austerity posed a challenge for broadcasters, manufacturers and the government. Ensuring that families would welcome this bizarre object into the intimate surroundings of the home depended not only on the existing domestic circumstances and lifestyles of families and households. TV's acceptance also depended on the material design, on commercial marketing and state promotion, and on wider popular meanings attributed to broadcasting before the technology's entrance into the home.

With a focus on TV, this chapter charts the key ways in which media technology was popularised for home use between the late 1930s and 1970s. It asks how TV became a taken-for-granted homogenising force. The successful entrance of early radio and TV into the home relied on the public fantasies and aspirations projected on to these media technologies to encourage people to buy them as 'domestic' artefacts. The concept of 'media imaginary' addressed in Chapter 1 is employed in this chapter to cast light on the emergence and negotiations of various social ideals and to explain the processes through which the acceptance of media technology in the home depended. During its inception, TV technology was popularised in the public imagination to ensure its social acceptance, eventually leading to widespread adoption in the home. Powerful public and popular representations of both broadcasting and domestic media appliances were involved in the establishment of the medium. These media imaginaries were centred on the family and domestic life.

As well as media institutions such as the UK's BBC and commercial broadcasting channels in the US, manufacturers of media technologies, advertisers and the government all had vested interests in the success of TV as a feature of home life. The chapter examines the complex roles played by design, marketing, advertising and popular media discourses at the stages before and during consumption in shaping images, meanings and values associated with radio and TV technology as well as programming. Media imaginaries that underpinned ideas about the home, families, public and private spheres are identified to indicate how they generated the desire for TV. This chapter is informed by and structured around an original study of the material form of the TV receiver between the 1930s and 1960s to show how the cultural process of designing and styling the TV set ensured its appeal to householders. The chapter indicates that TV sets were designed, promoted and publicised to become a part of domestic life yet also rapidly came to embody ideas of technological progress and imaginative mobility.

The social need for television

Early broadcasting became a key player in the history of social struggles about the meanings and changing organisation of public and private spheres of society. Critiquing earlier ideas of technology-driven social change, Raymond Williams emphasises that broadcasting technology was not just a symptom that determined wider social change. He argued that technologies are developed and used in direct response to perceived social needs and problems. Radio, and then TV, were media technologies designed to address a growing need for homes and households to be connected to the outside world. Williams (1974) developed the concept of 'mobile privatisation' to explain the rise of a social need for TV as a technology and cultural form. The social need for broadcasting emerged through two apparently contradictory yet interrelated trends in modern social life: 'geographic mobility', achieved through technologies of communication and transportation; and 'privatisation', realised through housing construction, domestic architecture and community planning.

By the 1920s and 1930s, the rise of smaller, nuclear families in western societies coincided with spatially and socially mobile lifestyles. A desire and need for information from beyond the home was generated by the fragmentation of traditional, tight-knit neighbourhoods into smaller, separate households, and the movement of people to housing estates and suburbs comprised of looser social ties. As Williams explains, broadcasting resolved this problem by bringing information from the outside world to this new kind of private home. The social motives for broadcasting in western societies such as the UK and USA evolved, then, as part of attempts to solve an underlying social problem of connectivity prompted by the mobility and privatisation of households. Not only did broadcasting address the practical problem of connecting isolated homesteads to a central communication source. It also solved an ideological problem of connecting the private sphere of home, domesticity and family with the public sphere of politics, the economy and news about national events.

Williams' concept of 'mobile privatisation' also invokes the idea of media as a form of 'travel' from the home. Referring to early TV in the US, Lynn Spigel explains: 'It gives people a sense of travelling to distant places and having access to information and entertainment in the public sphere, even as they receive this in the confines of their own domestic interiors' (2001: 391). In contrast to the earlier publicly situated mediums of cinema and theatre, radio and TV allowed family households to travel the world from the privacy of their living rooms by linking the outside world to the domestic context of the home. By broadcasting a flow of entertainment and education, the entrance of radio and TV in the home radically changed families' experiences of domesticity (Spigel 1992; 2001). This sense of travel has been ingrained not only in popular discourses about broadcasting and in programming, but also in the very shape of media equipment for home use.

After the Second World War, opponents of TV regularly drew on gendered discourses in their criticism of the medium. As a 'window on the world' beyond the home, TV was thought likely to breach time-honoured boundaries between the domestic and public spheres by offering women a taste and yearning for public life. It was feared that housewives might neglect their domestic duties by becoming distracted or 'passive viewers', or even restless seekers of adventure beyond the home (Andrews 2012; Spigel 1992; 2001). Likewise, it was feared that children might generate unruly behaviour in the home as distracted viewers. These cultural tensions coincided with social unease about changes in the relationship between the home and public spheres of life. In the early twentieth century, notions of 'domesticity' were underpinned by the ideological distinction between a feminine private sphere and masculine public sphere. Known as the 'separation of spheres', this gendered division of social spheres was characterised by the association of men with the public sphere and women with the private sphere. Men were traditionally engaged in paid work, politics and masculine leisure pursuits beyond the home while women were expected to be occupied in the home via housework, childcare, and feminine hobbies and pastimes (Vickery 1993).

Family togetherness and the changing nature of mediated household interaction formed key concerns since the very inception of broadcasting. Women's new civic status following universal suffrage challenged the traditional values anchored within separate spheres. However, the ensuing pressure placed on patriarchal principles was eased by boosting the Victorian idealisations of women: by locating women in the private sphere and referring to them as 'wives', 'mothers' and 'housewives' (Bailey 2009: 53). The ideological boundaries between public and private spheres were ruptured during the Second World War by the recruitment of women into full-time paid work. An explosion of popular and public discourses surrounded the role of the housewife in the immediate post-war period through broadcast programmes on both TV and radio, within a patriarchal drive to coax women back into the home.

TV was configured by reproducing powerful, traditional ideals of family life based on gendered and generational hierarchies. To combat public anxieties that TV might destabilise gender and generational relations, the emergent medium was promoted as a 'new hearth' that would bind the family together. Spigel (1992) emphasises the role of cultural fantasy that steered TV's integration into everyday family life. Captivating advertisements for TV and images in lifestyle magazines promoted family togetherness, depicting the 'family circle' gathered round the TV set, to convey the idea that the medium could reunite traditional families after the upheaval of war. The figure of the housewife and her domestic work in the home was also heavily endorsed in these popular discourses. Significantly, the post-war familial ideal was an image of an exclusively white, middle-class and nuclear model, evoking a traditional middle-class lifestyle that, for women, centred on the home. The design and marketing of the TV set as a domestic item was an important discursive site that presented a particular vision of the media home.

Designing media for the home

Against a backdrop of suspicion about TV's potentially disruptive effects on family life, the technology had to be carefully designed to fit into particular standards of home décor. Even though the medium was acclaimed as a 'window on the world' that could generate family togetherness, during the initial years of TV broadcasting TV receivers were regarded as inherently unattractive. While the 'window on the world' function was welcomed by many, the intrusion of the 'one-eyed monster' in the living room was not. How, then, did this bulky piece of equipment become a routine part of everyday life in the home? Ambivalent public and private responses to TV technology form part of a longer history. Although industrial capitalism was driven by an ability to invent and sell new products, western cultures of consumption showed a resistance to the 'newness' of technologies that stretched back to the eighteenth and nineteenth century (Forty 1986: 11). Until the 1920s, the living room was designated an intimate space for formal leisure and entertainment. Machinery such as sewing machines and electric lamps were decoratively styled to embody meanings associated with that sphere. New forms of electrical communications entering the home, such as telephone and radio, were viewed with a mixture of doubt and approval, prompting a questioning and re-evaluation of the private nature of that space (Spigel 1992; Marvin 1988; Susman 1984; Hirsch 1992; Morley 2007). This styling requirement was even more pertinent in the case of TV's entrance into the intimate space of the living room.

The reception of radio in the home provides a backdrop to the arrival of TV. In the 1920s, radio was initially perceived as a novel medium for technically proficient men who approached the 'crystal set' as a 'gadget' (Moores 1993). Comprising a rudimentary assortment of resistors, wires and valves, the first wireless sets to enter the home were viewed, particularly by women, as alien objects that looked incongruous in a domestic setting. And, as 'listening' required the use of individual headsets, early radio divided rather than united the family in the shared space of the living room. During this early phase, radio generally appealed to men, who viewed the equipment in terms of its technological qualities rather than the media content. As a 'masculine' technology involving technical skill to operate it, the wireless was often banned from the living room and consigned to the workshop or shed (see Boddy 2004; Moores 1993). Several technologies such as home cinema (Klinger 2006) and computers (Lally 2002; Ward 2006) have subsequently proceeded through this 'gadgeteer' phase before being domesticated. For instance, when the first personal computers (PCs) were bought, usually by men, they were mainly used for programming, motivated by the question: 'What can this thing do?' In the case of radio and then TV, the equipment had to be carefully designed for domestic use as a significant preceding stage of domestic adoption.

Keen to sell radios to families for use in the living room, by the late 1920s and early 1930s, manufacturers and broadcasters devised sophisticated solutions to market the product. As new objects, radio and then TV had to be adapted in terms of their physical, visual and audible presence. In the case of early radio, design formed a vital process in its mass acceptance in the home by transforming it from a 'gadget' for male enthusiasts to an entertainment unit for the family (Silverstone and Haddon 1996: 47). The cabinet in which the radio was housed took on visual features relating to other domestic objects so that they could look 'at home' in the living room by resembling a piece of furniture: a wooden or Bakelite cabinet to replicate antique or contemporary furniture (Forty 1986). By the late 1930s, radio was no longer viewed as an intrusive masculine gadget but as a medium and object that enhanced the attractiveness of a feminised living room. Radio shifted its status from that of an unwelcome visitor to become part of the family through design and via programming aimed at 'family audiences' (Moore 1993; Hollows 2008).

During the early years of radio up to the 1950s, the female listener and her perceived interests influenced the nature of broadcasting by dictating the tone and subject matter of the medium (Andrews 2012). This focus on the housewife underpinned the following media preoccupation with domesticity. For example, radio programmes during the 1920s and 1930s were aimed at women as homemakers by promoting and reflecting particular ideas about the female audience and about the domestic setting. Daily domestic advice programmes depicted women as dependent on radio for companionship and domestic guidance. In the UK, programmes such as *Common Sense in Household Work* (1929), *Household Talks* (1929), *Family Budgets* (1931), *How I Keep House* (1934), *Farmhouse Cookery* (1935) and *Housewives' Choice* (1946) categorised feminine interests with of those of home and family (Andrews 2012).

In the case of TV, the receiver did not pass through a gadgeteer phase. It was conceived, right from the start, as a commodity for mass consumption and domestic use. Broadcasting and domesticity reflected the rising consumerism of the 1950s in the US and UK, despite the continuing poverty and economic hardship experienced in post-war Britain. Fitting neatly into the economic framework of capitalism, it was designed as a 'mass-produced' commodity with standardised components for domestic consumption. Although Britain took the lead in TV manufacture in the 1930s, the sale of TV receivers to individual homes was inevitably slow. In 1936, less than 400 sets were available to receive the new service transmitted for only 30 miles from Alexandra Palace. A TV set cost £60, half the price of a small car (Bussey 1980). Limited transmission and the high price held back sales. By the start of the Second World War in 1939, the number of sets in use in Britain grew to around 23,000 (Scrine 1976). This was significantly higher than in the US and Germany, the two main rival countries involved in establishing TV broadcasting at the same time. But the manufacture of TV sets was halted by the British Government during the war. Wireless and TV factories were directed to produce communication machines for the war effort. This allowed the US to take a lead in TV cabinet design and manufacture.

Manufacturers recognised that the acceptance of this novel but unattractive technology in the home meant hiding the bulky valves and cathode ray tube in a cabinet. TV engineers, manufacturers and industrial designers, also known as product stylists in the US, led the process of its pre-domestication. The taming of this troubling yet desirable artefact was achieved by camouflaging the machine as furniture. Earlier radio cabinet makers and industrial designers performed a vital role in the media imagining of the TV's future place in the home by concealing the monster eye in a crafted wooden cabinet. Some sets even came with closing doors to conceal the gaping eye of the screen when not in use. This visual embellishment of the set as furniture, suited to the standards of décor of the living room, facilitated and stabilised the concept of 'family' viewing (Spigel 1992). Starting life as a piece of furniture for home use, the TV set gradually replaced the radio as the living room's central media apparatus in the post-war period. It even replaced the role of the hearth around which the family gathered. One particular design, the TV console, simulated a conventional hearth with a TV set placed inside a traditional fireplace frame (Chambers 2011).

At the time of writing, today's homes boast not only wall-mounted TV sets but even interactive wall-sized 'wallpaper screens' for what is advertised as a 'truly immersive experience'. But in the post-war period, manufacturers' industrial design departments initially served to express the idea of a tamed, domesticated machine to offer consumers a sense of control over what was a novel and alien technological experience. The use of wood to style the console was crucial in signifying aspirational domesticity. In the UK, contrasting surfaces of wood in natural colours and handicraft skills reminiscent of the British Arts and Craft Revival were used. Interior décor, furniture and architecture of early twentieth-century Britain was gradually influenced by the European Modern Movement. Famous and experienced designers were recruited by British manufactures to dress these machines in plastic moulding as well as wood and Bakelite, including Wells Coates for E.K. Cole Ltd., Victor Taylor for Ace Radio Ltd. and Richard D. Russell for Murphy Radio. When the project of modernism finally took hold in Britain in the interwar years, clean lines became synonymous with clean lives (Chambers 2011).

For example, as a pioneer of the Modern Movement in 1930s British architecture and design, Wells Coates worked with the radio manufacturing company, E.K. Cole Ltd. Coates addressed the popular demands for conventional, decorative craft styles in furniture by blending them with the more austere functionalism of the Modern movement through plastic moulding. In America, one of the most influential designers of TV sets was John Vassos who worked on the design of the first mass-produced TV set for RCA Corporation, debuted at the 1939 New York World Fair (Schwartz 2006). He designed RCA's 12-inch TRK-12 receiver for the Fair and even a 'phantom' version housed in a transparent Lucite plastic case. Vassos' design philosophy was unique in fusing the harsh Bauhaus functionalism and softer style of American streamlining with rich patinas and generous forms of classic case furniture in handcrafted, highly polished wood cabinets. These sets were aimed at the wealthy, inferred by advertisements depicting TV viewers dressed in evening suits and ball gowns. The luxury status of these TV sets was also signified by high prices from US$199.50 to $600 and also by sales in New York's luxury department stores: Macy's, Bloomingdale's and Wanamaker's (Schwartz 2006).

In the UK, exhibitions such as the 1936 Olympia and 1939 Radiolympia were major spectacles that dramatised and venerated the introduction of TV for home use. At the 1939 Radiolympia exhibition, every major radio manufacturer exhibited TV sets or combined radio and TV sets (On the Air[1]). However, the New York World Fair was staged on an altogether grander scale, reflecting Vassos' flamboyant designs. While war was waging in Europe, exhibition space for the new medium in the US nearly doubled at the 1940 New York World's Fair. The display featured Vassos' 'Television Suites', showcasing new models in ten different American home settings including receivers housed in stylish bleached mahogany modular furniture. During this period, major American designers such as Donald Deskey and Russell Wright, as well as Vassos, styled multi-unit display cabinets for the 1940 New York Fair's 'America at Home' pavilion, thereby confirming America's international lead in TV set manufacture and sales.

Family, nation and visions of progress

After a five-year break in TV broadcasting during the Second World War (1939–1945), a TV service was resumed in the UK in 1946. At this stage, less than two-thirds of its adult population had ever laid eyes on a working TV set (Hopkins 1961). It was not until 1952 that the signal could be received by 81 per cent of UK homes. By now, the US posed a serious threat to British TV manufacturing, being five years ahead in domestic product development. American TVs were marketed as multi-console sets with radio, TV and phonographs combined in luxurious and expensive wood cabinets for around $500 and also as cheaper table receivers for less than half that price (Kosareff 2005). Despite being weakened by war, progress in the UK was rapid. More than 93 per cent transmission coverage was achieved by 1957 (Hopkins 1961). At a cultural level, the state rebuilding of Britain's infrastructure entailed a new, positive vision of nation and family to be promoted through the medium of TV (Scannell 2000; Briggs 2000). TV was conceived as a medium to be consumed by families to be linked to the idea of 'a nation of families' (Morley 2002: 108).

For example, at national exhibitions of the early to mid twentieth century, the model home played a major role in promoting the family as the heart of the nation. Audiences were invited to sign up as members of this new nation as consumers of new products (Sparke 2004). In the 1950s, the institutions that promoted ideas about 'good design', the 'ideal home' and 'good living' in the US and UK, presented TV broadcasting and good design as moral vehicles of national improvement, framed within a growing commodity culture. In these ways, the physical presence and domestic design of the TV receiver became a national issue, proffering a moral good by revering the nuclear family home. In the UK, this national vision of good design and good living was fostered through an alliance between manufactures and government-sponsored organisations such as the Council of Industrial Design (COID). The COID's role was to advance British manufacturing and foster national pride through good design during a critical period of national reconstruction. 'Good design' was conceived as a patriotic endeavour (Jones 2003). National broadcasting formed part of domestic media imaginaries, summoning ideas of domestic cultures as family cultures, thereby marginalising and discounting those who were not part of traditional families (Hollows 2008: 108). The establishment of broadcasting helped to domesticate the nation and embrace a nation of families (Morley 2002: 107).

The popular media were paramount in domesticating the TV set, in alliance with industrial design, by associating the medium with middle-class ideals of family leisure and domestic technology innovation. Extensive marketing efforts were made to confirm TV as vital to the family's gaze. In magazines such as the *Readers Digest* advertisements promoted TV sets not only as cosy family-centred objects but also as symbols of luxury, leisure and sophistication. Advertisements of couples dressed in ball gowns and tuxedos were, incongruously, depicted in comfortable living rooms gathered round luxurious, quality wooden veneered sets (Chambers 2011). British and American advertisements managed to appeal to traditional family values at the same time as emphasising design features that signified TV as the pinnacle of progress and modernity. Advertisements also invoked the idea of immediate access to the public sphere from home (Morley 2007). For example, the UK's 1949 Baird Townsman console TV receiver with 12-inch cathode ray tube was dressed in a cabinet of polished walnut, with controls arranged at the sides of the unit. An advertisement for the product comprised a large aerial photograph of London showing the curve of the River Thames with views of the Houses of Parliament, Whitehall and Westminster Abbey displayed next to the TV set's specifications. The image signified direct communication between home and Parliament, the very heart of the public sphere. In small print, the advertisement claimed:

> The Townsman is a console of exceptionally dignified appearance . . . Designed with all the craftsmanship and finish that goes to the making of a piece of quality furniture, the Townsman will make an imposing and dignified addition to any room as well as a superlative example of television technique.[2]
>
> *(Chambers 2011)*

Women's lifestyle magazines of the 1950s conveyed TV as a technology of the hearth: as the focal point of family space (Spigel 1990). Affluent nuclear families were pictured gathered around the console, gazing into the glowing TV set reminiscent of the glowing hearth as an emblem of familial intimacy and harmony. Handbooks on interior décor of the late 1940s and 1950s advised readers how to position the appliance in the home and how to develop TV-viewing conventions.

In the UK, the design of the TV set was highlighted in COID publications and in the displays of furnished rooms designed for the 'Britain Can Make It' exhibition (Jones 2003; Maguire and Woodham 1997). Thus, on both sides of the Atlantic, the home came to represent a stage on which good taste in design and wholesome family values were played out (Spigel 1992). In time, TV overtook the radio's commanding position in the living room. It became the 'must have' appliance: the commodity that characterised the home. Ethnographies of families' uses of TV confirm that families negotiated their use of this novel equipment in the home both by incorporating it into domestic life and making home adjustments to suit the new medium (see Morley 2002; Morse 1990; Silverstone 1994; Fachel Leal 1990). By the late 1950s, the act of owning a TV set signified 'progress' and 'modernity' (O'Sullivan 1991).

Metaphors of 'home theatre' and 'window on the world' were drawn on by industry, advertisers, policy-makers, artists, critics, social scientists and engineers as well as in popular literature such as women's magazines to convey the idea of viewers being imaginatively transported across the world. The middle-class home had been imagined as a theatre since Victorian times and was subsequently articulated through modern housing design. US post-war housing design reflected earlier modernist homes that accentuated theatricality and visual features as key organising principles. TV was represented as a socially healthy version of theatre that could be enjoyed within the privacy of the home without the discomfort of mixing with the masses (Spigel 1992).

The theatre became an organising metaphor for the middle-class home, reflecting the performative dynamics of everyday life. Architects, plan-book writers, religious leaders, domestic engineers, women's magazines and books on interior décor were variously describing the home as a 'stage' on which conventional social roles are played out by family members. To avoid the risk of entering potentially infected public spaces outside the home, family audiences could stage this home theatre in an 'antiseptic electrical space' (Spigel 1992). While advertisements showing glamorously dressed couples conveyed an imaginary night out in town, the idea of the home theatre and images of families gathered together round the TV 'hearth' evoked a reinstatement of leisurely family values. Advertisers managed to imply that TV could reconcile the paired yet contradictory aspirations for engagement in the public and the private world of traditional family life. TV presented imaginary travel to urban spaces at the same time as allowing families to stay together in the safety of the suburban home. However, later sociological studies uncovered the isolation that women often felt in their new suburban TV homes (Freidan 1963).

TV rapidly became the main leisure activity for children who, by the late 1950s, were watching an average of almost two hours of TV a day (Himmelweit et al. 1958). This generated public anxieties that TV was likely to replace cinema going and socialising with friends. Women's magazines alerted parents about the dangers that TV might present for children in the form of passive addiction or unruly behaviour. In this respect, the idea of the home theatre was tied to both utopian fantasies and dystopian anxieties about the prospects of family life and of gender and generational relationships in the home.

The domestication of television programming

TV was not only rendered familiar and habitual through its styling to match the furniture of the home. It was also a receiver of programmes that reflected and reinforced the normality and inevitability of domestic family life and suburban living. Despite opportunities to discover the outside world from the privacy of the living room, TV programming was, like radio before it, preoccupied with everyday domestic life. This medium played a vital role in media imaginaries of domestic space (as well as of travel away from home, addressed below). In the US, TV network advertisements offered women advice on how to juggle TV viewing with housework. Daytime TV was built around the imagined domestic routines and appropriate pastimes of housewives (Spigel 1992). Programmes such as soap operas comprised a series of short segments so that women could watch TV in a distracted manner while going about their household chores. Ideas about women's interests were promoted via variety and magazine TV programme formats centred on domestic life and providing advice to women about how to perform their housewife roles.

Daytime soap operas were initially introduced on US commercial TV to support and slot in between advertisements for soap. Together with situation comedies, these genres produced narratives involving family life that contributed to the domestication and normalising of TV within domestic routines (Spigel 1992). These programmes included series such as *I Love Lucy* (1951–1960, CBS), *Leave It to Beaver* (1957–1963, CBS/ABC), *The Adventures of Ozzie and Harriet* (1952–1966, ABC) and *Father Knows Best* (1954–1960, CBS). The scheduling of programmes around domestic daily routines in the home also promoted ideas of a 'family audience'. Spigel's reference to the theatricalisation of the home front suggests that, through both the promotion of family TV viewing and TV programmes, families themselves were conceived as a new and desirable spectacle. Hollywood stars were transported from the public movie screen to the sphere of the home through TV. This facilitated the negotiation of Hollywood's involvement in TV and consolidated its assimilation into the routine, everyday life of the housewife (Mann 1992).

When TV broadcasting was resumed in 1946 after the Second World War in the UK, it consisted only of public service broadcasting via the BBC. Unlike the US, no commercial TV was allowed until 1955. Initially, the BBC offered a series of specialist afternoon magazine programmes for women, with titles focusing on home and family life including *Designed for Women* (1947), *For the Housewife* (1948), *Leisure and Pleasure* (1951), *About the Home* (1951) and *Women's Viewpoint* (1951). These programmes were broadcast in an early-afternoon slot to attract female audiences. The content of these programmes played a major part in circumscribing women's roles and responsibilities in the home. From the mid twentieth century, national exhibitions were overtaken by TV programmes that influenced the institutions that promoted ideas about 'good design', the 'ideal home' and 'good living'. Model homes were now presented to audiences via TV programmes in their living rooms (Sparke 2004). Programmes such as *Designed for Women* and *Leisure and Pleasure* were typically located in cosy, feminised TV studio settings set up as comfortable, middle-class living rooms to present a traditional middle-class lifestyle centred on the home (Irwin 2015: 165). In 1953, the BBC appointed a dedicated head of TV programmes 'for women' (Irwin 2015; Andrews 2012). Exemplifying media imaginaries of early TV, the normalisation of the housewife role and the universalising of middle-class values as ideal lifestyles was a recurring theme throughout the early history of domestic media.

Women's magazines corresponded with TV programmes to cultivate domestic and consumer identities. As part of the early process of mediatising the home, TV formed the backcloth for a flood of popular discourses about the home, set within an explicit consumerist framework. In the UK, *House and Garden* displayed pictures of opulent home interiors while *Woman* magazine depicted the lifestyles of celebrities including Princess Margaret and famous actors (Irwin 2015: 166). Contrasting with women's lifestyle magazines of the period, certain TV programmes such as the BBC's *Wednesday Magazine* (1958–1963) conceived a female audience as perceptive and discriminating with an interest in the public world of the arts. These programmes addressed their female audiences not only as housewives and consumers but also as citizens and voters (Leman 1987; Irwin 2015). Topics such as architecture were repositioned within a domestic framework to provide cultural signifiers of the 'ideal' house and home. For example, Irwin (2015) provides an analysis of a specific episode of the *Wednesday Magazine* programme on the design and building of the new modernist house, Edritt House, in Mill Hill, North London. The programme moved between the domestic/ private and cultural/public divide but, significantly, kept returning the topic to domesticity. Irwin explains that:

> This is a transitional stage in the process of establishing a style of cultural television for a female audience. The house offers a look at a very aspirational and affluent lifestyle, especially so in a late 1950s Britain just emerging from a period of scarcity and austerity.
>
> *(Irwin 2015: 168)*

A whole discourse was created through TV programming to frame domesticity, femininity and aspirational home living, as Irwin (2015) confirms. Today, programmes such as *Grand Designs* (Channel 4, 1999–) that feature unusual and often elaborate architectural projects and series about house-hunting, such as *Location, Location, Location* (Channel 4, 2000–), are described as 'property porn',[3] providing a continuing focus on home to articulate consumerism and aspirational living in contemporary TV (also see Chapter 8).

David Morley (1992) emphasises the power of media texts to bring public life into domestic cultures and to actually shape those domestic cultures as national cultures. In the case of early TV, the experience of a 'public' realm was fostered in the context of private, domestic life by conveying a sense of belonging to a nation. For example, in the early 1950s the UK TV industry needed something more than product styling and persuasive magazine features to boost sales. It came in the form of the Coronation of Queen Elizabeth II in 1953, a major public event that won millions of households over to the new medium. Although there were only about two and a half million sets in use in the UK at the time, an estimated 20 million people watched at least part of the Coronation on TV on sets of friends, neighbours and in shop windows (Bussey 1980; Briggs 2000). Through scheduling and by broadcasting national events, the content of media are centrally involved in creating and communicating powerful ideas of the nation, of distant 'homelands' and of domestic space, thereby evoking both traditional and new imaginings of 'home' (Morley 1992; Hollows 2008; also see Chapter 7).

Benedict Anderson (1991) advanced the influential idea of the modern nation-state as an 'imagined community' to explain the need for a common understanding between the citizens in order to engage in a national consciousness. Despite not knowing their fellow citizens, members of a community form an idea of a communion with these strangers through the ritual of newspaper reading, listening to radio and watching TV to generate a sense of collective experience. Explaining that the development of the national newspaper laid the foundations for this imagined nation, Anderson states:

> It is imagined because the members of even the smallest nation will never know most of their fellow-members, meet them, or even hear of them, yet in the minds of each lives the image of their communion.
>
> *(Anderson 1991: 6)*

In the same way, the establishment of a national system of early broadcasting nurtured a sense of collective experience with other anonymous listeners and viewers, evoked through the content of broadcasting and by the weaving of TV schedules into households' daily routines. The programming of key items such as the news and soap operas at specific times of the day creates a sense of a common nation by collectively structuring the daily schedules of individual households across the country. However, this imagined community represents a particular version of family and nation: mainly white, middle class and heteronormative. Households and social groups that do not conform to these types of families and identities can become marginalised or excluded through these powerful media imaginaries (Hollows 2008). In terms of broadcasting schedules, the term 'dayliness' developed by Paddy Scannel (2000) describes how broadcasting contributes to the shaping of everyday routines. Radio and TV schedules slot into and shape daily routines in such a way as to confirm the ordinariness and inevitability of broadcasting and of those domestic routines. These schedules become so natural that audiences come to structure the temporal patterns of the day, week and year in a way that connect these domestic temporal rhythms with practices that traverse the nation

(Scannel 2000: 19–21; Gauntlett and Hill 1999). As a feature of the early stages of the mediatisation of the home, this form of assimilation can be identified as a 'normalisation of social practice' (Jansson 2013; see Chapter 1).

Domesticity, progress and portable TV

TV viewing was gradually integrated into family routines and into the spatial geography of the home, with the TV set rapidly becoming a mundane, 'tamed' item (Barthes 1977). But by the end of the 1950s, a new set of metaphors emerged to describe home as a place for travel. During this period of the 1950s and 1960s when TV gradually became a taken-for-granted medium, the TV console began to embody the social tensions associated with two apparently conflicting ideas: domesticity and progress. Spigel (1992) explains that the framework of 'theatricality' was connected with and gradually fed into the idea of 'mobility'. She refers to these new ideas about mediated travel away from home through the term 'mobile home' to suggest that watching TV encouraged audiences to cultivate a preoccupation with the potential of space travel and satellite technologies. The idea of TV as 'travel' was expressed through programmes about far away places and voyages of adventure and by its new material design as a portable set (Spigel 2001). This preoccupation corresponded with the introduction of cheaper, portable radios and second TV sets from the late 1950s and early 1960s. From an early stage, TV receiver design had signified the contradictions between a craft aesthetic and newly emerging styles associated with mass production, between styles of craftsmanship and the artistic principles of modernism. The arrival of portable TV promised something more exciting. Allowing more flexibility in styling, slimmer TV cabinets offered manufacturers a major opportunity to reconfigure the meanings of the TV set and increase sales through lower prices.

The TV set was liberated from its permanent place in the living room to convey an imaginative mobility. The TV set entered new imaginative territory by moving beyond the living room into kitchens, studies and bedrooms. This new item could now be positioned almost anywhere around the home, leading to the weakening of communal viewing habits. Yet, as Morley (2002: 92) reminds us, in terms of family household dynamics, communal family viewing was never an activity that occurred 'naturally'. Family-oriented viewing had to be carefully negotiated as part of family life, with evening meals often planned to coincide with regular TV programmes (Gauntlett and Hill 1999). Communal family viewing in the living room was therefore short-lived. Yet this idea has lingered as a powerful fantasy to this day (Morley 2002).

In 1956, a new portable set launched in the UK was advertised in the *Wireless and Electrical Trader* magazine with a clumsy but intriguing caption: 'ANNOUNCING CARRY-IT-AROUND TV'.[4] The 9-inch Ekco portable with FM radio sold for 66 guineas. It was placed in a moulded plastic box designed by E.K. Cole Ltd., operated by mains or 12-volt car battery, with built-in collapsible aerial (Chambers 2011). The handle on the top of the console resembled a suitcase handle. A mobile 'personal TV' was born, designed to be carried around like a piece of luggage. Recommendations for use were listed to help customers decide what to do with the gadget: 'IN THE HOME; AS A SECOND SET; IN SICKROOMS OR HOSPITALS; IN THE OFFICE OR BOARDROOM; IN HOTELS OR GUESTHOUSES; ON PICNICS; IN CARAVANS; ON HOLIDAYS AND MOTOR TOURS'. Householders were enticed, through design and lowered prices, to purchase second and third sets for use around the home. Yet the impulse to push the technology outdoors and mobilise it was striking. Two years later, in 1958, a 17-inch Ferguson portable TV set was named 'Flight 546' to emphasise its mobility. The advert displayed a picture of a portable TV set with a passenger aeroplane on its screen. Costing 58 guineas, the portable boasted a gold-plated telescopic aerial, and an 'ELEGANT CABINET, ONLY 14" DEEP OVERALL, COVERED WITH SIMULATED PIGSKIN, WEIGHT 31 ½ lbs ONLY' (Chambers 2011).

Needless to say, portable TV sets were seldom moved around the house, let alone outside the home. Awkward and heavy, these machines either had to be plugged into the mains or weighed down with heavy batteries. And outdoor reception quality was very poor. Nevertheless, portable TV in the 1960s captured the public imagination by triggering new metaphors of home and travel. The naming of these new portable designs was pure fantasy. In the US, by now the vanguard of portable TV engineering design, Philco launched a transistorised and battery powered portable set called the 'Safari' model, evoking images of embarking on an African hunting expedition, accompanied by the portable TV. The naming of these models was as crucial as the styling, capturing the idea of mobility and exotic outdoor adventure. General Electric produced the 'Adventurer', Zenith created the 'Jetliner' and RCA the 'Globe Trotter' with their stress on imaginary travel away from the home. Later, more practical mini portables were advertised in the US, using metaphors of transport. The idea of mobility and adventure associated with TV symbolised positive notions of portable culture (Spigel 2001). Portables designed with sun shields were advertised positioned beside swimming pools and at picnic sites to evoke an indoor–outdoor aesthetic.

During this period, futuristic designs associated with portability were inspired by the dawning of space travel in the US. A mobile notion of domesticity was conveyed via 1960s images that even depicted the home as a rocket. Spigel (2001) argues that the portable TV set expressed a 'privatised mobility'. The imagery of space-age domesticity signalled a break with the past, corresponding with ideas of the New Frontier promoted by President Kennedy's emphasis on space travel as a supreme sign of national progress. The high-tech world of telecommunications transformed ideas about private and public space: the metaphor of home as 'theatre' was overtaken by the idea of the home launched 'in orbit' (Baudrillard 1985; Spigel 2001). Inverting Williams' (1974) concept of mobile privatisation that described the reconnection of the privatised home with the public sphere, Spigel emphasises the aspirations of progressive family lifestyles and glamour of escape or travel away from the home conveyed in the popular media.

Shifting from feminine to masculine aspirations and identities, portable TVs implied a move away from ideas of home as a decorative feminine space for the pursuit of trivial pastimes in favour of a masculine, scientific space associated with elevated goals of national supremacy and citizenship (Spigel 2001: 390). The TV set now signified technological progress, mobility, modernity and adventure rather than cosy domesticity and family togetherness. The fantasies of portability in both design and in advertisements of the 1960s conveyed, then, an emergent set of gender and generational relations. A masculinisation of the technology was effected via associations with mobility and scientific progress.

In addition to masculine images of mobility and progress, the portable TV signified social class distinctions. In the UK, portable TVs often replaced large-screened sets in middle-class homes. Public debates about the potentially harmful effects of TV viewing in the 1960s, such as Mary Whitehouse's 'Clean-up Campaign',[5] coincided with widening accessibility to TV to influence class attitudes to the technology. Kudos was now attached to 'low' viewing. The middle classes expressed themselves as 'selective viewers'. A gradual switch occurred in terms of the relationship between social status, size of set and its prominence as an object in the living room. By the early 1970s, working-class homes were seen to possess the largest sets with the middle classes hiding portables discreetly among bookshelves.

Class distinctions in taste were also found by Ondina Fachel Leal (1995) in her study of the meaning of TV in Brazil. Like the British experience, the TV set in upper-class Brazilian homes was positioned more discretely, away from public view. Among the urban working classes, the TV set was regarded as a treasured possession with the set's status reflected by its prominent positioning in the lounge to show off the owners' successful 'modern life'. The TV set in working-class homes was surrounded by other meaningful ornaments to encourage the 'watching' of TV not only by members of the household but also by passers-by on the street, whether the set was switched on or off (Fachel Leal 1995). A contrasting trend was observable in the US, where large-sized sets were universally esteemed in living room settings. And, among large-screened sets in the UK, the concealment of the screen in a wooden cabinet, often with closing doors, persisted as a design theme right up to the 1980s alongside futuristic portable designs. Advertisements mirrored these contradictory images of craft tradition and scientific progress by mixing futuristic ideals of progress with highly sentimental images of home and nature (Kosareff 2005). This brings to mind Bruno Latour's observation, that 'modernity' represents the construction of systems that, incongruently, fuse together technology and nature (Latour 1993).

From communal to individual viewing

Portable designs not only reflected ideas about travel and adventure. They also corresponded with new TV-viewing habits during a period when, on both sides of the Atlantic, the home's 'aura of sharing and communality' was wearing thin (Cieraad 2006). As mentioned earlier, the position of receivers in the home branched out from the lounge to kitchens and bedrooms along with the growth in viewing, improvements in programmes, reliability of sets and, importantly, the introduction of domestic central heating. By the early 1960s, open-plan kitchens and living rooms were featuring in modern home architecture and design. The opening up of communal living space allowed housewives to supervise children, chat with husbands and watch TV while preparing meals (Cieraad 2006; Morley 2007). Yet open-plan architecture and family TV viewing began to clash with the individual projects of household members. It sparked domestic tensions about programme preferences and multiple uses of these communal spaces.

The arrival of a range of electronic products in the home from the 1960s onwards fostered home-based but separate, individualised tasks and undermined the ideals of shared use of space (Hirsch 1992; Silverstone 1991). Imaginative media mobilities that embraced the social tensions associated with domesticity and progress corresponded with a shift in emphasis from familialism to individualisation (Giddens 1992; Beck and Beck-Gernsheim 1995). As a feature of individualisation, family members' understanding of their social position and their interactions with other people is guided less by traditional duties and more by active personal choice and negotiation between individuals. The portable set was gradually designed to signify sole use through the production of more individualised devices with the addition of remote controls, headphones and muting switches. The device was marketed as a remedy for family fights over programme choice (Cieraad 2006). Advances in cable, satellite and video confirmed the demise of family-centred viewing and rise of more private, individualised viewing (Hirsch 1992). By the 1980s, children were regularly watching TV in their bedrooms and parents watched in the living room, with 80 per cent of British household TV viewing becoming dispersed (Gauntlet and Hill 1999). Portability and mobility came to symbolise the contradictions between passive, individualised 'bedroom viewing' and active, mobile viewing (see Chapter 4). Following the rise of portable TV, more personalised, communication technologies came to represent the tensions and pressures involved in managing the familiar binaries of personal/private and public/outdoors. This occurred during a period when traditional family values were being re-evaluated in relation to aspirations towards a democratisation of intimacy (Chambers 2012).

Initial representations of TV in advertisements and magazines as a 'harmonising' force were gradually overtaken by alternative visions of individuals being entertained separately, as isolated audiences. Families were depicted at home together yet apart: watching their chosen programmes on separate TV sets around the home. Spigel explains that these contradictory discourses about domestic media reflected the ideological tensions of the era. Critics and commentators maintained that TV might pose a danger to family life and did not belong in the family home (Spigel 1992). To promote family togetherness, TV was often conveyed as an ideal form of family leisure and useful medium to draw children into the home and spend more time in the company of the family. Yet, at the same time, children were depicted as potential prey to the power of TV. Such contradictory discourses and anxieties have also been triggered in connection with later technologies such as video games, mobile phones and computer tablets, as indicated in the following chapters.

Conclusion

This chapter indicates that early domestic technology broadcasting was propelled by a combination of commercial and idealistic impulses. The chapter has also identified some of the principle ways in which radio and TV are distinguished from other kinds of objects by chronicling the history of the design and styling of the technology for home use in relation to wider popular discourses that comprised media imaginaries of the time. With a focus on TV, the chapter indicates that early twentieth-century domestic media technologies comprised a vital stage of interpretative flexibility during which a range of media imaginaries were generated, deliberated and projected about their uses and adaptation to the home. The TV set's placement in the home in the 1950s comprised the beginning of the mediatisation of the home as an evolving process (Peil and Röser 2014: 237). TV manufacturers, designers, advertisers and popular media played a vital role alongside programming in this cultural process by presenting early versions of the apparatus as a device for embellishing the décor of the family home, elevating domestic femininity and fostering family togetherness. Characterised by ambivalent social attitudes towards newer media technologies, negative social responses posed challenges for the government, manufactures, designers and advertisers of TV receivers whose aim was to persuade households to embrace the equipment as both a domestic commodity and a moral worth.

The chapter has identified the key ways in which early television was distinguished from other kinds of objects by examining the intersecting roles of industrial design, marketing and programming in shaping the social meanings of TV sets during its early adoption. The expression of post-war national and familial values of good design and good living associated with the advancement of television technology in the UK was signified through a combination of TV content and console design. The medium was venerated via the aesthetic and material symbolism of the TV set, from craft-styled wooden consoles to 1960s' portable designs and also displays of these products at national exhibitions to promote 'good design'. Positioned within a domestic framework, British 1950s programmes on architecture and home design endorsed the object's status by providing cultural signifiers of the 'ideal' home and by conflating ideas about 'audience', 'consumer' and 'nation'. Portable TV designs invoked a sense of travel and personalised use, undermining notions of family togetherness associated with earlier notions of TV as the family 'hearth'. Through a focus on the relationship between design, programming and wider popular discourses, the chapter builds on the seminal work of scholars such as Morley, Spigel, Scannel, Moores and Hollows who have advanced understandings of the role of domestic media in communicating powerful ideas of nation, family and 'home'.

Social concerns about mobile forms of domestic leisure embodied in portable TV are indicative of more recent changes in work and leisure (Spigel 2001). The ideals of mobility, freedom and progress remain central themes in contemporary imaginaries of new digital technologies and domesticity, reflecting anxieties about individualisation and changing family life. Today, these concerns are conveyed through ideas about the movement of information between homes and work, exemplified by the introduction of the computer and then the rise of the digitally connected contemporary home explored in later chapters.

Notes

1 *On the Air*, the online radio and TV history centre, available at: *http://www.vintageradio. co.uk/htm/tvhistory.htm*, accessed 5 December 2015.
2 Available at: *www.thevalvepage.com/tv/baird/townsman/brochure.htm*, accessed 25 May 2010.
3 For an example of debates in the press about property porn, see London, B., 'Property Porn: The UK's Favourite New Guilty Pleasure', *The Daily Mail*, 10 September 2012, available at: *http://www.dailymail.co.uk/femail/article-2200949/Property-porn-The-UKs-favourite-new-guilty-pleasure.html*, accessed 25 May 2010.
4 Wireless and Electrical Trader 1956, available at *http://www.rewindmuseum.com/vintagetv. htm*, accessed 15 September 2010.
5 See Thompson (2012) for a study of Mary Whitehouse's campaigning activities.

References

Anderson, B. (1991) *Imagined Communities: Reflections on the Origin and Spread of Nationalism*, London: Verso.

Andrews, M. (2012) *Domesticating the Airwaves: Broadcasting, Domesticity and Femininity*, London: Continuum.

Bailey, M. (ed.) (2009) *Narrating Media History*, London: Routledge.

Barthes, R. (1977) *Image-Music-Text*, London: Fontana.

Baudrillard, J. (1985) 'The Ecstasy of Communication', in Hal Foster (ed.) *Postmodern Culture*, London: Pluto Press, pp. 126–134.

Beck, U. and Beck-Gernsheim, E. (1995) *The Normal Chaos of Love*, Cambridge: Polity Press.

Boddy, W. (2004) *New Media and Popular Imagination: Launching Radio, Television and Digital Media in the United States*, Oxford: Oxford University Press.

Briggs, A. (1979 [2000]) *The History of Broadcasting in the United Kingdom, Vol. 4: Sound and Vision*, Oxford: Oxford University Press.

Bussey, G. (1980) 'Vintage Television Receivers', in *The Great Optical Illusion*, Science Museum, London (A Philips Industries publication in Conjunction with Thorn Consumer Electronics for the Special Exhibition on Television, March to September).

Chambers, D. (2011) 'The Material Form of the TV Set: A Cultural History', *Media History* 17 (4), pp. 359–375.

Chambers, D. (2012) *A Sociology of Family Life: Change and Diversity in Intimate Relations*, Cambridge: Polity Press.

Cieraad, I. (2006) 'Introduction: Anthropology at Home', in Irene Cieraad (ed.) *At Home: An Anthropology of Domestic Space*, Syracuse, NY: Syracuse University Press, pp. 1–12.

Fachel Leal, O. (1990) 'Popular Taste and Erudite Repertoire: The Place and Space of Television in Brazil', *Cultural Studies* 4 (1), pp. 19–29.

Friedan, B. (1992 [1963]) *The Feminine Mystique*, Harmondsworth: Penguin.

Forty, A. (1986) *Objects of Desire: Design and Society Since 1750*, London: Thames and Hudson.

Gauntlett, D. and Hill, A. (1999) *TV Living: Television Culture and Everyday Life*, London: Routledge.

Giddens, A. (1992) *The Transformation of Intimacy: Sexuality, Love and Eroticism in Modern Societies*, Oxford: Polity Press.

Himmelweit, H.T., Oppenheim, A.N. and Vince, P. (1958) *Television and the Child: An Empirical Study of the Effect of Television on the Young*, London: Published for the Nuffield Foundation by Oxford University Press.

Hirsch, E. (1992) 'New Technologies and Domestic Consumption', in Roger Silverstone and Eric Hirsch (eds) *Consuming Media Technologies: Media and Information in Domestic Spaces*, London: Routledge, pp. 208–226.

Hollows, J. (2008) *Domestic Cultures*, Maidenhead: Open University Press.

Hopkins, H. (1961) *The New Look: A Social History of the Forties and Fifties*, London: Secker and Warburg.

Irwin, M. (2015) 'BBC's Wednesday Magazine and Arts Televison for Women', *Media History* 21 (2), pp. 162–177.

Jansson, A. (2013) 'Mediatisation and Social Space: Reconstructing Mediatisation for the Transmedia Age', *Communication Theory* 23 (3), pp. 279–296.

Jones, M. (2003) 'Design and the Domestic Persuader: Television and the British Broadcasting Corporation's Promotion of Post-war "Good Design"', *Design History* 16 (4), pp. 307–318.

Klinger, B. (2006) *Beyond the Multiplex: Cinema, New Technologies and the Home*, Berkeley, CA: University of California Press.

Kosareff, S. (2005) *Window to the Future: The Golden Age of Television Marketing and Advertising*, San Francisco, CA: Chronicle Books.

Lally, E. (2002) *At Home with Computers*, Berg: Oxford.

Latour, B. (1993) *We Have Never Been Modern*, London: Harvester Press.

Leman, J. (1987) 'Women's Programmes: Why Not?', in Helen Baehr and Gillian Dyer (eds) *Boxed In: Women and Television*, London: Pandora, pp. 84–92.

Maguire, P. and Woodham, J. (1997) *Design and Cultural Politics in Post-war Britain: The 'Britain Can Make It' Exhibition of 1946*, Leicester: Leicester University Press.

Mann, D. (1992) 'The Spectacularisation of Everyday Life: Recycling Hollywood Stars and Fans in Early Televison Variety Shows', in Lyn Spigel and Denise Mann (eds) *Private Screenings: Television and the Female Consumer*, Minneapolis, MN: University of Minnesota Press, pp. 41–70.

Marvin, C. (1988) *When Old Technologies Were New: Thinking about Communication Technologies in the Late Nineteenth Century*, Oxford: Oxford University Press.

Moores, S. (1993) *Interpreting Audiences: The Ethnography of Media Consumption*, London: Sage.

Morley, D. (1992) *Television, Audiences and Cultural Studies*, London: Routledge.

Morley, D. (2002) *Home Territories: Media, Mobility and Identity*, London: Routledge.

Morley, D. (2007) *Media, Modernity and Technology: The Geography of the New*, London: Routledge.

Morse, M. (1990) 'An Ontology of Everyday Distraction: The Freeway, the Mall, and Television', in Patricia Mellencamp (ed.) *The Logics of Television*, Bloomington, IN: Indiana University Press, pp. 193–221.

O'Sullivan, T. (1991) 'Television Memories and Cultures of Viewing 1950–65', in John Corner (ed.) *Popular Television in Britain*, London: British Film Institute, pp. 169–174.

Peil, C. and Röser, J. (2014) 'The Meaning of Home in the Context of Digital Mediatisation, Mobilization and Mediatisation', in Andreas Hepp and Friedrich Krotz (eds)

Mediatised Worlds: Culture and Society in a Media Age, Basingstoke: Palgrave Macmillan, pp. 233–252.

Scannell, P. (2000) 'For Anyone-as-Someone Structures', *Media, Culture and Society* 22 (1), pp. 5–24.

Schwartz, D. (2006) 'Modernism for the Masses: The Industrial Design of John Vassos', *Archives of American Art Journal* 46 (1–2), pp. 4–24.

Scrine, R.C. (1976) 'Milestones in Television History', *The Technical Journal of Rediffusion Engineering* 2 (5), pp. 142–147.

Silverstone, R. (1991) 'Beneath the Bottom Line: Households and Information and Communication Technologies in the Age of the Consumer', PICT Policy Research Papers, No.17, Oxford: PICT.

Silverstone, R. (1994) *Television and Everyday Life,* London: Routledge.

Silverstone, R. and Haddon, L. (1996) 'Design and the Domestication of Information and Communication Technologies: Technical Change and Everyday Life', in Roger Silverstone and Robin Mansell (eds) *Communication by Design: The Politics of Information and Communication Technologies*, Oxford: Oxford University Press, pp. 44–74.

Sparke, P. (2004) 'Studying the Modern Home', *The Journal of Architecture* 9 (4), pp. 413–417.

Spigel, L. (1990) 'Television in the Family Circle, the Popular Reception of a New Medium', in Patricia Mellencamp (ed.) *Logics of Television: Television, Essays in Cultural Criticism*, London: BFI Publishing, pp. 73–97.

Spigel, L. (1992) *Make Room for TV: Television and the Family Ideal in Postwar America*, Chicago, IL: University of Chicago Press.

Spigel, L. (2001) *Welcome to the Dreamhouse: Popular Media and Postwar Suburbia*, Durham, NC: Duke University Press.

Susman, W. (1984 [1973]) *Culture as History: the Transformation of American Society in the Twentieth Century*, New York: Pantheon, 1973, reprinted 1984.

Thompson, B. (2012) *Ban This Filth!: Letters from the Mary Whitehouse Archive*, London: Faber and Faber.

Vickery, A. (1993) 'Golden Age to Separate Spheres? A Review of the Categories and Chronology of English Women's History', *The Historical Journal* 36 (2), pp. 383–414.

Ward, K. (2006) 'The Bald Guy Just Ate an Orange: Domestication, Work and Home', in Thomas Berker, Maren Hartman, Yves Punie and Katie Ward (eds) *Domestication of Media and Technology*, Maidenhead: Open University Press, pp. 145–164.

Williams, R. (1974) *Television: Technology and Cultural Form*, London: Fontana.

3

THE DOMESTICATION OF MEDIA TECHNOLOGY

Introduction

Dominant meanings of 'home' suggest a calm haven away from outside disruptions, underpinned by notions of its privacy and separation or retreat from an 'outside' world. Yet, the media technology entering that space can often be an irritating reminder that home is a place of continuous change (Morley 2003). Chapter 2 has explained how the television (TV) set was historically marketed, designed and shaped for ease of acceptance within the household as part of a wider set of discourses that promoted a particular version of 'home' and 'family'. Production, design and advertising comprise powerful media imaginaries that attempt to 'pre-domesticate' technologies to conform to domestic values and meanings. However, these preceding processes cannot predict how media and communication technologies will be adopted or integrated within households once they cross the threshold. Further stages of domestication occur after the purchase of media equipment to ensure the equipment is tailored to the demands of the household (Silverstone 1994; Hollows 2008). Between the 1970s and 1990s, a range of new home entertainment and information communication technologies were entering the home including cable, TV, DVD, playstations and multimedia personal computers (PCs). By the late twentieth century, it was becoming clear that the home was no longer a retreat from technological change but, instead, a dedicated space for that change. The spread of PCs from workplaces to homes generated new opportunities for homeworking, thereby blurring and challenging traditional divisions between and meanings of 'work' and 'home'. From the 1980s onwards, PC connection to the internet could provide home access to a range of services including shopping, banking and information. From the 1990s, the home was gradually being defined by the technology within it.

The domestication approach uncovers the ways in which the cultural and social space of the home and social dynamics of the household are reconfigured by media and information technologies. When domestic media technologies are acquired and moved into the home, they are inscribed with meanings that allow them to be incorporated into the everyday routines of the household. Key decisions must be made about where media equipment should be positioned, when and how it should be used, by whom and for what length of time. Silverstone (2006) explains that media domestication is an evolving process involving a dynamic trajectory of evaluation and adjustment by household members. Through positioning and regular use, the technology is gradually integrated and contained. It steadily loses its strangeness or exotic status to become a routine piece of equipment embedded in everyday life (Silverstone and Haddon 1996). This process of integrating media technology into the everyday rhythms of the household is the subject matter of the domestication debate.

Through a focus on the micro-dynamics of media use in the home, the concept of domestication has been important in refuting arguments that new media, particularly the internet, represent a globalised space of flows and standardised set of media experiences. Domestication has approached media and equipment within the home as visible, physical objects as well as media content (Morley 2002, 2003). This chapter begins by explaining the conceptual and theoretical tools developed by the domestication approach. Second, it outlines the findings of a series of studies that show how media technologies are incorporated into everyday lives. The third section provides a critical review of the applicability of the approach in the context of mobilisation, personalisation and mediatisation.

The domestication of media technologies approach

Situated in the British and European cultural media studies tradition, the theoretical framework of 'domestication' critiqued earlier reductionist approaches to media. First, by stressing the active role of users in the process of media adoption, it challenged technological determinism, the media-centric model that assumed media to be the cause of particular societal changes (Morley 2006a: 28). Second, it critiqued media textual studies that neglected the everyday activities and contexts in which people viewed the media texts. The narrow scope of these approaches overlooked the complex social relations involved in using media. Work in the social sciences and media studies countered technological determinism by emphasising the importance of user needs and user engagement in the advancement of media technologies. Silverstone and Haddon took these aims a step further by identifying the technology's transformed meaning when it became a familiar everyday object in the home, as a process of integration of technological objects (Haddon 2003; Silverstone and Haddon 1996). Underpinning the domestication model, social constructivism addressed those aspects of social change relating to technological developments (Berker et al. 2006; Silverstone and Haddon 1996) and the study of technology (Latour and Woolgar 1979; MacKenzie and Wajcman 1985; Pinch and Bijker 1987; Williams and Edge 1996). 'Domestication' sought to identify the processes through which consumers and households assign meaning to media technologies in their efforts to 'manage and control their own electronic spaces and to make mass-produced objects and meanings meaningful, useful and intelligible to them' (Silverstone 1994: 64). With its focus on agency, domestication has also aimed to uncover the power struggles between householders involved in using the technology in the home.

The domestication approach initially built on and advanced research in the 1980s by David Morley on the *Nationwide Audience* (1980) and *Family Television* (1986). Highlighting questions of household composition and domestic viewing practices, Morley's groundbreaking study of family TV uncovered significant gendered patterns of media use. By shifting the focus from individuals to families, these studies confirmed that watching TV involves gender and generational frictions that influence the status and positioning of TV in the home. Morley's (1986) research described the family living room as a communal context in which a gendered power imbalance is confirmed by the father's domination over individual family members' programme preferences. The remote control tended to be used by men to control not only channel selection but also viewing decisions of the household involving the main TV in the shared space of the living room. Building on these findings, a series of studies conducted in the 1990s focused on the role of TV, telephone and teleworking in UK households. These involved research on the use of information and communication technologies (ICTs) by single parents and the young elderly (Silverstone 1999; Haddon 2000). In their study of single-parent families, Haddon and Silverstone (1995) distinguished between the 'household' and the 'home' to differentiate between the organisation of daily routines relating to material resources and the emotional idea of home as a place of belonging, security or anxiety. Initially, domestication researchers conceptualised distinctive stages in the domestication process that explain the dynamics involved in integrating media technologies in the home: commodification, appropriation, objectification, incorporation and conversion.

A pre-adoption phase of 'commodification' occurs when the potential owner may search for details about the features and facilities of the item and make plans in advance about its position and role in the home. 'Appropriation' deals with the whole process of consumption, particularly the point at which the object enters the home, is placed in a particular position and initiated through use. Yet the meanings attributed to the item are not fixed at this initial adoption phase. 'Objectification' focuses on the ways the object is used, including not only its functional use but also the way the object is aesthetically assigned a place in the home. The concealment of a TV set behind cocktail cabinet doors indicates a particular attitude to the technology which differs from that in a home where the TV set is proudly on display in the centre of the room. This objectification phase may involve exploring the features and potential of the technology. 'Incorporation' addresses a following phase when the object is assimilated into the temporal routines and everyday rituals that comprise the home, including how the object is used. For example, watching TV involves household routines about the type and sequence of programmes to watch and at what times of the day. Here, the device is gradually incorporated within the daily customs and rhythms of the household. 'Conversion' refers not only to the next 'taken-for-granted' stage but also to the symbolic enhancement of the household's public image. This may involve, for example, flaunting the new TV set or computer to neighbours and visitors. A process of 'continuous negotiation' occurs during this phase of conversion (Mansell 1996; Silverstone 2006). The meanings associated with the object may gradually stabilise during this phase, leading to near 'closure' (Pinch and Bijker 1987). At this point, the device may become a familiar, taken-for-granted object, integrated into the daily routines of the household. A phase of redefinition might occur if the device is integrated into another device within the process of technological conversion, such as a radio combined with a record player or, more recently, the combining of the TV set with internet use, via smart TV.

The domestication approach draws attention to the fluid or 'organic' nature of media adoption in the home as the meaning of the media technology may change over time (Mansell 1996: 26; Silverstone 2006; Wirth et al. 2008). For instance, a TV set may be moved from its central position in the living room into a bedroom and replaced by a newer set that then takes on the meaning of family viewing. In its new context in the bedroom, the meaning of the old set is likely to differ considerably by transforming into a more private and individual viewing device, as suggested in Chapter 2. Eventually, the device will take on meanings of oldness (Quandt and von Pape 2010).

Double articulation

Silverstone and Haddon (1996) added further theoretical features to the concept of domestication, namely 'double articulation' and 'moral economy'. The concept of double articulation of media technologies reminds us that the technology is an object and conveyor of media messages. Silverstone and Haddon (1996: 62) explain that meaning creation in relation to media technologies occur on at least two interdependent levels. The first articulation of media technologies involves the technology as object and its role as a consumer object: for example, the radio, TV set, computer, video game console or tablet computer. The second level of articulation addresses the use of and engagement with media in daily life, involving the texts, and patterns and social organisation of use including programmes, schedules, genres and software. The technical levels communicate the 'meaning of the commodity as object' while 'the texts and communications of these technologies' comprise the symbolic dimension in the sense of generating the messages. Thus, the concept of double articulation highlights the household's transformative relationship with the outside world (Peil and Röser 2014: 236). This conceptual tool was shown to be particularly effective in considering the whole process of the technology's integration in the home and for understanding media change.

As Silverstone and Haddon (1996) emphasise, the technologies as 'objects' need to be articulated first. They create connections between the outside world, households and individual household members, 'doubly articulated into public and private cultures' (Hartmann 2006: 86). For example, a study of the adoption of computers in the home by Leslie Haddon (1992) demonstrated that the technology did not simply add an extra object and facility to an existing range of objects and functions in the home. As a new media object, the computer affected the entire communication framework and all social interactions in the household. A further study by Haddon and Vincent (2004) on the introduction of mobile phones into the home found the same level of impact in terms of the mobile phone's role in managing all of the household's communication.

The second sense of the term 'double articulation' involving media content also concerns the ways in which the public and private spheres are interconnected and how they are manifested and expressed. The technological object and media messages are inscribed with public values and meanings that then become part of the private sphere of the household. This second level of articulation of media technologies involves a linking of the private worlds of users with the public worlds outside the home. Providing opportunities for constructing meanings and values in the private context of home, media draw householders into an expansive space of public and communal values. This second level of articulation provides individuals with the critical resources for developing an understanding of all elements of contemporary culture (Silverstone 1994: 123).

Moral economy

Domestication research also drew attention to the economic constrains and moral judgement involved in householders' constructions of domestic media spaces. Silverstone et al. (1992) found that the presence of media gadgets in the home poses a number of challenges in terms of regulating and maintaining boundaries between family activities. Major decisions are made by parents about what media to allow in the home, what kind of content is suitable for their children, and when and where it is appropriate for them to access it (see Chapter 4). Silverstone and colleagues explained that households comprise 'moral economies' which determine the way media objects are incorporated and used in the home. The household involves a series of delicate negotiations and exchanges or 'economies' at a moral level, through which household members deal with and negotiate challenges to their wellbeing (Silverstone 1994; Silverstone and Haddon 1996; Silverstone et al. 1992). The media forms one of the most active challenges to the household's moral economy. Through householders' negotiated practices, the moral economy involves navigation of and adaptation to these challenges. The household's moral economy aims to shield the home, and its members, against the disruptions that might be experienced through the introduction of media technologies in the home.

A range of technologies trigger moral exchanges about their use. Examples addressed in depth in Chapter 4 concern children's uses of media in the home and parental regulation. Parents with young children aim to protect their children from inappropriate content and establish an appropriate balance between the educational and entertainment uses of media by their children. This can involve a range of rules and inducements. Moral exchanges are prompted by questions about, for example, the number of hours children should be allowed to watch TV or play computer games; the use of smart phones by children; how to deal with online risks (also see Chapter 4). Thus, the transition of the media object from the 'formal' economy of the market place to the 'moral' economy of the household involves the perceived need to defend and preserve the ontological security of household members against the threat of mediatised change.

The values and ethics comprising a household are bound to be challenged and altered by the entrance of media technology in the home. The arrival of TV in the home from the 1950s, video games and PCs during the 1980s and 1990s, and, more recently, smart TV and computer tablets, have forced households to tackle a whole range of difficulties generated by the presence of these media objects in the home. These challenges include the reaffirming or disturbing content emitting from these objects as media texts. And, in terms of use, the layout of the home circumscribes the characteristics of the media in terms of use. For example, a TV or desktop computer located in the living room is likely to be domesticated differently from one placed in the bedroom or kitchen. The positioning influences the amount and type of media use by adults as well as children (see Chapter 4 and 5).

Early domestication research of the 1990s

The 1990s formed an important period when PCs were being introduced to the home. Empirical studies of the domestication of technology by Haddon included households of communal students, young adults, single parents and older people. The complexity of household composition in many homes prompted Haddon to consider the nature of the boundaries around them. New demands are made on ICTs when households are undergoing transition from one form to another, for example through divorce or when children enter or leave the home (Haddon 1992, 2000, 2006: 109). Haddon's studies of computer use uncovered the significance of the meanings attributed to computers from outside the home, in the workplace, before they entered the home as a domestic technology (Haddon 1992: 86). Like early radio, computers were initially used by gadgeteers who focused on the technological qualities of the hardware rather than the affordances of the software. This contrasts with the trajectory of the TV set which, as shown in Chapter 2, was designed and marketed exclusively for the home (Williams 1974).

By the early 1990s, computers were marketed not only as office equipment but also as domestic appliances to become an integral part of family life (Lally 2002). Yet they were not designed to look domesticated in the same way as early TV sets. Home computers continued to resemble workplace technologies. A few manufacturers tried to domesticate computers in a manner similar to wooden TV cabinet but, interestingly, these failed to appeal to householders. At the time, computers were viewed as a work technology rather than a leisure technology for home use. Wrapped in a coloured case, the Apple iMac eventually found one way of surmounting the problem. However, popular images of computers' domestic uses also supported their adoption in the home. Computer periodicals and women's magazines showed how the technology could be incorporated into household agendas by compiling household budgets, recipes and eventually by providing educational uses for children as well as adults (Lally 2002).

The arrival of 'interactive technologies' in the 1980s was accompanied by the claim that a large number of white-collar workers would, in future, work at home (Hamill 2011). A study of paid office work conducted from home involving computers, known as 'teleworking', was conducted in 1992 by Haddon and Silverstone to explore the relationship between home and paid work. A range of motives for teleworking were identified, including the desire to avoid commuting, support alternative work or entrepreneurship, and as a response to work problems, as a way of dealing with redundancy. Haddon and Silverstone (1992) found significant gender differences in use. It was predominantly women who tended to take up teleworking as a strategy to deal with the tensions emerging between their domestic and paid work role. Teleworking allowed women to prioritise their domestic role by fitting their paid work in with housework and childcare.

In addition to the structuring of time at home, the researchers found that work seeped into the home in a number of ways, not just as telework but also through the overspill of work into the home or through second jobs. It leads to a de-synchronisation of a person's free time from that of other household members and their social networks (Haddon and Silverstone 1993, 1995). In cases where people brought work home or initiated or received work-related messages at home, this often led to the entrance of ICTs into the home to support work, either by bringing a laptop home or the reduplication of work facilities in the home such as the PC. Some mobile workers either had their next day's work faxed to them at home or relayed to them as a phone message. More flexible working hours and 24-hour organisational operations led to more flexible time to consume ICTs. While teleworkers were constrained by the encroachment of paid work into home life, time-shifting technologies such as videocassette recorders (VCRs) and answering machines available by the early 1990s enabled people to cope better with the problem of being out of synch with conventional leisure schedules. Once placed in the home, use of the equipment extended from the teleworker to other family members who could then familiarise themselves with the technology by experimenting and developing their competences. This extension of office work into the home was, then, one of the major ways in which ICTs became domesticated and embedded in everyday home life. Conducting paid work at home could also change the experience of existing ICTs.

These teleworking studies uncovered the active yet also complex role played by home-workers in organising the computer to manage work from home, and the tensions involved (Silverstone 1994; Lie and Sørensen 1996; Lally 2002).

Teleworking domesticated the computer by shaping and constructing its everyday meanings in a household context. Yet, at the same time, the domestic arrangements of teleworkers are, to an extent, reconfigured by ICTs and work. In terms of the moral economy of the household, the domestication process is often problematic, not always seamless and sometime unsuccessful. With the PC viewed as a work tool, household tensions emerge when the technology starts to represent work or when other householders encroach on its use. Elaine Lally's (2002) research on home computers in Australia addressed the ways that the first generation users of computers at home integrated the technology within the everyday routines of the household and into the spatial arrangements of the home. Some households embraced and actively domesticated the technology, with users checking emails over a coffee. In other cases it took time for the household to incorporate the computer into the temporal rhythms of the home. Some households domesticated the technology by rearranging furniture and rooms to fit the technology into the home environment. Other domesticating practices included adornment of the machine with ornaments or cuddly toys or by making a decorative cover for the screen.

Several studies demonstrated that the domestication of these technologies reproduces conventional gender relations through the structuring of domestic routines. A Dutch study by Bergman and van Zoonen (1999) revealed that women used ICTs as an extension of their feminine roles by maintaining personal and family networks, and fostering community sharing and communication. They viewed internet communication as a virtual translation of feminine interests in personal contact, sharing, social networking and the sustaining of community. Another Dutch study of busy households found that ICTs can have almost contradictory roles that generate tensions relating to the acceptance of the medium (Frissen 2000: 70). ICTs are viewed as flexible tools that help manage mobility and everyday social interactivity. Yet they are also often seen as the reverse: time-consuming technologies that actually reduce adaptability and control. The range of research that drew on the domestication approach from the 1990s provided insights into the customs and practices of everyday life involving media technologies that were hitherto overlooked. The study of single-parents' uses of ICTs by Haddon (2000) highlighted social class as well as gendered and generational issues. Lone mothers with limited financial resources were constrained in their uses of media technologies. Most were anxious about the expense associated with their landline telephone use and felt the need to restrict use to cheap tariff periods (Haddon and Silverstone 1995). In the 1990s, telephone stamps offered a sense of control in saving for and spreading the cost of the phone bills. Telephone stamps were bought by lone parents to spread the costs of bills and offer some self-restraint. Haddon (2000) found that the landline phone was more significant to the young elderly.

Within these studies of the micro-social customs and practices of everyday life in the home, the domestication research perspective emphasised individuals' and households' 'agency' involved in the processes of integrating media artefacts in the home. These studies focused on the ways in which families and household members embedded media goods with existing household meanings and customs (Berker et al. 2006). Domestication research findings indicate that families and households often adjust to and appropriate media technologies in the home in ways that differ considerably from public discourses about media consumption.

Domestication research from 2006

Three decades after the initial work on the domestication of media and technology, a new corpus of work published by Thomas Berker and colleagues built on the initial domestication studies. This later research confirmed the central importance of place, with its focus on home. In the 1990s, arguments about the internet and new media heralded ideas about the rise of a placeless mode of communication and globalised, homogenised media experiences. However, by the first decade of the twenty-first century, domestication research was confirming that 'home' continues to be a germane concept in the context of new technologies and globalisation. Morley points out that while global media offer access to previously unknown places, 'place' remains paramount even in an age of global experiences. Morley (2010: 5) states that 'Cyberspace still has a very real geography', confirmed by the centrality of location within so many mobile connections. The domestication approach was applied through a set of case studies in more varied settings, from the traditional household to the small business. Researchers concurred that even after the technologies had been bought by the household, making them meaningful and slotting them into the space and life of the householders are 'ongoing processes rather than being a one-off event' (Haddon 2006: 196).

Building on the work of Haddon (1990), a study of the role of media technology in single-parent households in the UK by Anna Maria Russo Lemor (2006) demonstrates the hardships associated with lone parenthood. She draws on the sense of 'home' used by Haddon and Silverstone (1995), that is, the emotional and conceptual notion of a residence as a place of belonging and, at times, a space that may confer either security or anxiety. Russo Lemor also highlights the influence of public discourses of 'family' for single-parent families who are compelled to negotiate and contest domestic cultural ideals and notions of family life. In her sample of six single fathers and 16 single mothers, the children lived with their single parents for at least 40 per cent of the time with no other adults in the house. Single parents perceived 'home' as a dynamic and fluctuating set of relations and interactions between ex-partners, extended family and friends. These perceptions of home influenced the ways parents made decisions about their children's uses of media.

The single parents confirmed that economic, spatial, time management and psychological issues all impinge on the positioning and use of TVs and computers in the home. Their main concern was to forge a meaningful and secure setting for their children by sustaining rules and routines that the children had experienced before the break-up with the ex-partner. The aim of single parents was to balance their responsibilities and roles as caretakers, breadwinners, nurturers, disciplinarians, parents and playmates. One single parent placed the computer in the kitchen so that she could oversee her children's use of the internet and work while they played in the next room. Russo Lemor (2006) found that lack of time affected parents' use of media, particularly the use of computers. Computers were viewed as useful and affordable technologies for sustaining contact with friends and family or developing new acquaintances. Yet single parents often lacked time to socialise as a result of demands relating to household chores and childcare. In terms of leisure, single parents were constrained by limited financial resources, particularly in the cases of divorce and separation. This restricted the purchase of technologies for the home and, in turn, limited the role played by media in the home.

Single-parent families often form part of extended households, which involve parents' ex-partners and new partners (Russo Lemor 2006). Children whose parents are divorced or separated regularly access media across more than one household and are therefore more likely to engage with media within two distinctive moral economies (Lally 2002). Moreover, boys participating in computer gaming often move between groups of households as part of 'boy cultures' (Haddon 1992, 2006; Wheelock 1992; Furlong 1995). These empirical observations challenge the idea of households as static, unchanging units each with their own moral economies. Even within a single household, there may be 'multiple' homes (Lally 2002: 38). These studies have prompted the consideration of differing and conflicting moral economies rather than a single moral economy of the household (Green 2001: 182).

In her research on householders' uses of the internet, Maria Bakardjieva (2006) highlights the issues of household agency but also of unstable, blurred boundaries between public and private. Rather than acting as consumers of the internet, in the manner of conventional TV viewing, the householders she interviewed performed as active users, as producers. She also observed an unstable moral economy in which the family members were combining and blurring work and family practices in the home. The boundaries around domestic values and spaces are also explored by other authors such as Wellman and Haythornthwaite (2002) who suggest that blurring boundaries have become embedded into community building, family connections, education, complementing individual's existing networks, attitudes, behaviours and experiences.

Taking this a step further, Katie Ward (2006) refers to the 'domesticated internet' to emphasise that domestication is a non-linear process involving household agency. In interviews with families from north Dublin about their uses of technology at home, she found that integration of the computer and internet media into the household and family routines is a dynamic process. The technology is afforded a degree of agency that often generates conflicts over children's uses of the computer and over the organisation of spatial and temporal routines in the household. Those working from home differentiated between 'home' and 'work', explaining that their work and the technology became closely associated with one another. For Ward, the computer is ascribed status within an economy of meaning relating to the organisation of home, work and leisure; time and space.

The presence of ICTs in the home came to represent work to the families, with access to the computer facilitating 'home-work'.

A study of the role of media in Welsh homes by Mackay and Ivey (2004) found that the PC remained a 'hidden' medium, likely to be hidden away in a bedroom or office rather than displayed in shared living room spaces. This ambiguous relationship with the computer was also evident in Ward's study. She found that most users made attempts to balance the technology's ability to 'intrude' and 'disrupt' the household's value systems. Some families made clear distinctions between work and family life. Some did so by establishing rules and patterns surrounding the use of physical location of the computer. But working from home requires a degree of skill in management of physical and symbolic boundaries relating to the public and private spheres and work and family life. Ward emphasised the fragility of these home-work boundaries. With work and home overlapping, it became difficult to distinguish where one ended and the other began.

Domestication is, then, a dynamic process sometimes generating discord among family members (Ward 2006: 156). The strategies used to manage and accommodate the technology and to distinguish work from home, leisure and family space involved creating symbolic boundaries within the home through time, space and meanings attributed to the technology. Space and domestic and technological objects were carefully organised. Some subjects divided the household into zones. Spatial symbolism was used – when used upstairs the computer symbolised work, when used downstairs it symbolised leisure. For example, laptops were often positioned in upstairs studies to emphasise this distinction. These symbolic boundaries were also conveyed through two separate email addresses. The division of time into 'work' and 'family/leisure' and the attachment of specific meaning to all household media also helped distinguish work and leisure activities. For example, the TV symbolised leisure while the laptop symbolised work. Such strategies indicate the intrusion of technology and how its presence can incite certain behaviour. In today's era of mobile domestic technologies involving media convergence and mobile technologies, issues of 'intrusion' and 'interruption' are likely to be redefined and renegotiated within the framework of a new multi-screen home (see Chapter 6). The mobile quality of touchscreen technology prompts a reassessment of the strategies of domestication, confirming the dynamic process of accommodation and management emphasised by past studies such as Ward's.

An investigation of Chinese households by Sun Sun Lim (2006) extends what have been mainly western case studies. Through interviews with parents and children in 20 one-child families in Shanghai and Beijing, she considers the intricate relationship between China's one-child policy, growing consumerism and the values that urban middle-class families assign to new ICTs. Chinese consumerism is a relatively recent phenomenon with significant growth in personal incomes and ready access to material goods in China's urban cities in the 1990s (Lu 2000). The functional and symbolic value of ICTs has made them prized objects of this consumerism. Expanding consumerism has facilitated the expression of individuality through consumption, allowing urban Chinese households to ignore or negotiate ideological indoctrination by the state (Wei and Pan 1999). New consumer desires stimulated by advertising have heightened pressure to keep up with peers (Gamble 2003). It has been said that before the rise of urban Chinese affluence, individuals aspired to four status symbols: bicycles, watches, sewing machines and radios (Yan 1994). More recent status symbols associated with affluence were VCRs, TVs, washing machines, cameras, refrigerators and electric fans. By 2003, this list of desired objects also included newer ICTs such as computers, mobile phones and digital cameras (Euromonitor 2003). Once a compelling status symbol, the smart phone became a common and familiar personal gadget.

ICTs are no longer regarded as luxuries in urban China but as essential components of the home space. These communication technologies are seen as integral to social advancement yet also as potentially addictive. Parents become active mediators of their children's ICTs use. Lim (2006) found that parents moderated their enthusiasm for new ICTs in their efforts to control children's uses within the moral economy of the household. The dual qualities of ICTs as shared and communal, and as individuated and personal, enabled negotiation of the domestic private–public boundaries to harmonise with families' priorities. The control that parents attempted to exert over their children's ICTs uses confirmed both the compartmentalisation of children's leisure time and the high regard for educational achievement in Chinese culture. The use of ICTs for social advancement, connecting the family with its guanxi network[1] and facilitating social inclusion by one's peers, were symptomatic of the growing importance of ICTs in Chinese society today. In these ways, urban Chinese families' processes of ICTs domestication navigated two paradoxical cultural trends: the unpredictable forces of modernisation and the enduring values of tradition (Lim 2006).

In a German study of media's entrance into the household, Quandt and von Pape (2010) demonstrate that gendered distinctions between shared and personal devices continue to structure the entrance of media in the home. Men are still regarded as the gatekeepers in terms of bringing the new device into the home, although this can vary according to media type. The future user of the technology is not inevitably the person who makes the purchasing decision. The researchers discovered that highly personalised gadgets such as mobile phones tend to be selected by the user while shared media devices such as computers are likely to be chosen by men and used by other household members. Although this is now being challenged by a growing personalisation of media gadgets such as computer tablets, Chapter 6 indicates that advertisements of mobile domestic technologies continue to promote gender differences in household routines.

Quandt and von Pape combined their ethnographic observations with additional photographic documentation of the positioning of media equipment in the household. Computers were often placed in rooms that lacked clearly organised arrangements and integration rules and even in spaces that were ergonomically awkward. Quandt and von Pape state: 'They [computers] are a source for "pollution" of the home environment.' This was particularly the case when computers were positioned in the study, the most obvious place to find them. These rooms were usually badly organised with a muddle of material and devices. Compared to other rooms, studies were more likely to be 'sloppy' or even dirty with 20 per cent of studies in this state. By contrast, the researchers found that TV sets are usually positioned in settings designed specifically for TV viewing in a social and leisure context. The majority of the living rooms, two-thirds of them, contained special TV furniture with the chairs positioned around the TV set in a conventional manner. The TV set was typically housed in a large cabinet with a large sofa opposite, facing it, which Quandt and von Pape call the 'TV shrine', echoing earlier notions of the TV set as the new hearth.

In the past, older media devices remained in the home while they continued to be workable. Householders were usually unwilling to spend money on updating and replacing devices for the sake of it. Nowadays, new and cheaper personalised devices are sought more frequently since they generally offer superior affordances and ease of use as well as the kudos associated with innovative items and early adoption. Nonetheless, certain studies have identified the co-existence of old (analogue) and new (digital) technological devices (Mackay and Ivey 2004; Quandt and von Pape 2010). For example, Quandt and von Pape (2010) found that certain traditional equipment such as TV sets and stereo systems were replaced more slowly than personalised items, being regarded as long-term investments. In time, these 'duels' between old and new would be won by the 'new' devices, according to Quandt and von Pape (2010: 338). Although the industry's drive towards more personalised objects leads to more rapid generational change, it only occurs when the newer devices have obvious user advantages. While laptops present in households were mostly current models, desktop devices tended to be older models, lagging one or two generations behind the current technology (Quandt and von Pape 2010: 339). The cheaper, more mobile and more personalised the technology, the stronger the willingness to replace it.

As yet, little research is available on patterns of media use among lesbian, gay, bisexual and transgender (LGBT) households. Nonetheless, studies of the household expenditure of LGBT consumers in the US indicate that gay male households have the highest disposable income among LGBT households, reflecting the higher incomes of men in general (see the 2013 *LGBT Report* by Experian). Household income among partnered lesbians falls short of all partnered women, since the latter includes the income of men (Experian 2013). The higher discretionary spending among gay male households indicates that these households are likely to be rich in media equipment. Notable research by Stonewall (2011) on the portrayal of LGBT youth on TV in the UK has found that ordinary gay people are almost invisible on the 20 most popular programmes watched by youth in the UK. Out of 126 hours of output, only 46 minutes represent gay people positively and realistically. In 2010, three-quarters of the portrayals were confined to only four programmes on Channel 4 and ITV1 programmes: *I'm a Celebrity, Get Me Out of Here*; *Hollyoaks*; *Emmerdale*; and *How to Look Good Naked*. On BBC 1, there were just 44 seconds of positive and realistic portrayals of gay people in over 39 hours of output. These disturbing findings are likely to affect the choices made by LGBT households in their media habits, indicating that they are more likely to access media content more selectively through the use of new media devices in the home. American findings suggest that LGBT consumers tend to focus on LGBT-focused media sites (Experian 2013). These emerging findings provide indications that LGBT households are likely to display certain distinctive features when it comes to the domestication of media in the home.

Domestication and mediatisation

While acknowledging the vital role of the domestication perspective in media research, a group of scholars regard the use of the central term 'domestication' to be analytically ambiguous. Helle-Valle and Slettemeås (2008) argue for an uncoupling of 'domestication' from the domestic and the private in order to facilitate use of the term to understand 'acts' of domestication. They argue that processes of 'taming the wild' occur in wider contexts to highlight broader processes of enculturation. Joanne Hollows (2008) also extends the concept of domestication to address important ways in which aspects of the public sphere are 'domesticated' with, for example, office spaces and coffee shops styled to resemble living rooms. Although recognising that competing moral economies exist within one household, Hartmann (2009) suggests that the idea of household structure may now be obsolete, arguing that the sense of familiarity, belonging and ontological security associated with the use of media in the home now extends to mobile technologies such as the laptop or mobile phone rather than the home. 'A sense of continuity and order might indeed become more related to the actual objects in question' (Hartmann 2009: 233). Alternatively, suggests Hartmann, perhaps the Wi-Fi café or the individual programme or website may also gain significance in terms of evoking a sense of belonging. Hartmann argues that all these possibilities now require investigation in a world of mobile media.

The domestication approach has been questioned in more recent studies of mobile technologies in which the home is deemed less relevant (for example, Vuojärvi et al. 2010). On the one hand, the extensive use of mobile technologies such as smart phones and computer tablets in the home coincides with changing meanings of home, indicating that the home context remains pertinent in debates about the mediatisation of space (Lebfreve 1974; Jansson 2013; see Chapter 6). On the other hand, the vital role played by the mobile phone for new migrants in conferring a sense of normality is identified in Chapter 7. By supporting familial and intimate connections 'back home' while negotiating an alien space, this personal mobile device helps combat feelings of isolation and loneliness (Bonini 2011: Horst 2006). This indicates that a process of 'mobile domestication' is involved in individuals' relationships to the device to negotiate the challenges associated with being on the move and then settling in a new country.

Similarly, Neil Selwyn (2003) extends the domestication concept from the home to the individual user. He argues that ICTs are now less 'fixed' to the confines of particular spaces, institutions or power supplies for network connections. Selwyn states that:

> It can be argued that technologies go through a process of domestication into the 'moral economies' of people's lives as well as across all the institutional settings that they are brought into. Therefore each individual will be constantly negotiating the 'proper placement of technology' into their lives according to a range of personal and institutional factors.
>
> *(Selwyn 2003: 110)*

Thus, the accelerated growth of mobile, personalised media technology indicates a need to further reassess the domestication approach. Emphasising the formative power of personal media in everyday life, Terje Rasmussen (2014) argues that the concept of 'domestication' needs to be updated in line with recent social and technological change to understand current personalised media use. By linking the concept of domestication to the concept of lifeworld, Rasmussen addresses domestication more specifically as 'personalisation'. Together with media convergence, these trends correspond with key changes in household compositions and family structures. These changes include transnational families created through cross-border migration as well as increases in other types of households such as households comprised of older people, single people, single parents and households containing adult children associated with the life phase of 'extended youth' and 'boomerang generation'.

Revising the five stages of the domestication process of commodification, appropriation, objectification, incorporation and conversion, Katie Ward (2006) identified a sixth prior stage of domestication, 'imagination'. This stage of the process of household integration is linked to but precedes commodification. After the stage of production and before the potential consumer reaches the point of buying the media artefact, Ward argues that the consumer enters the phase of 'imagination', where advertising stimulates a desire for the media object. The initial stage of imagining is, then, when the technology is enculturated into the wider social imagination and, indeed, into the national consciousness. It forms the public representation of mediated intimacy involving the cultural work during the period of initiation through design and marketing strategies to overcome the potential fears and anxieties about the new product whether it be a TV set, music system, PC or tablet. Ward's stage of 'imagination' resonates with the concept of 'media imaginary' I have adopted and introduced in the previous two chapters and used to explore early TV. This is not just an initial phase of domestic adoption of media technologies in the home. It also forms a powerful discursive frame around the whole process of media adoption. Media imaginaries about home and domestic space play a key role in defining that space not only through wider discourses about media but also via media content, indicating the need for an understanding of the dialectical relationship between home and media content.

Likewise, Hartmann (2009) advocates the assignment of a renewed emphasis on 'imagination' as a preceding phase of the domestication process. Related to this, she proposes adding another level to the process of domestication: the idea of 'discursive domestication'. She explains that this is the least material dimension of the process, given the imaginative work undertaken by potential or actual consumers in their media participation. Integrated into the moral economies as justifications for media acquisition, uses, and whole lifestyles, these discursive appropriations occur at many levels: societal, organisational, youth cultural, familial, and at the level of individuals and so on. Hartmann asserts that this imaginative work is everywhere. It involves the whole discursive construction around new media including the utopian and dystopian debates and the possible social consequences of media advancement in institutional and everyday life. At a societal level, imaginative work is involved in visions such as the 'information society' or 'information highway'.

The growing mediatisation of home and everyday life means that the characteristics and sense of our existence in the world is increasingly multifaceted and complicated. Explaining how mediatisation and domestication are interlinked, Hartmann (2009: 234–235) states that the domestication process demonstrates at a micro-level what mediatisation conveys at a meta-level. The current escalation in the digitisation and mobilisation of media involve major shifts in the uses and roles of media in and beyond the home. As Hartmann states, domestication plays a vital role by acting as a 'coping mechanism' to deal with mediatisation. Referring to mediated domestication and a domesticated mediatisation, Hartmann also emphasises that mediatisation cannot occur without domestication, since mediatisation progresses through the routine, everyday mediated activities as well as via global institutions.

Domestication is therefore situated in broader historical and national cultures. Taking part in a collective experience of the nation is cemented through major events such as national ceremonies, events in the national calendar such as Thanksgiving and Christmas and through everyday routines such as watching soap operas, as mentioned in Chapter 2. In these ways, broadcasting has performed a major role as part of multiple popular discourses, in shaping and fixing people's conceptions of the relationship between the ideological constructs of 'public' and 'private'. This process has not only functioned by experiencing the 'public' realm via media content in a domestic context but also by the domestication of the public sphere itself (Andrews 2012; Hollows 2008; Morley 1992: 285). Concurrently, the media domestication of the public sphere ensures the socialisation or regulation of the private realm. Media technologies facilitate the extension of social relationships outwards in terms of time and space as a feature of late modernity. These dialectical cultural processes are features of mediatisation that form macro-social dimensions of a domestication of the public sphere. While media imaginaries entail the construction of the 'public' and 'private', householders engage with media through routines that negotiate imaginaries in the context of the social constraints and opportunities involved in their daily lives.

Conclusion

To summarise, the domestication approach has contributed to an understanding of the role played by media and information technologies in the home in several key ways. First, the approach has circumvented the technological determinism of past media studies by providing an intellectual awareness of the co-determined, co-constructed nature of the dynamics between practices in the home and media technology (Silverstone 2006: 230). Second, this was achieved by emphasising householders' agency in domesticating media technologies and the ways that they integrate them into existing meanings, values and everyday practices. Findings confirmed that this process of appropriation can be unpredictable by diverging from the intensions of producers, advertisers and overt popular discourses surrounding media technologies. Conversely, the research also revealed the active role that these home-workers played in shaping and constructing, domesticating and organising the computer to contain and organise work. Third, the approach uncovered the moral economy of households and negotiated practices involved in the integration of media and ICTs in the home. Researchers found that the domestication process is problematic, not always seamless and sometime unsuccessful. A particular focus on home-workers in the 1990s, a time when computers were being introduced into the home, indicated that women were centrally involved in home-working as a way of managing their domestic and work duties. Research confirmed that new technologies play a central role in reinforcing gendered roles and hierarchies. The domestic arrangements of home computer users are, to an extent, reconstituted by ICTs and work.

A fourth feature of the domestication approach is the concept of double articulation that identifies the ways in which media technologies are experienced both as consumer objects and in terms of the patterns and social organisation use that include media content and software. Related to this, a fifth attribute of domestication research is that it highlights the fluid nature of the boundaries of a household or a family. The approach contributed to an understanding of the ways in which traditional boundaries between home and work, between the private and public spheres, are both evoked and breached by media and ICTs. Finally, researchers identified the role of media in both confirming and contesting the constructed meanings of the 'domestic' as a set of spaces and practices. The approach emphasises the ways in which the technology has the capacity to sustain, reflect and reform domestic arrangements. As Morley states, in his discussion of the domestication of electronic technologies via the 'smart house': 'technologies are no longer merely supplementary to, but constitutive of what the home itself now is' (Morley 2006b: 214).

The chapter has also addressed critiques and advancements of the domestication approach. The roles played by today's personalised mobile technologies such as smart phones and computer tablets indicates the need to advance the domestication beyond the household to understand the implications of the continuous traversing and reshaping of public and private spheres through mobile media. This indicates the need to consider the mediatisation of society and everyday life as a social process linked to domestic life through a digitalisation and mobilisation of personal and familial relationships. By highlighting the media saturation of society, the concept of mediatisation engages with the macro-social ways in which 'the home' is mediatised. Domestication operates as a set of household strategies to deal with this diffusion of media throughout all institutions and social exchanges. The following chapters explore these emerging themes and concerns through topics which include children's uses of home-based media and media parenting; the roles played by media and communication technologies among migrants and transnational families; and through case studies of video gaming, mobile domestic media such as computer tablets and visions of the technologised 'smart home' and 'connected home'.

Note

1 A guanxi network refers to personalised networks of influence or network of social contacts in Chinese society.

References

Andrews, M. (2012) *Domesticating the Airwaves: Broadcasting, Domesticity and Femininity,* London: Continuum.

Bakardjieva, M. (2006) 'Domestication Running Wild: From the Moral Economy of the Household to the Mores of a Culture', in Thomas Berker, Maran Hartmann, Yves Punie, and Katie Ward (eds) *Domestication of Media and Technology,* Maidenhead: Open University Press, pp. 62–79.

Bergman, S. and van Zoonen, L. (1999) 'Fishing with False Teeth: Women, Gender and the Internet', in John Downey, and Jim McGuigan (eds) *Technocities,* London: Sage, pp. 91–108.

Berker, T., Hartmann, M., Punie, Y. and Ward, K.J. (2006) 'Introduction', in Thomas Berker, Maran Hartmann, Yves Punie, and Katie Ward (eds) *Domestication of Media and Technology,* Maidenhead: Open University Press, pp. 1–16.

Bonini, T. (2011) 'The Media as "Home-making" Tools: Life Story of a Filipino Migrant in Milan', *Media, Culture & Society* 33 (6), pp. 869–883.

Euromonitor (2003) Consumer Lifestyles in China (February 2003).

Experian, (2013) *The 2013 LGBT Report,* Experian Marketing Services, available at: *http://www.experian.com/assets/simmons-research/white-papers/2013-lgbt-demographic-report.pdf,* accessed 5 December 2015.

Frissen, V.A. (2000) 'ICTs in the Rush Hour of Life', *The Information Society* 16 (1), pp. 65–75.

Furlong, R. (1995) 'There's No Place Like Home', in Martin Lister (ed.) *The Photographic Image in Digital Culture,* London: Routledge, pp. 170–187.

Gamble, J. (2003) *Shanghai in Transition: Changing Perspectives and Social Contours of a Chinese Metropolis,* London: Routledge Curzon.

Green, E. (2001) 'Technology, Leisure and Everyday Practices', in Eileen Green and Alison Adam (eds) *Virtual Gender: Technology, Consumption and Identity,* London: Routledge, pp. 173–188.

Haddon, L. (1990) 'Researching Gender and Home Computers', in Knut Sørensen and Anne-Jorunn Berg (eds) *Technology and Everyday Life: Trajectories and Transformations*, Trondheim: University of Trondheim, pp. 89–108.

Haddon, L. (1992) 'Explaining ICT Consumption: The Case of the Home Computer', in Roger Silverstone and Eric Hirsch (eds) *Consuming Technologies: Media and Information in Domestic Spaces,* London: Routledge, pp. 82–96.

Haddon, L. (2000) *Old and New Forms of Communication: E-mail and Mobile Telephony,* a report for British Telecom, November.

Haddon, L. (2003) 'Domestication and Mobile Telephony', in James Katz (ed.) *Machines That Become Us: The Social Context of Personal Communication Technology*, New Brunswick, NJ: Transaction Publishers, pp. 43–56.

Haddon, L. (2006) 'The Contribution of Domestication Research to Home Computing and Media Consumption', *The Information Society* 22 (4), pp. 195–203.

Haddon, L. and Silverstone, R. (1992) 'Information and Communication Technologies in the Home: The Case of Teleworking', *Working Paper 17*, SPRU CICT, University of Sussex: Falmer.

Haddon, L. and Silverstone, R. (1993) 'Teleworking in the 1990s: A View from the Home', *SPRU/CICT Report Series*, No. 10, University of Sussex, Falmer.

Haddon, L. and Silverstone, R. (1995) 'Lone Parents and Their Information and Communication Technologies', *SPRU/CICT Report Series*, No. 12, University of Sussex: Falmer.

Haddon, L. and Vincent, J. (2004) 'Managing a Communications Repertoire: Mobile vs Landline', Fifth Wireless World Conference Managing Communications, University of Surrey, 15–16 July.

Hamill, L. (2011) 'Changing Times: Home Life and Domestic Habit', in Richard Harper (ed.) *The Connected Home: The Future of Domestic Life*, London: Springer, pp. 29–58.

Hartmann, M. (2006) 'The Triple Articulation of ICTs: Media as Technological Objects, Symbolic Environments and Individual Texts', in Thomas Berker, Maren Hartmann, Yves Punie, and Katie Ward (eds) *Domestication of Media and Technology*, Maidenhead: Open University Press, pp. 80–102.

Hartmann, M. (2009) 'Everyday: Domestication of Mediatisation or Mediatized Domestication?', in Knut Lundby (ed.) *Mediatization: Concept, Changes, Consequences*, New York: Peter Lang Publishing, pp. 225–242.

Helle-Valle, J. and Slettemeås, D. (2008) 'ICTs, Domestication and Language-Games: A Wittgensteinian Approach to Media Uses', *New Media and Society* 10 (1), pp. 45–66.

Hollows, J. (2008) *Domestic Cultures*, Maidenhead: Open University Press.

Horst, H.A. (2006) 'The Blessings and Burdens of Communication: Cell Phones in Jamaican Transnational Social Fields', *Global Networks* 6 (2), pp. 143–159.

Jansson, A. (2013) 'Mediatisation and Social Space: Reconstructing Mediatisation for the Transmedia Age', *Communication Theory* 23 (3), pp. 279–296.

Lally, E. (2002) *At Home with Computers*, Berg: Oxford.

Latour, B. and Woolgar, S. (1979) *Laboratory Life: The Construction of Scientific Facts*, Princeton, NJ: Princeton University Press.

Lefebvre, H. (1974/1991) *The Production of Space*, Oxford: Blackwell.

Lie, M. and Sørensen, K.H. (1996) 'Making Technologies Our Own? Domesticating Technology into Everyday Life', in Merete Lie and Knut H. Sørensen (eds) *Making Technologies Our Own? Domesticating Technology into Everyday Life*, Oslo: Scandinavian University Press, pp. 1–30.

Lim, S.S. (2006) 'From Cultural to Information Revolution: ICT Domestication by Middle-class Chinese Families', in Thomas Berker, Maran Hartmann, Yves Punie and

Katie Ward (eds) *Domestication of Media and Technology*, Maidenhead: Open University Press, pp. 185–204.

Lu, H. (2000) 'To Be Relatively Comfortable in an Egalitarian Society', in Deborah Davis (ed.) *The Consumer Revolution in Urban China*, Berkeley, CA: University of California Press, pp. 124–144.

Mackay, H. and Ivey, D. (2004) *Modern Media in the Home: An Ethnographic Study*, Rome: John Libbey.

Mackenzie, D. and Wajcman, J. (eds) (1985) *The Social Shaping of Technology*, Buckingham: Open University Press.

Mansell, R. (1996) 'Communication by Design', in Robin Mansell and Roger Silverstone (eds) *Communication by Design*, Oxford: Oxford University Press, pp. 15–43.

Morley, D. (1980) *The 'Nationwide' Audience: Structure and Decoding*, London: BFI.

Morley, D. (1986) *Family Television: Cultural Power and Domestic Leisure*, London: Comedia.

Morley, D. (1992) *Television, Audiences and Cultural Studies*, London: Routledge.

Morley, D. (2002) *Home Territories: Media, Mobility and Identity*, London: Routledge.

Morley, D. (2003) 'What's "Home" Got to Do With It? Contradictory Dynamics in the Domestication of Technology and the Dislocation of Domesticity', *European Journal of Cultural Studies* 6 (4), pp. 435–458.

Morley, D. (2006a) 'What's "Home" Got to Do With It? Contradictory Dynamics in the Domestication of Technology and the Dislocation of Domesticity', in Thomas Berker, Maran Hartmann, Yves Punie, and Katie Ward (eds) *Domestication of Media and Technology*, Maidenhead: Open University Press, pp. 21–39.

Morley, D. (2006b) *Media, Modernity and Technology: The Geography of the New*, London: Routledge.

Morley, D. (2010) 'Domesticating Dislocation in a World of "New" Technology', in Chris Berry, Soyoung Kim and Lyn Spigel (eds) *Electronic Elsewheres: Media Technologies and the Experience of Social Space*, Minneapolis, MN: University of Minnesota Press, pp. 3–16.

Peil, C. and Röser, J. (2014) 'The Meaning of Home in the Context of Digital Mediatisation, Mobilization and Mediatisation', in Andreas Hepp and Friedrich Krotz (eds) *Mediatised Worlds: Culture and Society in a Media Age*, Basingstoke: Palgrave Macmillan, pp. 233–252.

Pinch, T. and Bijker, W. (1987) 'The Social Construction of Facts and Atifacts: Or How the Sociology of Science and the Sociology of Technology Might Benefit Each Other', in Wiebe Bijker, Thomas Hughes, and Trevor Pinch (eds) *The Social Construction of Technological Systems: New Directions in The Sociology and History of Technology*, Cambridge, MA: MIT Press, pp. 17–50.

Quandt, T. and von Pape, T. (2010) 'Living in the Mediatope: A Multimethod Study on the Evolution of Media Technologies in the Domestic Environment', *The Information Society* 26 (5), pp. 330–345.

Rasmussen, T. (2014) *Personal Media and Everyday Life: A Networked Lifeworld*, Basingstoke: Palgrave Macmillan.

Russo Lemor, A.-M. (2006) 'Making a "Home": The Domestication of Information and Communication Technologies in Single Parents' Households', in Thomas Berker, Maran Hartmann, Yves Punie, and Katie Ward (eds) *Domestication of Media and Technology*, Maidenhead: Open University Press, pp. 165–184.

Selwyn, N. (2004) 'Reconsidering Political and Popular Understandings of the Digital Divide', *NewMedia and Society* 6 (3), pp. 341–362.

Silverstone, R. (1994) *Television and Everyday Life*, London: Routledge.

Silverstone, R. (1999) *Why Study the Media?* London: Sage.

Silverstone, R. (2006) 'Domesticating Domestication: Reflections on the Life of a Concept', in Thomas Berker, Maran Hartmann, Yves Punie, and Katie Ward (eds) *Domestication of Media and Technology*, Maidenhead: Open University Press, pp. 229–247.

Silverstone, R. and Haddon, L. (1996) 'Design and the Domestication of Information and Communication Technologies: Technical Change and Everyday Life', in Roger Silverstone and Robin Mansell (eds) *Communication by Design: The Politics of Information and Communication Technologies*, Oxford: Oxford University Press, pp. 44–74.

Silverstone, R., Hirsch, E. and Morley, D. (1992) 'Information and Communication Technologies and the Moral Economy of the Household', in Roger Silverstone and Eric Hirsch (eds) *Consuming Technology: Media and Information in Domestic Spaces*, London: Routledge, pp. 115–131.

Stonewall (2011)' Unseen on Screen, Research into the Representation of Lesbian, Gay and Bisexual People on Youth Television', available at: *https://www.stonewall.org.uk/resources/unseen-screen-2011*, accessed 5 December 2015.

Vuojärvi, H., Isomäki, H. and Hynes, D. (2010) 'Domestication of a Laptop on a Wireless University Campus: A Case Study', *Australasian Journal of Educational Technology* 26 (2), pp. 250–267.

Ward, K. (2006) 'The Bald Guy Just Ate an Orange: Domestication, Work and Home', in Thomas Berker, Maran Hartmann, Yves Punie, and Katie Ward (eds) *Domestication of Media and Technology*, Maidenhead: Open University Press, pp. 145–164.

Wei, R. and Pan, Z.D. (1999) 'Mass Media and Consumerist Values in the People's Republic of China', *International Journal of Public Opinion Research* 11 (1), pp. 75–96.

Wellman, B. and Haythornthwaite, C. (2002) *The Internet in Everyday Life*, Oxford: Blackwell.

Wheelock, J. (1992) 'Personal Computers, Gender and an Institutional Model of the Household', in Roger Silverstone and Eric Hirsch (eds) *Consuming Technologies: Media and Information in Domestic Spaces*, London: Routledge, pp. 97–116.

Williams, R. (1974) *Television: Technology and Cultural Form*, London: Fontana.

Williams, R. and Edge, D. (1996) 'The Social Shaping of Technology', *Research Policy* 25 (6), pp. 865–899.

Wirth, W., von Pape, T. and Karnowski, V. (2008) 'An Integrative Model of Mobile Phone Appropriation', *Journal of Computer-Mediated Communication* 13 (3), pp. 593–617.

Yan, R. (1994) 'To Reach China Consumers, Adapt to Guo-Qing', *Harvard Business Review* 72 (5), pp. 66–74.

4

MEDIATISED CHILDHOODS AND MEDIA PARENTING

Introduction

Relationships with parents at home play a major role in shaping children's informal media engagement. The home continues to be the most predictable location for young people's internet use. However, children's access to numerous media appliances in the home has complicated relationships between parents and children. Parent–child relationships and ideas of home are being reconfigured by children's growing agency and media literacy (Bovill and Livingstone 2001; Livingstone 2004). Teenagers born at the turn of the millennium are the first generation able to take advantage of broadband and digital communication while growing up. The UK communications regulator, Ofcom states in a recent report, 'As a result of growing up in the digital age, 12–15-year-olds are developing fundamentally different communication habits than older generations, even compared to the advanced 16–24 age group' (Ofcom 2014a). While young people tend to be typecast as 'digital natives', at the same time, they are portrayed as antisocial family members immersed in media. Despite dramatic differences between young people and adults in terms of digital media experiences, young people spend more time in the home now than at any other time in the history of media communication technologies.

Children's media-related tasks in the home are shaped by several factors including changing public and parental attitudes to children's agency, parents' perceptions of the risks associated with children's access to new technologies, changing types of households, and major transformations in the ways childhood is conceived and galvanised through new media consumption patterns. The rise of single-parent households, dual-career parents and reconstituted or 'blended' families, and rising unemployment among youth are among structural shifts generating new family dynamics around children's uses of media in the home.

Growing financial constraints are prompting young people to delay leaving home, leading to an 'extended youth' since the late 1990s with 26 per cent of adults aged between 20 and 34 in the UK living with a parent or parents in 2013 (ONS 2014). In the US, the term 'empty nest syndrome' has been replaced in popular media debates by the 'crowded nest syndrome' (see for example, Shaputis 2004). The related trend of adult children returning home has been highly popularised in the US and UK as the 'boomerang generation'. Young people leave home at a later age and while at home they spend greater amounts of time indoors, engaging with media. Unsurprisingly, conflicting expectations about the amount of time young people should spend using media and the degree of parental guidance, surveillance and disciplining involved can create tensions within the household.

Parental decisions about the role to be played by media technologies in the home are influenced by contradictory trends. Parents are concerned about how the technology can enhance their children's educational progress. Yet they also harbour fears about the potential dangers of media technology for children and family life (Buckingham 2000; Seiter 2005). In a relatively new era of digital media technologies, parents face the challenge of being unable to draw on their own childhood experiences or memories as a guide for supervising their children's digitalised lives and associated moral compass (Buckingham 2011; Livingstone 2006: 166). Parenting is now viewed as a negotiation between parents and children. Among American families, 'reflexive parenting' indicates new dynamics in parenting strategies (Alters 2004; Lareau 2003). Companionship rather than authoritarian approaches to child socialisation are favoured (Jamieson 1987, 1998).

The key themes addressed by contemporary research on children's media in the home include the media practices and literacies of young people, the major opportunities and risks that they must navigate, and the role of domestic media in connecting or fragmenting families. This chapter charts the changes in relationships between parents and children corresponding with the introduction of media equipment in the home. It shows how parental values and the ways parents monitor and regulate their children's uses of media are affected not only by media technologies and content but also by economic imperatives, social class and gender roles, and by broader cultural changes in parenting styles. Drawing on a range of research, the chapter is arranged around four themes. First, the chapter enquires into children's access to media equipment, their current media habits and ways that they navigate their uses of media in the home. Second, it highlights the parental anxieties and discourses of risk associated with the use of new media technologies by children. Third, it looks at how parents deal with the rapidly expanding role of media in the home. It explains 'media parenting' in the era of digital media, that is, the parental strategies used to monitor children's engagement with media in today's media-laden homes. Finally, the chapter addresses issues of media literacy in a commercially driven media environment.

Patterns of domestic media use by children

In western and other countries, family households with dependent children tend to evolve into child-centred and media-rich spaces. The type and range of media technologies present in the home reflects the central place occupied by children in the emotional life of the home (Jamieson 1987, 1998; Beck and Beck-Gernsheim 1995). Parents are willing to create a media-rich environment for their children, believing that the educational value of the technologies will enhance their children's chances in life (Buckingham 2000, 2007; Livingstone 2009). The accumulation of media equipment in their bedrooms has generated a new kind of mediatised childhood since the late twentieth century: one firmly rooted in the home yet with the prospect of connections with networks of friends and information on a global stage. This new childhood is characterised by a new type of parenting. Livingstone and Das (2010) refer to the emergence of the 'special child' to explain the tendency for parents to spend more money on each child or, indeed, on a sole child as family sizes shrink.

The idea of the special child is also a growing feature of smaller urban Chinese families influenced by the one-child policy, introduced in 1979. A privatisation of childhood associated with consumerism is exemplified in urban China where there has been a huge growth in luxury children's goods market (Zhao and Murdock 1996). Chinese children's access to media in the home has been influenced not only by the one-child policy but also by significant growth in personal incomes in the 1990s and ready access to material goods in China's urban cities (Lu 2000). With most urban Chinese families comprising one-child families, a considerable proportion of their household purchases are devoted to the single child, with about half the luxury goods sold in China bought for the child (Yan 1994; Chan and McNeal 2004). Young Chinese people who grew up in the 1980s and 1990s were born into an era of affluence and have high consumer demands. They are most responsive to advertising and actively acquire branded goods in ways that contrast with older generations who tend to be oblivious to advertising. As mentioned in Chapter 3, urban Chinese parents' attempts to exert control over their children's engagement with media technologies reflects the compartmentalisation of children's leisure time and a high regard for educational achievement in Chinese culture. However, investment in media products and digital gadgets for children of affluent middle-class Chinese families can undermine parental authority and values (Lim 2005).

Similarly, media consumption saturates children's relationships in contemporary Europe and North America. Media appliances, electronic games and other commodities are now treated as indispensable aspects of a child's socialisation and integration into a peer group. Children place great pressure on parents to buy media gadgets. In turn, parents complain about the quantity of items that children say they need, but they also lament the extent to which generational relations are mediated through the commercial market (Clark 2013). A major factor related to children's media use within households is age, with children spending time online at earlier ages (Livingstone and Bober 2005: 221). A child's movement through the key stages of childhood is now symbolised by the use of certain brands, personalised mobile media devices such as tablets and mobile phones and use of social network sites. The assimilation of consumption into children's play and relationships generates tensions about the way parents supervise children's media engagement (Layard and Dunn 2009; Pugh 2009). Parents bemoan the mediation of generational identities through the marketing of toys and media content (Childwise 2015).

The dominance of television (TV) in children's lives in the 1990s has not been overtaken but, rather, added to by the growth in internet use and the widespread take-up of mobile phones and computer tablets. Children in the UK continue to watch over 14 hours of TV a week and access internet mainly from home (Ofcom 2014b). Children under the age of 5 years have traditionally had little engagement with media in the home except indirectly in the background. However, an extension of the marketing of digital toys to very young children, a rise in marketing 'educational toys' and growth in pre-school TV has changed this pattern (Livingstone 2007). A new category of childhood has been invented through consumer advertising strategies. Pre-adolescent children are labelled 'tweens' or 'teenies' within global markets to denote distinctive pre-teenage interests and seek out markets in toys, comics, TV programmes, video games and other interactive media (König 2008; Sargeant 2010). Mobile phones are targeted at children as young as eight and, as highlighted in Chapter 6, touchscreen computer tablets are also specifically designed and marketed to parents as educational toys for toddlers. In the UK, 40 per cent of children aged 3–4 years who cannot yet read or write are now using tablets at home. Among children aged 5–15 years, tablet use at home doubled from 2013 with one in three children aged 5–15 years owning their own tablet computer by 2014 (Ofcom 2014b; Livingstone 2014).

Such trends are global, as the research from China confirms. Research in Germany also shows how the movement from one age group to the next is handled and exhibited by children through their choice of consumer goods in highly individualised and unequal societies (König 2008). Now commonplace among teenagers in most countries, internet use is accelerating mostly among eight-year-olds. Engagement with electronic games and TV programmes in the home becomes pervasive when children first go to school. In the US, 95 per cent of children have internet access by the age of eleven (Clark 2013). Despite the accelerated use of mobile communication technologies, young people remain more likely to log on at home (87 per cent) (Livingstone and Wang 2011). Ofcom has assessed the media used by children aged 5–15 years at home between 2007 and 2014, including games consoles/games players, internet – personal computer (PC)/laptop/netbook-based, digital video cassette recorders (VCRs), DVD players/recorder/blu-ray recorders. Ofcom found significant differences in adoption and use according to socio-economic groupings. Higher levels of household adoption of media devices occur among children aged 5–15 years in affluent AB households (upper middle and middle class) and lower levels of adoption occur in DE households (working class and lowest levels of subsistence) (Ofcom 2014b: 36–37). These figures demonstrate not only the increasing centrality of home-based media in young people's lives but also that inequalities in household incomes affect children's access to media devices.

In the UK, the tablet computer appears to be replacing other devices such as games machines and smart phones in children's bedrooms (Ofcom 2014b). The rise in use of such mobile devices indicates that children are less likely to be monitored by parents when using the internet. The privacy of the children's bedroom is therefore a major concern for parents. While TV remains a dominant medium, older children are spending more and more time online and favour smart phones to support their social activities. Adolescents use media to express their individuality at the same time as immersing themselves within the culture of their peer group. By their late teenage years, young people are navigating their way through an extensive range of communication, information and media literacy functions as part of the experience of transferring from school to college or employment (Livingstone and Das 2010).

Children's media-oriented bedrooms

Mounting restrictions on children's physical mobility outside the home since the late twentieth century correspond with a belief that children should have a personal and private space in the family household. Comprising this private space, the child's bedroom is becoming more and more media-centred, often crammed with new communication appliances that sustain individual, privatised media use. Changes in children's relationship to public and private spaces correspond to the rise of youth-centred media and a screen-based 'bedroom culture' (Bovill and Livingstone 2001; Lincoln 2004; Lincoln 2012; Livingstone 2009). In affluent parts of Europe, this bedroom culture is characteristically rich in media (Livingstone and Das 2010). Relating to the proliferation in media devices in children's bedrooms, and at younger ages, teenagers are spending less leisure time in the communal, family spaces of home and more leisure time in the privacy of their bedrooms (Bovill and Livingstone 2001; Livingstone 2002). However, a study comparing 6–17-year-old children's uses of media in their bedrooms by Bovill and Livingstone (2001) found that children are using media dynamically, to express their identities.

Children's use of the home to develop a bedroom culture has been prompted by four major trends. The first is a withdrawal of young people into the home in response to increased surveillance of outside spaces which were once a focus of parental anxiety and also because young people themselves are regarded as a threat or nuisance in public spaces. The second trend has involved an individualisation of family members' personal interests. Families no longer share similar preferences in music, TV or even mediums. Whether this trend will continue or not depends on how media convergence and use of mobile devices in the home are played out (see Chapter 6). Third, the drop in price and size of media equipment allows items such as TVs, music systems, games and mobile gadgets to be bought by relatively low-income families and to be used in small bedrooms. A fourth trend relates to the notion of childhood agency mentioned above: the 'cultural repositioning of the child as a person in their own right' (Livingstone and Das 2010: 31). This focus on children means that they now have a claim on a major share of a family's household financial resources.

These trends involving the media-rich child's bedroom coincide with other dynamics of media use in family households identified by Livingstone and Das (2010). The home-based leisure of families has become more compartmentalised (Van Romaey and Roe 2001), with families more likely to be 'living together separately' (Flichy 1995). Related to this compartmentalisation, time spent collectively as 'a family' becomes a task involving careful and conscious planning. The media-rich bedroom also means that even when children are not in the physical presence of their friends, their leisure and entertainment time and activities involve their friends and peers more than parents (Ito et al. 2010; Livingstone 2009; Livingstone and Das 2010). Children's interest in using their bedroom is often motivated by their lack of autonomy to select media content in communal settings. The bedroom's significance also relates to personal identity, reflected through styles of bedroom shaped by personal taste.

How the bedroom is equipped, in terms of media resources, becomes a major issue for children and parents (Livingstone and Das 2010). Bedroom culture has particular resonance for girls who value this private space for internet connection with friends, exploring their sexuality and feminine identities, and engaging in cultural consumption activities (Elm 2009; Kearney 2007; Buckingham and Bragg 2003; Nayak and Kehily 2008; Wang 2010). The internet tends to be perceived as a private space that augments the physical experience of privacy in the bedroom. Comprising a major dimension of media in the home, young people's bedroom culture drives change by contributing to the blurring of public and private boundaries. This bedroom culture indicates not only children's desire for mediatised sociality but also a strong desire to be alone as a way of coping with difficult circumstances (Livingstone 2005).

Personalised media devices in children's bedrooms are organised to ensure their privacy, often by barring parental and sibling intrusion. While parents often respond to these as unsociable practices, they reflect the limited means available to young people to manage and evade the potential for parental scrutiny and regulation associated with the communal areas of domestic space (Livingstone and Bober 2005). Bedroom culture therefore provides a way for children to manage individual interests. Despite the solitary use of new media devices in the bedroom, virtual communication managed through bedroom privacy facilitates collective identities with friends, bypassing co-present family members (Livingstone 2005). Social media allow children to be 'at home' and 'away from home' at the same time. The rise in personalised media use within an individual, privatised domestic space affords a context through which the outside world is brought indoors in a controlled way (Bovill and Livingstone 2001).

Parents view media technologies as a potential threat to their children with regard to inappropriate content, even though equipment is usually purchased by parents for its educational value as well as sensible recreational use (Lally 2002;

Murdock et al. 1992; Wheelock 1992). Children's access to media in the home is related to parental education and income, but it is not simply the more affluent middle-class households that offer children more access to media (Clark 2013; Livingstone and Das 2010; Buckingham 2000). Reflecting higher incomes, two-parent households and families with working mothers are more likely to create a media-rich home for their children. However, lower-income and single-parent households also aspire to provide their children with media-rich bedrooms, indicating the lengths that single-parent families go to in facilitating children's media use (Livingstone and Das 2010). Nevertheless, differences in media equipment, location of devices and type of access are evident.

Children from lower-income homes are more likely to have access to a TV or games machines in their bedrooms. Highly educated and higher-income parents are more likely to give their children access to a computer away from the bedroom and access to books in their bedroom rather than placing a TV or VCR in children's bedrooms (Livingstone and Das 2010; Cédric Courtois et al. 2012). Social class distinctions in media consumption also contribute to distinctions in children's social standing among peers and in terms of social capital (Clark 2013). While parental social capital and income is pertinent, family values also have a significant influence on purchasing choices, types of technologies that children are allowed to use, and the ratio of traditional and technological toys and activities available to children (Plowman et al. 2008). Inequalities in children's access to media-rich bedrooms and in their freedom to engage meaningfully with media lead to significant distinctions between teenagers in terms of their level of autonomy to develop self-defining media repertoires and to use them to define themselves. These inequalities relate to and reflect wider inequalities in other spheres of children's lives (Buckingham 2011; Livingstone and Das 2010).

For parents, this personalised, individuated and privatised use of media can indicate a fragmentation of family-centred domestic leisure. Within the moral economy of the household, new kinds of household interaction emerge based on parental rules. These involve complicated child–parent negotiations in applying those rules by parents wishing to curb time spent by children on mobile phones, tablets, computer games and so on (Haddon 2004; Livingstone 2002; Silverstone and Haddon 1996). Parents feel obliged to make contracts with their children to control when and where they can play computer games, for example, after finishing school homework (Silverstone 2006). Most parents believe that children's TV and digital media time should be curtailed, and that violent video games have a negative impact on children (Layard and Dunn 2009).

Media socialisation and media risks

The growing amount of new media equipment in children's bedrooms at younger ages has generated public fears about the negative effects of media on children (Livingstone 2009; Rohloff 2013). Media panics about socially disengaged young people replacing human contact with virtual contact correspond with concerns that 'youth' is increasingly disconnected from family life. Such fears are acknowledged in government reports including 'Safer Children in A Digital World' for the UK Council for Child Internet Safety (UKCCIS) (Byron 2008). Today's parents find themselves pulled in opposite directions. An empirical study of the ways families in the US negotiate media use by Lynn Schofield Clark (2013) records the stories of many parents who bemoan the widespread use of mobile phones, texting and social network sites by their children. She found that parents also express concerns about the role of gaming, TV programmes and music in children's lives.

Much past scholarship about families and media focused on media and socialisation to identify the level and effects of children's exposure to media (see Messenger Davies 2010 for a review). Socialisation involves the social processes through which individuals learn about their culture and develop meanings, norms and values to participate and negotiate that culture (Signorielli 2000; Maccoby 2007; Arnett 1995). Within a media-centred and positivist perspective, children have been identified as a vulnerable group at particular risk from media influences. Problems such as aggressive behaviour, early sexuality and obesity are identified as social problems that emerge during childhood caused by negative media influences. Supporters of the socialisation approach argue that research needs to identify causes through precise testing to tackle empirical problems. By contrast, an alternative child-centred and constructivist approach emphasises children's agency by examining how children engage with and gain pleasure from media. By focusing on the skills and strategies children adopt on managing the role of media in their lives, the constructivist approach examines what children acquire from media use (Livingstone 2007: 5). It critiques the media-centred perspective as a simplistic causal theory which gives rise to moral panics by approaching the child as a 'victim'.

Past socialisation research focusing on media effects has been influenced by a stimulus-response approach (Valkenburg 2000: 54), suggesting that contact with advertising has a direct effect on the consumer behaviour of very young children. However, more recent theories of media effects address children as active agents who engage dynamically with media. Although there are methodological and theoretical weaknesses in relation to findings, a review of research on media effects found evidence that depictions of violence on TV, film, video games/DVDs and electronic games can, indeed, have a harmful effect on the behaviour and attitudes of children, particularly for boys (Millwood et al. 2009). In developed countries, labelling, age limits and scheduling restrictions are applied in response to such concerns. The greater potential for negative effects seems to occur when children view material that is unsuitable for their age because it is aimed at an older age group. However, the link between effects of exposure to the particular features and age associated with the content is often inadequately argued. By contrast, critiques of the media effects model arising from socialisation studies emphasise the importance of the cultural context of children's media use. The media is said to impart the cultural assumptions or ideologies that allow people to comprehend the social world. Exposure to media accounts for only small amounts of change in beliefs and outlooks with other dynamics also influencing children's attitudes. The challenge for researchers is that the effects of the media coalesce with multiple other social factors and influences that are often detectable only as protracted changes in habits and customs over time.

Despite the shortcomings of the socialisation approach, Livingstone and Das (2010) warn against abandoning the question of media effects entirely, arguing that overemphasising children's agency 'risks an over-celebration of agency' at the cost of questions about differences in age. 'The balance is delicate and the question of effects still contested' (Livingstone 2007: 10). A risk-based approach is recommended by Livingstone to examine the range of factors that combine to inform certain social patterns and trends involved in children's engagement with media. Recognising that the media are not the sole cause of change, constructivist approaches emphasise that the media contribute to ongoing trends. They mediate, and through certain technological affordances, help to reinforce some social practices and make others seem less attractive.

Parents are pressured to furnish the home with media-based leisure equipment to make up for deteriorating public facilities such as schools and public libraries. In terms of negotiating rules about children's uses of media in the home, these social trends combine to create tensions in parenting. Children are likely to be unmonitored when using social media, since they are usually engaged with this in the privacy of their bedrooms or while they are on the move. One of the most rapidly growing media practices adopted by children is social networking. Among 12–15-year-olds who go online, 70 per cent have a social media profile and most access their profiles from their mobile phones (Livingstone et al. 2014). However, parental control is declining as the technology becomes more complicated and unfamiliar (Livingstone 2009). Emphasising that media are one of the main ways in which young people obtain the customs and beliefs of the everyday culture in which they live, Arnett (1995) states that there has been a significant decline in the family's role as an agent of socialisation and simultaneous increase in adolescents' autonomy (Arnett 1995: 529). Parents are concerned about their lack of knowledge and control over young people's use of digital media (Fromme 2003; Livingstone 2007; Lincoln 2012). Positive research findings suggest internet use generates greater teen autonomy, greater teen choice and enhancement of peer group relations (Buckingham 2007; Cheong 2008; Heim et al. 2007; Livingstone 2009; Patchin and Hinduja 2010). Nevertheless, tensions between parents and children over young people's uses of new media are accelerating. Parents are concerned about losing control over children's lives and being unable to protect them against problems such as cyberbullying, sexting and game violence.

The idea of a risk-averse culture is supported by certain negative research findings. Moreover, extensive use of information communication technologies (ICTs) by young people has been associated with poor health, low educational achievement, the decline of face-to-face communication, social isolation, low self-esteem and social incompetence (Gentile et al. 2004; Strasbourg and Wilson 2002; Vandebosch and Van Cleemput 2009; Subrahmanyam and Greenfield 2008; Drotner et al. 2008). For example, research in San Diego by Tanton et al. (2012)

highlights the problems of children's increasingly sedentary lives in the home. Their study of children aged 6–11 years indicates that children in households of lower socio-economic status are more likely to be overweight or obese. These children had greater media access in their bedrooms (TV 52 per cent vs. 14 per cent, DVD player 39 per cent vs. 14 per cent, video games 21 per cent vs. 9 per cent) but lower access to portable play equipment (bikes 85 per cent vs. 98 per cent, jump ropes 69 per cent vs. 83 per cent) compared to higher-income children. They also found that lower-income family households maintained more restrictive rules about physical activity in the home. Parents from lower socio-economic groups watched TV/DVDs with their children more often (3.1 vs. 2.5 days per week). Concluding that lower socio-economic status home environments provide more opportunities for sedentary behaviour and fewer opportunities for physical activity, the researchers recommend that chronic disease risk can be reduced by removing electronic media from children's bedrooms. A UK study of 14-year-olds' physical activity and media habits that compared their GCSE[1] results at age 16 found a drop in as much as two grades among those adolescents spending an extra hour a day on screens such as watching TV and playing video games (Corder et al. 2015).

A number of stakeholders are engaged in safeguarding children online at national, European and international levels. For example, in the UK, the NSPCC has developed an online guide called *Net Aware*[2] to help parents stay up to date with the range of websites, apps and games used by children. The guide provides key information and addresses safeguarding issues to give parents confidence to engage in balanced conversations about how their children use the internet and understand the appropriateness of popular sites for their children. In addition, a whole industry has emerged around commercial self-help literature to supply guidance to parents about children's media uses. Advice manuals involve counteractions to dystopian visions of negative effects of digital media on children's lives.

Today, parents are addressed by health advisors, counsellors, teachers and other experts through magazines, books, TV and radio and, as Nicolas Rose states: 'through the unceasing reflexive gaze of our own psychologically educated self-scrutiny' (Rose 1999: 213). This family self-surveillance is prompted by the ambition to be a 'good family', and a central feature of this ambition is the 'correct' family regulation of today's mediated childhood through conduct and practices that show both respect for and control of children. Parenting advice manuals usually address middle-class parents and, more specifically, mothers. Typical titles include *A Parent's Guide to Understanding Social Media: Helping Your Teenager Navigate Life Online* (Oestreicher 2012), *The Parent's Guide to Texting, Facebook, and Social Media: Understanding the Benefits and Dangers of Parenting in a Digital World* (Edgington 2011); *Is Your Child Safe Online? A Parent's Guide to the Internet, Facebook, Mobile Phones and Other New Media* (Whitby 2011) and *The Big Disconnect* by Steiner-Adair and Barker (2013). Such advice manuals typically begin by referring to the astonishing pace at which technology is changing people's lives and the negative impact of the digital revolution on parents and children. They then offer sympathetic advice regarding this unprecedented 'revolution in the living room'. Promoting a discourse of parental anxiety through a string of provocative questions, the front flap of *The Big Disconnect* is characteristic of the approach:

> Have iPads replaced conversation at the dinner table? What do infants observe when their parents are on their smartphones? Should you be your child's Facebook friend? As the focus of family has turned to the glow of the screen – children constantly texting their friends, parents working online around the clock – everyday life is undergoing a massive transformation. Easy availability to the Internet and social media has erased the boundaries that protect children from the unsavoury aspects of adult life. Parents often feel they are losing a meaningful connection with their children. Children are feeling lonely and alienated. The digital world is here to stay, but what are families losing with technology's gain?
>
> *(Steiner-Adair and Barker 2013)*

Media parenting strategies

In the context of today's media-saturated homes, a new kind of parenting involves parents negotiating with their children about how and when media should be used. While parents acquire the duty to protect children from risk, they are also expected to ensure children's participation in major decisions within a family based on today's 'pure relationship' (Giddens 1992). This parenting approach contrasts with traditional authoritarian parental roles based on hierarchical relations between the generations. However, children often delight in exploring and flouting the norms of public and private boundaries by harnessing digital media's power to permeate private spaces and to construct 'publics' (Ito et al. 2010; Livingstone 2006). Their curiosity and naivety can draw them into costly consumerist activities and the endorsement of powerful commercial ventures. Frictions between parents and children often occur in the context of the purchase and use of new media in the home and also typically centre on their children's uses of media technologies in relation to wider issues of communication, disclosures, surveillance and privacy (Gillies et al. 2001; Jamieson 1999). The gradual retraction of state involvement in regulating the media places more and more responsibility on parents and teachers to guide and regulate children's use of media.

The moral panics about media effects are indicative of a risk society (Beck 1992). Clark (2013) argues that within economically difficult circumstances, parents feel pressured to work longer hours to provide a quality of life for their children in order to lessen risks in their lives. The commercialisation of media and the privatisation of home life are among wider social processes that impinge on parent–child relationships in the home. Parents adopt a range of strategies to manage their children's educational and leisure activities at the same time as negotiating the demands of their own work commitments. On the one hand, the growing use of media by young people corresponds with the demands of parents' work lives. On the other hand, parents are compelled to supervise and micro-manage their children's escalating media use (Clark 2013). This is not only a problem associated with families on low incomes. In the US, UK and Europe, the sense that middle-class incomes have fallen as a result of the economic crisis heightens parental anxieties about preparing their children to compete in a more competitive global economy.

The extension of children's education into late teenage years and rising competition for jobs compels parents to invest in media technologies to enhance children's informal learning at home. However, Livingstone et al. (2014) that found that while parents are attempting to regulate their children's digital activities, they tend to view these as opportunities for rewarding or punishing rather than learning or creativity. They tend to place restrictions on use rather than steering children towards beneficial or more varied activities. Many parents look to their child's school for help, yet schools are only beginning to recognise young children's digital lives. Children are often using content designed for older age groups and free apps that have advertisements. This is because parents choose not to pay for such services. Many young children struggle with interfaces based on print or hard-to-use navigation. A new initiative by ParentZone called 'Parent Info'[3] is an example of the provision of high-quality information to parents and carers about their children's wellbeing and resilience.

YouTube's new service designed especially for children is proving to be contentious. A complaint filed with the Federal Trade Commission (FTC) by Campaign for a Commercial-free Childhood (CCFC) and other leading advocacy groups in the US is requesting an investigation of Google's dedicated YouTube app directed at children, YouTube Kids app.[4] The FTC has been called upon to investigate whether Google's YouTube Kids app violates Section 5 of the FTC Act, which prohibits unfair and deceptive marketing practices. It points out that the videos provided for children on YouTube Kids combine commercial with other content in ways that are misleading to children and that would not be allowed to be screened on broadcast or cable TV. Several video segments endorse toys, sweets and other consumer products that appear to be 'user-generated' but which have undisclosed relationships with product manufacturers that may violate the FTC's guidelines concerning the use of endorsements and testimonials in advertising. However, in marketing the app to parents, Google claims that all advertisements are pre-approved by YouTube's policy team to ensure compliance with the app's rigorous advertising policy. This example is indicative of the kinds of commercial pressures that have become normalised within children's media experiences.

Family arrangements are significant in shaping individuals' attitudes towards media and their consumption practices in the contexts of everyday life. Within the wider trend towards informality and the adoption of a more consultative approach, parental mediation can vary according to social class, gender issues, family household type, and religious and cultural values. The emotion work involved in monitoring children's media-related activities in the home seems to fall disproportionately on mothers. Mothers are more likely to engage in reflexive parenting.

Women have traditionally taken on both the 'second shift' involving the work of organising the household and the 'third shift' – the emotion work involved in caring for and facilitating children's safety. This responsibility intensifies with the new and ongoing demands of digital and mobile media. A new kind of childcare, characterised as 'intensive parenting' is often triggered by the time constraints and stress involved in juggling work with parental mediation (Liss et al. 2012). This intensive parenting may place pressure on partner relationships in the home. These parental mediation issues are compounded by present-day flexible working patterns and the always-connected workplace, which leads to the expansion of the role of work as a major organising influence in family life (Clarke 2013: 215–216).

The rise of the so-called information and digital era coincides with today's reflexive parenting (Hoover et al. 2004). Parents, particularly mothers, are expected to make conscientious decisions about the uses of digital and mobile media as well as all other aspects of the child's life. These decisions are not based on a rational assessment of risk but on enhancing their children's wellbeing as a 'good parent'. Drawing on the term 'emotion work' coined by Arlie Russell Hochschild (1979), Lynn Schofield Clark (2013) extends the idea of reflexive parenting to highlight the intensified emotion work involved in parenting in 'the digital age'. Clark explains that today's media-saturated environment requires an intensified level of emotion work by both parents and children in their relationships with each other. Parenting advice books, mentioned above, are good indicators of the 'emotion work' involved in parents' attempts to navigate information overload in the digital age (2013: 93). Margaret Nelson (2010) goes a step further, suggesting that the intense pressure placed on parents and children have led to a new kind of 'parenting out of control'. Preparing their children for competition and new life challenges leads parents among 'elite' and well-resourced families to hover, interfere and guide the child within a form of 'helicopter parenting' which is now out of control. Nelson contrasts this 'helicopter parenting' with 'parenting with limits'. Helicopter parenting relies on enormous amounts of time and money to support an elite style of care. New technologies such as smart phones, social networking sites and GPS devices provide parents with more opportunities to communicate with, supervise and spy on their children, yet these often contribute to this 'out of control' parenting. The effect is persistent control of a highly personalised, negotiated and continuous nature.

Social class and ethnic differences are significant factors influencing how families and households approach and incorporate digital, mobile and entertainment media into their lives. Lynn Schofield Clark (2013) found that families adopt communication ethics that differ according to social class, and to a lesser extent, according to race and ethnic identity. She describes two distinct patterns of parenting in a digital era: an 'ethic of expressive empowerment' and an 'ethic of respected connectedness' which correspond with family class differences. For Clark, 'ethic' relates to the idea of the moral economy of the household employed within domestication theory by referring to the body of principles and values distinctive to a particular group (Clark 2013: 133). Upper-middle-class and middle-class families have an ethic of expressive empowerment, meaning they encourage children's media use for learning, expression and personal development, and deter distractive and time-wasting media use (as they perceive it). For these families, who engage with media extensively in the home, good parenting is associated with raising children who are 'self-confident, caring, self-resilient, honest, and capable of expressing their views and emotions while expressing self-control' (Clark 2013: 16). Ironically, children demonstrate their self-reliance by regularly calling their mothers for advice, resonating with Annette Lareau's 'concerted cultivation', Sharon Hays' (1998) 'intensive mothering' and Nelson's 'helicopter parenting'. The parental aim to help middle- and upper-middle-class children gain independence generates opposite consequences.

Clark (2013) confirms that affluent parents, mobile phones and social media are fostering the 'helicopter parenting' identified by Nelson (2010), allowing parents to hover over their children, spy on their online profiles and intervene sometimes in inappropriate ways. Such families rarely watch films or TV together. This is because today's upper-middle-class family usually owns several types of portable devices, ranging from e-readers and tablets to laptops and smartphones, which may encourage fragmented and individualised media practices. Their wider options for media use when at home also militate against shared screen time except on rare occasions. The demands of family life, particularly the need to balance ever-increasing work demands with the demands of the individual children's enrichment activities, means that communication between family members is judged by efficiency: media is used for home–life management by scheduling and communicating details of transportation with demands placed mainly on mothers to be constantly available for such communication.

Children living in poorer households are technologically deprived compared to children who have access to a wealthier and media-rich parent (usually the father), which may lead to expressions of dissatisfaction (Haddon 2006). However, Clark found that lower-income families with fewer economic and cultural resources embrace an 'ethic of respected connectedness' in their style of family communication that guides how they think about the potential risks of digital and mobile media. The emphasis among these families is on media use that is respectful, compliant and family-focused. These 'would-be-middle class' families would have had higher income levels, more purchasing power and better housing if they had not experienced intervening circumstances such as divorce, ill heath or unemployment. They regard good parenting as raising children who are 'loyal, respectful, patriotic and caring toward both their families and communities' (Clark 2013: 16). Among these households, family bonds are viewed as the greatest defence against risk. Children and teenagers in these families tend to have more unstructured leisure time, occupying smaller family quarters. They often spend more time with siblings and other relatives, reinforcing a sense of family connectedness. Parents go to great lengths to help their children develop their abilities, for example by enrolling their children in special programmes for high achievers or to develop computing skills. Yet most parents in these families lack the resources needed to pursue the kinds of intensive extra-curricular schedules that pattern the lives of pre-teens and teens in the middle and upper-middle families of Clark's study.

Among upper- and middle-class families, parenting in a non-authoritarian manner means favouring their children's individual rights over those of family members, posing challenges about the appropriateness of asserting parental authority. Less advantaged parents are less knowledgeable about digital and mobile media than upper-middle-class parents. Parents' lack of familiarity with the equipment becomes a further source of friction (Clark 2013: 205). Clark found that, among less advantaged and would-be middle-class families, parents tended to engage in stronger parental authority, perhaps in response to the heightened risks that their children encounter. Siblings are often expected to look out for one another and these families learned to rely on one another during crises. This insularity means that they had fewer resources available to support them when they experienced unfamiliar circumstances, such as those involving digital and mobile media. They rely on those they know. Clark explains that the media uses of more privileged children resonate with the values of school or other institutions, while those of poorer families are less valued, thereby exacerbating social inequalities. Sherry Turkle (2011) coined the phrase 'alone together' to highlight the tendency for people in the same space to use technologies to connect with people from a distance. Clark (2013) suggests that being 'together alone' describes would-be middle-class and less advantaged families.

Tensions in parenting are also said to be associated with a decline in family stability and rising divorce rates, a decline in children's respect for their elders and the rise of youth culture (Jenks 1996; Kehily 2010). The impact of single-parent households is as marked as social class as a factor of social inequality. Significant challenges in parental mediation for single-parent households have been uncovered by domestication research (addressed in Chapter 3). Reduced income resulting from divorce or separation complicates media parenting for single parents. Research demonstrates that the lack of economic resources in single-parent households affects the time available to spend with children, the level of adult mentoring and children's access to educational opportunities (Russo Lemor 2006). Despite limited time and resources, sole-parent households are likely to go to great lengths to maintain media-rich bedrooms for their children. Earlier studies by Haddon and Silverstone emphasise that, for single parents, creating a feeling of 'home' is an achievement in itself, involving the process of domesticating media technologies as well managing issues of time and space (Haddon and Silverstone 1995: 15).

The complexities of parenting practices in single-parent households highlight the moral economy of the household regarding the dynamics of adoption and use of media (Russo Lemor 2006). When children identify with two different households due to separation, divorce or remarriage, the family dynamics associated with children's negotiation of privacy via their media use in the home can differ considerably (Hoover and Clark 2008). 'Media parenting' after divorce often involves protracted discussions and joint efforts about decisions concerning the amount of time children should spend on video gaming, watching TV and using mobile phones. Media parenting decisions depend on the estranged parents sustaining amicable relations with one another. And parenting post-divorce can also be complicated by the arrival of a new partner whose presence in the household affects the already fragile relations established between the two parents (Clark 2013). For single parents, the monitoring of children's home-based media practices can be highly challenging if it involves even more than two households, including that of grandparents. Each household is likely to have its own independent yet interconnected moral economy that places pressure on parents' attempts to establish rules and routines for the children, including media uses.

Children tend to play a more significant role in household decisions about family activities in single-parent households, where parents have to juggle the role of caretaker and breadwinner. Single-parent households can pose particular problems for parental mediation through the need to negotiate children's media habits with ex-partners. Ex-partners may be either stricter or more lenient about children's access to the equipment (Haddon and Silverstone 1995; Russo Lemor 2006). Almost all the parents interviewed in a US study by Russo Lemor (2006) spoke of problems in adapting to the other parent's ideas and practices in relation to their children's media activities, whatever the custody arrangement. In most cases, the ex-partner is depicted negatively as a heavy user of media and ICTs and as overly thoughtless about their children's media consumption. Parenting after divorce makes media parenting even more of a burden because parents feel that they have to compensate for the other parents' (perceived) ineptness for the sake of the children.

Children's media literacy and commercial media

With new technologies reshaping family life, media literacy is now an important issue on the policy agenda, one that not only relates directly to media skills developed in school but also in children's home lives. As the home becomes an increasingly central space in which children are experimenting with new media, that space needs to be recognised as a major learning space by policy to tackle issues of media literacy (Rudd et al. 2006). However, media policies based on a home–school link are particularly challenging because the internet is used very differently in each context (Livingstone and Bober 2005; EU Kids Online 2014). In countries such as the US and UK, social uses of digital and mobile media and the emphasis on individualism and achievement that underpin the current technological environment have deepened social divisions. Differing levels of media access and user skills are major ways in which inequalities between children are reproduced. While having children in the household is a key enabler of media literacy, family households are major perpetuators of social inequalities of class, gender and generation. Reflecting these markers of social inequality, the main barriers to media literacy are age, socio-economic status, gender, disability, ethnicity and proficiency in English. Families have differing levels of access, as exemplified by studies of single-parent and lower-income households, and not all young people are 'digital natives'. Families' views about how the home is to be organised to foster children's media literacy are related to major questions about who, in contemporary society, is ultimately responsible for regulating children's skills in using new media (Livingstone 2005).

Commercial industry self-regulation is rapidly replacing state-imposed media regulation as part of a shrinking public sector and welfare provision. This shift is characterised by a reduction in government support for media literacy initiatives to develop children's media knowledge and skills in order to participate within a new digital media environment. Indeed, as technological convergence and transnational media markets become more complex, media regulation by individual states becomes more challenging and almost unfeasible. Policies such as the promotion of media literacy endorse the lack of commercial regulation of media by placing the responsibility to deal with media risks on parents' shoulders. The transfer of responsibility for regulating children's media uses from the state to parents, teachers and children reflects a privatisation of regulation. This situation results in ongoing interpersonal frictions with parents and children within attempts to employ blunt or ingenious strategies about where to position the computer and how to restrict use of content and services. The commercialisation of media and the related pressure placed on parents to take charge of regulating children's media habits is part of a wider set of trends (see Chapter 9). This principle of self-regulation removes responsibility from the commercial media industry by demanding that individuals regulate themselves: by becoming a 'good parent' to ensure safety provisions for media content and adhere to trade restrictions or other obligations that serve children's interests. It ensures that private, commercial interests are served at the expense of public interests.

Conclusion

The chapter reveals that parenting practices have changed considerably, with parental media guidance and monitoring affected by social class, financial resources and type of household. Although having children in the household is a key enabler of media literacy, parents worry that bedrooms become the focal point of children's activities in the home. If new media devices are placed in children's bedrooms, children usually take control of the equipment and restrict access to others in the household. Within the moral economy of the home, parents monitor children's use by placing media devices in shared domestic spaces, such as hallways, kitchens and lounges, to allow parents to monitor the use of the equipment. However, the growing mobility of media devices is making it difficult for parents to monitor their children's media uses to protect them from risks.

The chapter confirms that the household is a key site of social difference with media playing a central role in that process (Livingstone 2006). The range of media parenting strategies reveal significant differences according to the social class and educational status of the families as well as the type of household. Strategies differ according to the level of family income and family structure. A lack of digital skills risks digital exclusion, consumer disadvantages, and low participation risks exacerbate social inequalities between children (Livingstone and Wang 2013). With media-rich homes and extensive use of new media by children in home, school and other contexts, media literacy has become a major policy matter. The issues raised in this chapter indicate the growing need for policy to attend to the home as an important learning space to provide support for parents and children in grappling with issues of media literacy in this context of privatised regulation.

Notes

1 GCSE is a qualification in a specific subject typically taken by school students aged 14–16 years in the UK, except Scotland.
2 Net Aware information is available from the NSPCC website at: *http://www.nspcc.org.uk/preventing-abuse/keeping-children-safe/share-aware/*, accessed 5 December 2015.
3 Information about Parent Info is available on the ParentZone website at: *http://www.theparentzone.co.uk/parent_info/4921*, accessed 5 December 2015.
4 See 'Campaign for a Commercial-free Childhood (2015) Advocates File FTC Complaint Against Google's YouTube Kids', available at: *http://www.commercialfreechildhood.org/youtubekids*, accessed 5 December 2015.

References

Alters, D.F. (2004) 'The Family in US History and Culture,' in Stewart M. Hoover, Lyn Schofield Clark and Diane F. Alters (eds) *Media, Home, and Family*, New York: Routledge, pp. 51–68.

Arnett, J. (1995) 'Broad and Narrow Socialization: The Family in the Context of a Cultural Theory', *Journal of Marriage and Family* 57 (3), pp. 617–628.

Beck, U. (1992) *Risk Society: Towards a New Modernity*, London: Sage.

Beck, U. and Beck-Gernsheim, E. (1995) *The Normal Chaos of Love*, Oxford: Polity Press.

Bovill, M. and Livingstone, S. (2001) *Children and Their Changing Media Environment: A European Comparative Study*, Mahwah, NJ: L. Erlbaum Associates.

Buckingham, D. (2000) *After the Death of Childhood: Growing up in the Age of Electronic Media*. Cambridge, UK: Polity Press.

Buckingham, D. (2007) *Beyond Technology: Children's Learning in the Age of Digital Media*, Cambridge: Polity Press.

Buckingham, D. (2011) *The Material Child: Growing Up in Consumer Culture*, Cambridge: Polity Press.

Buckingham, D. and Bragg, S. (2003) *Young People, Media and Personal Relationships*, London: BBC and Broadcasting Standards Commission.

Byron, T. (2008) 'Safer Children in a Digital World: The Report of the Byron Review', available at: *www.dcsf.gov.uk/byronreview*, accessed 3 August 2010.

Chan, K. and McNeal, J.U. (2004) *Advertising to Children in China*, Hong Kong: The Chinese University Press.

Cheong, P.H. (2008) 'The Young and Techless? Investigating Internet Use and Problem-Solving Behaviours of Young Adults in Singapore', *New Media and Society* 10 (5), pp. 771–791.

Childwise (2015) 'The Childwise Monitor Report – Children's Purchasing', Childwise, Research and Markets.

Clark, L.S. (2013) *The Parent App: Understanding Families in the Digital Age*, Oxford: Oxford University Press.

Corder, K., Atkin, A.J., Bamber, D.J., Brage, S., Dunn, V.J., Ekelund, U., Owens, M., van Sluijs, E.M.F. and Goodyer, I.M. (2015) 'Revising on the Run or Studying on the Sofa: Prospective Associations between Physical Activity, Sedentary Behaviour, and Exam Results in British Adolescents', *International Journal of Behavioural Nutrition and Physical Activity* 12, p. 106.

Courtois, C., Mechant, P., Paulussen, S. and De Marez, L. (2012) 'The Triple Articulation of Media Technologies in Teenage Media Consumption', *New Media and Society* 14 (3), pp. 401–420.

Drotner, K., Siggaard Jensen, H. and Schroder K.C. (2008) 'Conceptual and Relational Vagaries of Learning and Media', in Kirsten Drotner, Hans Siggaard Jensen and Kim Christian Schroder (eds) *Informal Learning and Digital Media*, Newcastle upon Tyne: Cambridge Scholars Publishing, pp. 1–10.

Edgington, S.M. (2011) *The Parent's Guide to Texting, Facebook, and Social Media: Understanding the Benefits and Dangers of Parenting in a Digital World*, Dallas, TX: Brown Books.

Elm, M.S. (2009) '"Teenagers Get Undressed on the Internet": Young People's Exposure of Bodies in a Swedish Internet Community', *Nordicom Review* 30 (2), pp. 87–103.

EU Kids Online (2014) written submission to the 'Committee on the Rights of the Child 2014 Day' of General Discussion Digital Media and Children's Rights, available at: *http://www.ohchr.org/Documents/HRBodies/CRC/Discussions/2014/line.docx*, accessed 5 December 2015.

Flichy, P. (1995) *Dynamics of Modern Communication: The Shaping and Impact of New Communication Technologies*, London: Sage.

Fromme, J. (2003) 'Computer Games as Part of Children's Culture', *Game Studies: The International Journal of Computer Game Research* 3 (1), available at: *www.gamestudies.org/0301/fromme*, accessed 5 December 2015.

Gentile, D.A., Lynch, P.J., Linder, J.R. and Walsh, D.A. (2004) 'The Effects of Violent Video Game Habits on Adolescent Hostility, Aggressive Behaviours, and School Performance', *Journal of Adolescence* 27 (1), pp. 5–22.

Giddens, A. (1992) *The Transformation of Intimacy: Sexuality, Love and Eroticism in Modern Societies*, Oxford: Polity Press.

Gillies, V., Ribbens McCarthy, J. and Holland, J. (2001) *Pulling Together, Pulling Apart': The Family Lives of Young People*, York: Family Policy Studies Centre/Joseph Rowntree Foundation.

Haddon, L. (2004) *Information and Communication Technologies in Everyday Life: A Concise Introduction and Research Guide*, Oxford: Berg.

Haddon, L. (2006) 'The Contribution of Domestication Research to In Home Computing and Media Consumption', *The Information Society* 22 (4), pp. 195–203.

Haddon, L. and Silverstone, R. (1995) 'Lone Parents and Their Information and Communication Technologies', *SPRU/CICT Report Series*, No. 12, University of Sussex, Falmer.

Hays, S. (1998) *The Cultural Contradictions of Motherhood*, New Haven, CT: Yale University Press.

Heim, J., Bae Brandtzæg, P., Hertzberg Kaare, B., Endestad, T. and Torgersen, L. (2007) 'Children's Usage of Media Technologies and Psychosocial Factors', *New Media and Society* 9, pp. 425–454.

Hochschild, A.R. (1979) 'Emotion Work, Feeling Rules, and Social Structure', *American Journal of Sociology* 85 (3), pp. 551–575.

Hoover, S. and Clark, L.S. (2008) 'Children and Media in the Context of the Home and Family', in Kirsten Drotner and Sonia Livingstone (eds) *International Handbook of Children, Media and Culture*, London: Sage, pp. 105–120.

Hoover, S.M., Clark, L.S. and Alters, D. (with Joseph G. Champ and Lee Hood) (2004) *Media, Home, and Family*, New York: Routledge.

Ito, M., Baumer, S., Bittanti, M., Boyd, D., Cody, R., Herr-Stephenson, B., Horst, H.A., Lange, P.G., Mahendran, D., Martinez, K.Z., Pascoe, C.J., Perkel, D., Robinson, L. and Tripp, L. (2010) *Hanging Out, Messing Around, and Geeking Out: Kids Living and Learning with New Media*, Cambridge, MT: MIT Press.

Jamieson, L. (1987) 'Theories of Family Development and the Experience of Being Brought Up', *Sociology*, 21 (4), pp. 591–607.

Jamieson, L. (1998) *Intimacy: Personal Relationships in Modern Societies*. Cambridge and Malden, MA: Polity Press.

Jamieson, L. (1999) 'Intimacy Transformed? A Critical Look at the "Pure Relationship"', *Sociology* 33 (3), pp. 477–494.

Jenks, C. (1996) *Childhood*, London: Routledge.

Kearney, J. (2007) 'Productive Spaces: Girls' Bedrooms as Sites of Cultural Production', *Children and Media* 1 (2), pp. 126–141.

Kehily, M.J. (2010) 'Childhood in Crisis? Tracing the Contours of "Crisis" and its Impact upon Contemporary Parenting Practices', *Media, Culture & Society* 32, pp. 171–185.

König, A. (2008) 'Which Clothes Suit Me? The Presentation of the Juvenile Self', *Childhood* 15 (2), pp. 225–237.

Lally, E. (2002) *At Home with Computers*, Berg: Oxford.

Lareau, A. (2003) *Unequal Childhoods: Class, Race and Family Life*, Berkeley, CA: University of California Press.

Layard, R. and Dunn, J. (2009) *A Good Childhood: Searching for Values in a Competitive Age*, London: Penguin.

Lim, S.S. (2005) 'From Cultural to Information Revolution: ICT Domestication by Middle-class Chinese Families', in Thomas Berker, Maran Hartmann, Yves Punie, and Katie Ward (eds) *Domestication of Media and Technology*, Maidenhead: Open University Press, pp. 185–204.

Lincoln, S. (2004) 'Teenage Girls' Bedroom Culture: Codes Versus Zones', in Andy Bennett and Keith Kahn-Harris (eds) *After Subculture*, London: Palgrave Macmillan, pp. 94–106,

Lincoln, S. (2012) *Youth Culture and Private Space*, Basingstoke: Palgrave Macmillan.

Liss, M., Schiffrin, H.H., Mackintosh, V.H., Miles-McLean, H. and Erchull, M.J. (2012) 'Development and Validation of a Quantitative Measure of Intensive Parenting Attitudes', *Journal of Child and Family Studies* 22 (5), pp. 621–636.

Livingstone, S. (2002) *Young People and New Media: Childhood and the Changing Media Environment*, London: Sage Publications.

Livingstone, S. (2004) 'Media Literacy and the Challenge of New Information and Communication Technologies', *Communication Review* 1 (7), pp. 3–14.

Livingstone, S. (2005) 'In Defense of Privacy: Mediating the Public/Private Boundary at Home', in Sonia Livingstone (ed.) *Audiences and Publics: When Cultural Engagement Matters for the Public Sphere*, Changing Media – Changing Europe series (2), Bristol: Intellect Books, pp. 163–185.

Livingstone, S. (2006) 'Drawing Conclusions from New Media Research: Reflections and Puzzles Regarding Children's Experience of the Internet', *The Information Society* 22 (4), pp. 219–230.

Livingstone, S. (2007) 'From Family Television to Bedroom Culture: Young People's Media at Home', in Eoin Devereux (ed.) *Media Studies: Key Issues and Debates*, London: Sage, pp. 302–321.

Livingstone, S. (2009) *Children and the Internet*, Cambridge: Polity Press.

Livingstone, S. (2014) 'Digital Media and Children's Rights', blog post, LSE Media Policy Project, available at: *http://blogs.lse.ac.uk/mediapolicyproject/2014/09/12/sonia-livingstone-digital-media-and-childrens-rights/*, accessed 5 December 2015.

Livingstone, S. and Bober, M. (2005) 'UK Children Go Online Project: Final Report of Key Project Findings 6', London School of Economics and Political Science, available at: *http://eprints.lse.ac.uk/399/*, accessed 5 December 2015.

Livingstone, S. and Das, R. (with contributions from Myria Georgiou, Leslie Haddon, Ellen Helsper and Yinhan Wang) (2010) 'Media, Communication and Information Technologies in the European Family', Working Report (April 2010), Family Platform, Existential Field 8, available at: *http://eprints.lse.ac.uk/29788/1/EF8_LSE_MediaFamily_Education.pdf*, accessed 5 December 2015.

Livingstone, S., Haddon, L., Görzig, A. and Ólafsson, K. (2011) 'EU Kids Online II: Final Report', London: LSE, available at: *http://eprints.lse.ac.uk/39351/1/EU_kids_online_final_report_%5BLSERO%5D.pdf*, accessed 5 December 2015.

Livingstone, S., Mascheroni, G., Ólafsson, K. and Haddon, L. (2014) *Children's Online Risks and Opportunities: Comparative Findings from EU Kids Online and Net Children Go Mobile*, LSE, London: EU Kids Online.

Livingstone, S. and Wang, Y. (2013) Media Literary and the Communications Act, Media Policy Brief 2, London School of Economics and Political Science, available at: *http://www.lse.ac.uk/media@lse/documents/MPP/LSE-Media-Policy-Brief-2-Updated.pdf*, accessed 5 December 2015.

Lu, H. (2000) 'To Be Relatively Comfortable in an Egalitarian Society', in Deborah Davis (ed.) *The Consumer Revolution in Urban China*, Berkeley, CA: University of California Press, pp. 124–144.

Maccoby, E. (2007) 'Historical Overview of Socialization Research and Theory', in Joan Grusec and Paul Hastings (eds) *Handbook of Socialization: Theory and Research*, New York: Guilford Press, pp. 13–41.

Messenger Davies, M. (2010) *Children, Media and Culture*, Maidenhead: Open University Press.

Millwood Hargrave, A. and Livingstone, S. (2009) *Harm and Offence in Media Content: A Review of the Empirical Literature* (2nd edn), Bristol: Intellect Press.

Murdock, G., Hartmann, P. and Gray, P. (1992) 'Contextualizing Home Computing: Resources and Practices', in Roger Silverstone and Eric Hirsch (eds) *Consuming Technologies: Media and Information in Domestic Spaces*, London/New York: Routledge, pp. 146–160.

Nayak, A. and Kehily, M.J. (2008) *Gender, Youth And Culture: Young Masculinities and Femininities*, Basingstoke, Palgrave Macmillan.

Nelson, M. (2010) *Parenting out of Control: Anxious Parents in Uncertain Times*, New York: New York University Press.

Oestreicher, M. (2012) *A Parent's Guide to Understanding Social Media: Helping Your Teenager Navigate Life Online*, Lawrenceville, GA: Group Simply Youth Ministries.

Ofcom (2014a) The Communications Market Report, 'Techie Teens Are Shaping How We Communicate', *Context, The Communications Market 2014* available at: *http://stakeholders.ofcom.org.uk/market-data-research/market-data/communications-market-reports/cmr14/uk/*, accessed 5 December 2015.

Ofcom (2014b) Children Parents: Media Use and Attitudes Report, October 2014, available at: *http://stakeholders.ofcom.org.uk/binaries/research/media-literacy/media-use-attitudes-14/Childrens_2014_Report.pdf*, accessed 5 December 2015.

Office for National Statistics (ONS) (2014) 'Large Increase in 20-34-year-olds Living with Parents Since 1996, 2011', released 21 January 2014, available at: *http://www.ons.gov.*

uk/ons/rel/family-demography/young-adults-living-with-parents/2013/sty-young-adults.html, accessed 5 December 2015.

Patchin, J.W. and Hinduja, S. (2010) 'Trends in Online Social Networking: Adolescent Use of MySpace over Time', *New Media & Society* 12 (2), pp. 197–216.

Plowman, L., McPake, J. and Stephen, C. (2008) 'The Technologisation of Childhood? Young Children and Technology in the Home', *Children & Society* 24 (1), pp. 63–74.

Pugh, A. (2009) *Longing and Belonging: Parents, Children and Consumer Culture*, Berkeley, CA: University of California Press.

Rohloff, A. (2013) 'Moral Panics as Civilizing and Decivilizing Processes? A Comparative Discussion', *Politica y Sociedad* 50 (2), pp. 483–500.

Rose, N. (1999) *Governing the Soul: The Shaping of the Private Self* (2nd edn), London: Routledge.

Rudd, T., Gifford, C., Morrison, J. and Facer, K. (2006) *What If . . . Reimagining Learning Spaces*. Bristol: Futurelab.

Russo Lemor, A.-M. (2006) 'Making a "Home": The Domestication of Information and Communication Technologies in Single Parents' Households', in Thomas Berker, Maran Hartmann, Yves Punie, and Katie Ward (eds) *Domestication of Media and Technology*, Maidenhead: Open University Press, pp. 165–184.

Sargeant, J. (2010) 'The Altruism of Pre-adolescent Children's Perspectives on "Worry and Happiness" in Australia and England', *Childhood* 17 (3), pp. 411–425.

Seiter, E. (2005) *The Internet Playground: Children's Access, Entertainment, and Mis-Education*, New York: Peter Lang.

Shaputis, K. (2004) *The Crowded Nest Syndrome: Surviving the Return of Adult Children*, Olympia, PA: Clutter Fairy Publishing.

Signorielli, N. (2001) 'Television's Gender Role Images and Contributions to Stereotyping: Past, Present and Future', in Jerome Singer and Dorothy Singer (eds) *Handbook of Children and the Media*, Newbury Park, CA: Sage Publications, pp. 341–358.

Silverstone, R. (2006) 'Domesticating Domestication: Reflections on the Life of a Concept', in Thomas Berker, Maran Hartmann, Yves Punie, and Katie Ward (eds) *Domestication of Media and Technology*, Maidenhead: Open University Press, pp. 229–247.

Silverstone, R. and Haddon, L. (1996) 'Design and the Domestication of Information and Communication Technologies: Technical Change and Everyday Life', in Roger Silverstone and Robin Mansell (eds) *Communication by Design: The Politics of Information and Communication Technologies*, Oxford: Oxford University Press, pp. 44–74.

Steiner-Adair, C. and Barker, T.H. (2013) *The Big Disconnect*, New York: Harper Collins.

Strasbourg, V.C. and Wilson, B.J. (2002) *Children, Adolescents and the Media*, London: Sage.

Subrahmanyam, K. and Greenfield, P. (2008) 'Online Communication and Adolescent Relationships', *Project Muse* 18 (1), pp. 119–146.

Tanton, P.S., Zhou, C., Sallis, J.F., Cain, K.L., Frank, L.D. and Saelens, B.E. (2012) 'Home Environment Relationships with Children's Physical Activity, Sedentary Time and Screen Time by Socioeconomic Status', *International Journal of Behaviour Nutrition and Physical Activity*, 9 (1), p. 88, doi: 10.1186/1479-5868-9-88.

Turkle, S. (2011) *Alone Together: Why We Expect More from Technology and Less from Each Other*, New York: Basic Books.

Valkenburg, P.M. (2000) 'Media and Youth Consumerism', *Journal of Adolescent Health*, 27 (2), pp. 52–56, 61–72.

Vandebosch, H. and Van Cleemput, K. (2009) 'Cyberbullying among Youngsters: Profiles of Bullies and Victims', *New Media & Society* 11 (8), pp. 1349–1371.

Van Rompaey, V. and Roe, K. (2001) 'The Home as a Multimedia Environment: Families' Conception of Space and the Introduction of Information and Communication Technologies in the Home', *Communications* 26 (4), pp. 351–369.

Wang, Y. (2010) 'Special Focus: Girl Culture and the Web', in Sonia Livingstone and Ranjana Das (eds) Existential Field 8: Media, Communication and Information in the European Family Working Report, pp. 57–65.

Wheelock, J. (1992) 'Personal Computers, Gender and an Institutional Model of the Household', in Roger Silverstone and Eric Hirsch (eds) *Consuming Technologies: Media and Information in Domestic Spaces*, London: Routledge, pp. 97–116.

Whitby, P. (2011) *Is Your Child Safe Online? A Parent's Guide To The Internet, Facebook, Mobile Phones and Other New Media*, London: White Ladder Press.

Yan, R. (1994) 'To Reach China Consumers, Adapt to Guo-Qing', *Harvard Business Review* 72 (5), pp. 66–74.

Zhao, B. and Murdock, G. (1996) 'Young Pioneers: Children and the Making of Chinese Consumerism', *Cultural Studies* 10 (2), pp. 201–217.

5

FROM ARCADE TO FAMILY-CENTRED VIDEO GAMING

Introduction

This chapter addresses the historical and contemporary processes involved in the design and promotion of video game consoles for their installment in the home. The aim is to understand the conditions under which video gaming became a family-based domestic leisure activity. With some notable exceptions, a feature of much of the earlier literature on gaming cultures has been a relative lack of consideration of the locality of gaming in relation to its content, despite the recognition that bedroom culture plays a central role in teenagers' lives. By exploring the social dynamics involved in the household adoption of video gaming, this chapter investigates how families and young people are addressed and signified through the advertising of family-centred video gaming. The first section traces the dramatic changes in the meanings and values of gaming underpinning the rise of home-based 'family-centred' video gaming. The second section chronicles the gendered and spatial codes involved in the history of the design and promotion of video gaming during its migration from the public sphere of the arcade to the private context of family home. The third section focuses on the motives for cultivating a new kind of video gaming entertainment designed for family participation in the home as a mediating strategy for parents established in the first decade of the millennium. In the final part, the chapter addresses emerging patterns and dynamics of video gaming in the home.

Aspirations towards inter-generational family gaming

The accumulation of media-related equipment in children's bedrooms and the privatisation of children's home-based leisure have prompted parents to find ways to reconnect with children through shared media entertainment. Parents routinely search for ways to use home-based media to bring their families together and offset the individualising effects of today's media affordances. Taking pleasure in watching a film or television (TV) programme together with children in the shared space of the living room is viewed as 'good parenting'. However, it is significant that parents prefer shared activities that do not involve media, revealing the ambivalence felt by parents about the role of media in family relationships with their children. In a study of children's uses of digital technology, Livingstone et al. (2014) noticed that when parents wish to demonstrate 'good parenting', they mention shared non-media activities such as going to the park, sports or craft activities in the home. Nevertheless, with aspirations towards collaborative media engagement, parents purchase media gadgets aimed at facilitating sociable, shared media leisure activities in their efforts to prioritise parent–child time together. For example, research by Hoover et al. (2004) identifies family modes of media incorporation as part of the construction of family identity. Despite ambivalent attitudes, a high priority for parents is the fostering of inter-generational media activities by encouraging children's media play with parents, grandparents and siblings (Clark 2013). The multiple motives for drawing children into family-centred media activities include the promotion of children's health, education and play as well as the enhancement of family connectivity.

A study in the US by Clark (2013) reveals that parents often spend insufficient unstructured time having fun and interacting with their children, and often use media to fill that gap. She also found that parents' desire to prioritise parent–child time together varies according to social class. Middle and upper-middle class families often fall into a habit of rushing between scheduled activities and settling into separate media-related activities when at home together. Mothers voice concern about wasting time watching movies even though young people consistently mention 'movie night' as a time for family bonding. Among lower-income families, Clark found that shared media time occurs because parents could not afford to participate in other shared activities. In these circumstances, media can form a common bond that crosses generations (Clark 2013: 220). Many parents now attempt to apply media in positive ways, using entertainment media as a platform for discussions of morality and using mobile phones and social media as a pragmatic means to enhance communication with their children.

Clark's work confirms that parents are keen to identify ways of engaging children in parent–child computer games to foster and improve collaborative and participatory learning between parents and children and enable parents to learn along with their children. She provides advice to parents in her book, *The Parent App*, to find ways to encourage their children to participate in family-centred digital projects as well as movie nights. Clark suggests inviting children and possibly their friends to participate in activities such as Dance Revolution, Guitar Hero or Wii Sports; and to select TV programmes that everyone can watch, and make a commitment to viewing these together on a regular basis. Clark also recommends that parents engage in family-centred digital projects in which children are encouraged to take the lead. She advises, 'Let your teen walk you through *Halo*, *Super Mario Brothers* or *Fruit Ninja*, or have your younger child introduce you to the world of Club Penguin or Webkinz' and, 'Challenge your children to take the lead on family-related digital projects, whether it's documenting the family vacation or making a video holiday card and distributing it through YouTube' (Clark 2013: 221). As the following sections show, these are the kinds of suggestions which have influenced the design and promotion of today's home-based, family-centred gaming.

From arcade to home: the design of video gaming for the home

This section traces the history of gaming's entrance into the home, which underpins the rise of today's parent–child collaborative video gaming as a parental mediating strategy. The early adoption of video games in the home from the 1970s involved major struggles over the meanings and values of the shared space of the living room. The history of video game design highlights the tension between two types of media functions: a toy in the form of an action game and a screen-based educational tool in the form of a computer. Beginning as public forms of entertainment within the fairground and amusement arcade, early video games moved from this public environment to become a private mode of entertainment. The traditionally male-identified space of the arcade was to be imposed on a feminised space of domestic leisure emphasised by the earlier domestication of radio and TV (Flynn 2001).

Introduced to amusement arcades from the 1970s, video games began as popular entertainment among young adults, particularly men and adolescent boys. The reasons why early console-based video games did not immediately blend into the domestic environment of the home were not so much about the unattractiveness of the technology but more about the reputation of the preceding context of play. Framed by the disreputable masculine imagery of the arcade, bars and funfair, the video game console was viewed as some untamed beast brought in from the wild, disorderly spaces of the public sphere (Flynn 2003). As Silverstone (1994: 98) states: 'Domestication does, perhaps literally, involve bringing objects in from the wild; from the public space of shops, arcades and working environments; from factories, farms and quarries.' As screen-based technologies, the video game was an interactive version of the TV set. But in order for the technology to be domesticated, this interactive quality demanded a particular kind of communal interaction and physical movement and a major reorganisation of communal space in the home. The video game industry decided to design games for the home by fusing a tradition of entertainment and play with that of family learning and education.

The first home video game console, Magnavox Odysee, available in the US from 1972, was designed for the living room to form part of family pursuits and promoted as 'a total play and learning experience' (Lubar 1993). Attempts to domesticate the console were made by designing video games to be connected to the TV set and by using educational signifiers in the design of the visual features of the equipment. Although gaming was presented as an activity for fostering family togetherness, the manufacturer downplayed the entertainment aspect. This early stage of game design brought together a games console and office computer design style to signify educational use, with gaming expressed as a secondary theme. Programmable systems such as the Atari Video computer system 2600, released in 1977, and the Commodore 64, released in 1982, were also designed to resemble a computer with gaming capabilities rather than an entertainment system. Yet most consoles from this era were dedicated consoles – they could only play the games that came with the console.

Game titles gradually migrated from the fairground and arcade into the home during the 1970s, with Nintendo releasing the first home video game in Japan in 1976. Significant parallels can be found between the domestication of the game console and earlier processes of domestication relating to the radio and TV (Flynn 2003; Spigel 1988, 1990, 1992; Boddy 1994; Silverstone 1994, 1997). However, popular game titles were needed, as well as appropriate console design, for video gaming to succeed in overcoming the barriers to its acceptance into the home. It was not until 1980 that an adapted version of the arcade hit, *Space Invaders*, was released for the Atari 2600, acting as a springboard for the successful launch of the home console industry. The facility of playing this widely popular game at home was the key to the US Atari console's success. It triggered the trend of console manufacturers attempting to gain exclusive rights to popular arcade titles and the marketing of game consoles to claim that the thrill of the arcade experience could be brought into the home (Baer 2005).

The early 1980s came to be known as the golden age of arcade video games in terms of appeal and technological innovation. Between 1980 and 1982, the number of video games in North America more than doubled (Wolf 2008; Dillon 2011). By 1982, the US arcade video game industry's revenue outstripped the combined annual gross revenue of both pop music and Hollywood films that year. Sales of home video games were $3.8 billion in 1982, approximately half that of video game arcades (Rogers and Larsen 1984: 263). In the same year, 86 per cent of the US population aged 13–20 years had played some kind of video game and an estimated eight million US homes had video games hooked up to the TV set. However, the popularity of arcades prompted parental concerns that video gaming might be causing adolescent truancy from school (Fisher 1994).

In was in 1983 that Japanese toy manufacturer Nintendo launched the family computer and a video game system called 'Famicom', advertising it as a toy. This marked the moment when games graduated from educational titles to embrace the fantasy spectacles associated with the arcade but situated in the context of home family entertainment. Later known as the Nintendo Entertainment System, this innovation was followed by dedicated consoles including the Sega master system, which introduced titles such as *Super Mario Bro* (1985) and *Space Harrier* (1988). The early game magazine *Nintendo Power* emphasised the system's potential for family play (Boudreau and Consalvo 2014: 1119). In contrast to the earlier Atari and Commodore systems which emphasised a computer aesthetic, the Nintendo and Sega video games were visually presented as entertainment gaming machines. Evidence of their computer origins were minimised through the addition of joy-sticks and add–on devices including 3D glasses. The fantasy of combining the video game machine with the TV to create a central digital control system in the living room formed part of science fiction fantasies about the futuristic smart home (Finn 2002; Spigel 1992). Through these media imaginaries, the entertainment technology of gaming transformed the cultural meanings associated with the living room. However, as these machines and the games designed for them contained residual connotations of the arcade, they continued to appeal mainly to male youth and were appropriated for personal use in the context of the male bedroom. Much early 1980s research and design continued to focus on individual digital gameplay, with a particular emphasis on play by young children (Mitchell 1985; Flynn 2003).

By the late 1990s, video game arcades were closing down as the technology of home video game consoles started to rival arcade games. A steep rise in the sale of consoles, with 26 million in US homes by 1990 (Forester 1993) confirmed the technology's central place in the home. However, manufacturers were keen to safeguard the console machine's street appeal at the same time as transforming the device into 'a domestic dweller within the living room' (Flynn 2003: 556). The transfer of the games console, with the TV screen, from the bedroom to the communal space of the living room was not widespread until the first PlayStation was released in 1994. Representing a major change in the late 1990s, video game manufacturers joined forces with entertainment and communications companies to transform their manufacturing image from 'toy' to 'media entertainment tech-nology'. It enabled gaming to take centre-stage within the young, still mainly male, adult market. Console players now appealed to an average age of 22 years (Flynn 2003).

Within the design of gaming for the home, arcade imagery was now combined with new gaming themes and marketed via both the software and the visual design of the hardware. The popular arcade imagery of 'Shoot-Em-Up' action games involving gun fire, violence and sports, highly popular among young men and boys, was retained but also combined with updated games such as *Grand Theft Auto* (PS2), *Tony Hawk's Pro Skater* (Xbox, PS2) and *Max Payne* (Xbox, PS2). Incongruously, these new-style action games were designed for a home console to be placed in the heart of the living room. There are noticeable parallels between the domestic appropriation of the video game console and the domestic adoption of the TV receiver from the 1950s (see Chapter 2). However, from its inception, TV programming ensured the transmission of content suitable for a more feminised domestic and family audience. Although designed for home use, the Sony PlayStation console of the mid 1990s continued to be viewed as the preserve of teenage boys and men in their twenties with spare income and loose family ties. Importantly, gaming narratives tended to have masculine appeal, reflecting gender-specific characters in relation to game content (Jansz et al. 2010). Likewise, advertisements in gaming magazines such as *Playstation* from the late 1990s depicted youthful male players.

By portraying video gaming as a form of extreme sport, advertisements created futuristic fantasies of untamed, rebellious and boisterous game play in which the surroundings (living room or bedroom) would be blown up in the narrative. Instead of conveying the living room as a refuge and context for family togetherness, game advertisements conveyed this domestic communal space as a stifling and hideous context of monotonous routines, to be obliterated. Paradoxically, video gaming was promoted as a set of adventures initiating out-of-body experiences through bodily action that relied on condemning and obliterating domestic space. Video gaming was now marketed for domestic consumption, yet it thoroughly contradicted domestic sensibilities. PlayStation 2 used the tagline, 'the third place', to convey the idea of console and TV as a portal to cybernetic fantasies of speed, danger and freedom (Laurel 1993). The game formed an imaginary, theatrical space in which the body could be transported into outer-space on a screen. The living room could be blocked out or annihilated (Flynn 2003).

Aimed at men and boys, this advertising imagery and game content comprised a celebration of masculine technological innovation and virtual immersion. At the same time, the games offered a dream of escape from domesticity as a feminine space. These imaginaries bring to mind not only military and frontier imagery but also boys' adventure stories of the nineteenth century. Jenkins (1998) observes that video game play reproduces several features of traditional play for boys, such as colonising environments that were once unsupervised spaces outdoors. Now practised in the confined and monitored spaces of the home, video games extend the kinds of activities that boys once played regularly in public spaces. This migration of gaming into the home intensified the pressures placed on parents, particularly mothers, to monitor and regulate children's connections to popular culture.

The video console from the 1990s to around 2005 was represented as an alien object that gatecrashed the domestic harmony of 'home'. Addressing a female readership, lifestyle magazines in this period such as *Ideal Home*, *Homes and Gardens* and *Country Living* conventionally associated feminine identities within discourses of domesticity as family togetherness. In contrast, gaming magazines such as *GamePro*, *Video Games* and *Electronic Games* portrayed the video console by proposing an alternative world filled with aliens, monsters, warriors and the third space involving the obliteration of the living room (Flynn 2003). This generated gender and generational divisions and, in turn, posed a problem for gaming manufacturers intent on promoting family-centred social gaming. Video gaming's public image and content clashed with the moral economy of the household, impeding its integration into household routines (Silverstone 1994: 129; Flynn 2003). At the time, console manufacturers were reluctant to transform the video game console into a wholly domesticated artefact in case they lost their mainly masculine market. It was not until the games were extended to include less aggressive action that they started to appeal to a wider market, including girls, women and grandparents, thereby initiating multi-generational communal activities in the home.

Within the domestication approach, a series of sociological studies in the 1990s confirmed that computer gaming formed a central part of boys cultures, performed across a network of households (Haddon 1992; Wheelock 1992). A study by Ruth Furlong (1995) revealed that gaming was often used to contest and subvert parental definitions of 'suitable' media use among boys who move between households as a result of parental divorce. Moving between homes became a means of gaining 'spatial freedom', allowing boys to construct an alternative moral economy. Similarly, Bernadette Flynn (2003) found evidence of gender exclusiveness and exclusion in households where male access was privileged and girls were thought insufficiently skilled despite the console's domestic positioning. Studies indicated that family household relationships are significantly altered by their children's media engagement. The traditionally male-dominated public leisure space of the arcade is propelled into a traditionally feminised leisure space of the living room, filling the home with arcade activities and values (Flynn 2003: 569). The challenges of parental monitoring of children's video gaming confirmed that the layout of the domestic environment and the relations between household members play key roles in structuring individual and collaborative media engagement. For example, connecting the games console to the main TV set in the living room often triggers arguments between parents and children (Haddon 2006: 116). Related research confirmed that the home comprised a site of gendered struggles with video gaming providing a powerful technology and set of practices through which conventional gendered power relations are enacted and reinforced (Bryce and Rutter 2003; Schott and Horrell 2000).

Gender differences among domestic video console users

Although evidence that differences in amounts of male and female play are now slight, female game players have tended to be overlooked in studies of gaming communities (Bryce and Rutter 2003; Carr 2005; Jenson and de Castell 2005, 2010, 2011; Kafai et al. 2008; Krotoski 2004; Thornham 2008; Walkerdine 2006, 2007; Yee 2008). The traditional association of girls with bedroom culture and their lack of full access to public social spaces have deflected research attention. However, studies indicate that the meanings associated with domestic media use are influenced by and often reproduce wider power relationships between men and women, and between adults and children in the household as well as between social classes (Gauntlett and Hill 1999; Morley 1986, 2002; Lally 2002). Social gaming exemplifies this gendered struggle. Women and girls are now much more tech savvy with research showing that they made up over 52 per cent of internet users and 70 per cent of casual online gamers even by 2004 (Graner-Ray 2004). In relation to gender differences in game content, Sheri Graner-Ray (2004) draws attention to differences in reward systems, game play preferences and avatar selection criteria.

Girls and women game players continue to be marginalised by the main themes and genres of the games which address men through military, masculine adventure and action themes with titles such as *God of War*, *Manhunt* or *Stalker*. Not only are female characters persistently underrepresented in commercially available games, there is also a prevalence of highly stereotypical representations of men and women in games with hyper-masculinised and hyper-feminised images (Berrin and Standley 2002; Dietz 1998; Ivory 2006; Jansz and Martis 2007; Martins et al. 2009). As a result, women and girls tend to be marginalised as a 'non traditional market' (Graner-Ray 2004). Girls are also addressed directly by pink box titles such as *Rockett's New School, Barbie: Horseshow* or *Mary Kate and Ashley: Sweet 16.* Importantly, women have also tended to be peripheral to a gaming community that identifies with masculinity, the dynamism of the city and its associated alienation from the home, the domestic and the feminine (Schott and Horrell 2000; Jenson and de Castell 2011). Girls and young women's relationship to digital games is reflected not only in relation to game content but also in terms of the ambiguous relationship of gaming to the domestic sphere. However, there is growing evidence that women tend to participate in gaming within domestic contexts with friends, family and partners, demonstrating the importance of family and household relationships (Jenson and de Castell 2011).

From 2000, a new class of games consoles designed as entertainment units were marketed for their DVD and computer functions as well as their gaming abilities. Contrasting starkly with the science fiction visions promoted in the video game advertising of the late 1990s, Sony's video game marketing objective was to create a 'digital entertainment hub in the home for personal creativity as well as entertainment' (Flynn 2003). During this same period, Microsoft launched the Xbox, taking great care to ensure that it looked nothing like a desktop computer. By now, PlayStation's idea of a digital entertainment hub and Microsoft's vision of the digital living room were brought together to feed into modernist imaginings of the 'home of the future' (Flynn 2003: 559). Technological advances led to the integration of aspects of work and leisure in game consoles as they became multifunctioning set-top boxes facilitating video game play with online gaming, data processing and hard drive storage. The intention was to create a machine designed for the domestic and communal setting of the living room by designing video gaming as an activity that would appeal to the whole family. Thus, by the early twenty-first century, large media corporations such as Sony and Microsoft were targeting the living room as a family entertainment hub in the home. This shift revealed a significant weakening of the boundaries between paid work, the home office, and domestic leisure. Prophetically, Flynn states:

> Along with these technological innovations, shifts from public to private modes of social engagement indicate that the home will become more of an important site for personal and mediated forms of work and social connectedness, with the living room an increasingly contested and negotiated space within the home.
>
> *(Flynn 2003: 573)*

Games consoles are regularly moved into the private space of children's bedrooms after the initial placement in a communal space (Aarsand and Aronsson 2009;

BBC 2005). Since action games appeal mainly to boys and men, thereby acting as a barrier to adult group gaming, consoles quickly gravitated from the living room to teenagers' bedrooms (BBC 2005; Bovill and Livingstone 2001; Livingstone 2009). By 2009, 69 per cent of 5–16-year-olds had games consoles, radios and DVD players in their bedrooms (ChildWise 2009). Parents face the challenge of trying to restrict their children's video and computer game play to particular times of the day, such as after the completion of their school work. The living room becomes a site of intense parental supervision and regulation to curb gendered as well as generational tensions among siblings. Knowledge about parental controls is limited among some parents, despite parents' anxieties about the potential harmful effects of gaming on young people. Ulicsak and Cranmer (2010) found that few parents were aware of the age ratings guidance and the meanings of content icons. Some did not set up parental controls because they believed that their children would override the restrictions while others missed the instructions that came with the console. Research also confirms that teenage boys owning multiple game consoles tend to play violent video games only in the privacy of their bedrooms to avert negative reactions from family members in the living room (Courtois et al. 2012).

The launch of family-centred video gaming

From 2005, video game companies responded to public concerns that video and computer gaming cause addiction and introvert, solitary and uncommunicative behaviour among teenage boys who play violent games. A dramatic shift in console and game design towards family-centred gaming formed part of a drive to domesticate video and computer gaming by promoting the shared space of the living room as a sociable entertainment hub. Nintendo Wii, Microsoft Xbox 360 and Sony PlayStation 3 were new home video game consoles in this category. For example, Nintendo Wii was designed to target a broader demographic by transcending gendered and generational differences. This marked a new form of home-based entertainment for communal use in a living room context. The industry began to develop games not just for the home but specifically for the living room to encourage inter-generational and inter-gender activity through a range of games designed for play by the whole family, from young children to grandparents. At last, the game content, marketing and advertising no longer contradicted the manufacturers' aims of placing the technology in the living room. Instead, and against a background of public anxiety about media's role in fragmenting family-centred leisure, family gaming bucked the trend of personalised and segmented media-based home entertainment.

Signified by the games and design of the slim console, Nintendo Wii was marketed from November 2006 as a 'family' system in the first UK marketing campaign. Other platforms followed in promoting family-friendly games including Sony PlayStation 3's *LittleBigPlanet* (2007), *Rock Band* (MTV Games and Electronic Arts 2007) and its cross-platform *Guitar Hero* (Activision 2005) (Ulicsak et al. 2009: 8). By 2008, the market in the UK had expanded by 26 per cent

(Riley 2008). Representing a major shift in the meanings and uses of mediated home-based leisure, games console ownership continued to grow with an average of 2.4 consoles per UK household by 2009 (Ofcom 2009b). Such digital games were now encoded as family-centred devices in response to parental concerns about the disconnection of youth from family life. This allowed manufacturers to extend their markets beyond former perceptions of the standard male user. The launch of family-centred video gaming during a climate of moral uncertainty and familial changes has tremendous appeal, especially since the new youth leisure technology market is financed mostly by parents rather than schools or other public institutions. Parent–child collaborative play is now regarded as a major mediating strategy for parents (Nikken et al. 2007). Recommendations are made that parents keep the console in a shared space so that they can monitor children's activities (Clark 2013; Ulisack and Cranmer 2010).

The traditionally sharp gender differences in game preferences had to be addressed for the design of family-centred gaming, given that girls and boys approach computer play in different ways related to genre and specific elements of narrative, character and setting (BBC 2005; Bryce and Rutter 2006; Krotoski 2004). In terms of age, younger children of either sex tend to engage with puzzles and action adventure games with popular characters from film and TV such as *Bob the Builder* (BBC/Playstation 2002) and *Toy Story 3* (Disney Interactive Studios 2010). As they age, boys gravitate towards first-person shooters, racing and action games while girls continue with puzzles and simulations (Marsh et al. 2005). A large-scale content analysis of the gender, race and age of characters in popular video games in the US showed that stereotyping remains prevalent with systematic over-representation of males, white and adults and a systematic under-representation of females, Hispanics, Native Americans, children and the elderly (Williams et. al. 2009).

Nintendo Wii responded to these cultural barriers by creating new games to reduce differences in physical ability and computer dexterity. To overcome exclusionary representations and foster family-centred play, the designers needed to offer a varied choice of games and game characters (avatars). The control systems were developed for directed body movement, offering a range of levels of physical strength and styles of play in a format that can foster inter-generational users to compete on equal terms (Shinkle 2008). In these ways, home video games were designed specifically to encourage mixed age group play including parents and grandparents, to allow adults to compete equally with young people. Significantly, during the height of its popularity, the Nintendo Wii was used almost evenly by men and women in the UK. Over a 6-month period during 2008, 29 per cent of women and 32 per cent of men played on the Wii at least once with 15 per cent of users being between the ages of 45 and 64 (TNS 2008). By 2010, a quarter of British homes had a Nintendo Wii video game console (Ulicsak and Cranmer 2010). Nintendo's promotion of family gaming was exemplified by its successful release of *Wii Play* (2006), *Wii Sports* (2006) and *Wii Fit* (2007), designed to be easy to learn and group-oriented. To identify the Wii as family-centred, Nintendo combined body movement with character diversity to generate new kinds of interactive use.

Computer companies such as Apple and Microsoft are continuing to design computers as stylish multimedia entertainment devices, transforming the computer console into a 'digital hub', the central node of a networked home. For example, at the time of writing, the Microsoft gaming device Xbox One plays CDs and DVDs, connects to the online service Xbox live and is partially compatible with Apple's iPod. These companies have designed a seamless integration of functionalities within computer-based devices that no longer resemble traditional computers (Quandt and von Pape 2010). Other companies have concentrated on integrating telecommunications, broadband applications and entertainment media such as TV with 'triple play', offering telephone, TV and broadband internet within one service connection.

The Nintendo Wii TV commercials

Returning to the Nintendo Wii example, this console was first advertised on TV in the UK in the lead up to Christmas from 2006 to tap into the lucrative festive market for family games, once dominated by traditional board games. The commercials revealed a striking departure from the youthful, action-packed advertisement images of handheld devices such as the Apple iPod and iPod Touch (Jenkins 2008). They also differed from the early 1980s Atari advertisements that had used famous characters such as the Morecambe and Wise comedy duo[1] to highlight party fun rather than family togetherness. And in contrast to recent commercials for masculinised video games with strong military and male hero characters, the Nintendo Wii commercials accentuated family camaraderie and kinship bonding by showing teenagers and younger children playing sport video games with parents and grandparents in domestic settings. The phrase, 'the whole family' is emphasised over and over again as a core unit. For example, in the 'Mario Goes Multiplayer' commercial for *Super Mario Wii* screened in 2009,[2] a family of six made up of teenage boys and girls, younger children and two women (a mother and aunt or friend) are seated together in a spacious open-plan lounge playing *Super Mario* on a multiplayer console. The commercial is styled as a documentary, with the name of the narrator and his family subtitled ('Ricky Whiting and his family from Brighton'). In his late teens, Ricky refers to 'family' several times in the voice-over:

> Playing good classic *Mario* with *my family* is so much fun. It's the only multiplayer game I have ever played which we all work as a team. One of *my family members* can hang on to me and we can fly up (shows Ricky and his mother both shaking handheld devices). This is the first platform game I've played with *my mum*. She was loving it. We normally play *Mario Kart*, but that was playing against each other. I think it's going to be less rowdy and *more happiness in our house* when we *get together* (my emphasis).

With the emphasis on family bonding, the game is conveyed as collaborative rather than competitive. Advertisements for Nintendo Wii consoles in online shopping catalogues chime with the same message. For example, the online shopping webpage for gaming products in the chain of department stores, John Lewis, claims: 'With a huge range of games, from adventures to self improvement titles, *the whole family* will love getting together to see who's got the smoothest moves!'[3] (my emphasis).

Nintendo Wii commercials signify the console's rightful place in the communal space of the living room. The activity, whether sport or quiz game, is staged in the heart of an imaginary home: spacious, uncluttered, middle class and suburban. These open-plan display homes boast ample space for handheld controls and bodies to be swung around by players and their observer–competitors. The game is performed by all members of a nuclear-style family, by parents, children and even by visiting grandparents. The 'bedroom cultures' of children and the edgy, 'street' visions of youth are eliminated by this new vigour of kin-based leisure interaction. Instead, these imaginary gaming families echo an earlier family type: the 1950s nuclear family: white, middle class and suburban (Chambers 2001). Children are placed centre-stage in the Nintendo Wii commercials, shown instructing or negotiating with adults in the playing of games.

Research confirms that one of the attractions of competitive games enjoyed by families is that they are designed to allow adults and children to compete equally and reduce differences in physical ability (Ulicsak and Cranmer 2010). The commercials accentuate 'youth' as the vanguard of the new technology yet as firmly embedded in the heart of the family. Within this brave new family configuration, children and adolescents are refashioned as a new kind of innocent, innocuous and safe 'youth' through interchangeable clean-cut hairstyles, clothing and childlike exuberance. Such qualities contrast sharply with the 'cool' commercials for mobile new media technology such as the iPod silhouette commercials with the 'street' and 'hip' notions of youth (Jenkins 2008). Nintendo Wii commercials avoid using the youth codes of independence, street identity, self-control and self-absorption typical of commercials for mobile media gadgets such as the famous silhouette Apple iPod ads from 2003 onwards. The relocation of video gaming devices in the family living room fosters the idea that parents can resume control over youth, with a sense of reintegrating 'youth' within 'family'.

The launch of family-centred video gaming during a climate of moral anxiety about children's engagement with media has tremendous appeal. As mentioned in Chapter 4, children are remaining at home and financially dependent on parents for longer in an unprecedented period of 'extended youth'. This often generates tensions of youth dependence and independence articulated in the home setting. Seeing themselves as responsible for creating a cohesive family identity, parents attempt to forge familial bonds through negotiations involving new media (Hoover and Clark 2008). Home-based family-oriented gaming appears to offer parents opportunities for both family bonding and control of children's use of new media. These mediated family practices can be viewed as 'socially scripted behaviour' (Gagnon and Simon 1973: 262). Home-based leisure forms a key context in which family bonding is scripted, with gaming offering an important site for this expression of intimacy.

Emerging patterns and dynamics of family gaming

Not surprisingly, strong claims have been made by the consumer electronics industry that family-centred video gaming can have a positive influence on family life. After its launch in 2006, Nintendo Wii games claimed to foster family identities through play by offering a vital stage on which to perform 'family togetherness' in a progressive domestic communication technology context. Microsoft and the Interactive Software Federation of Europe (ISFE) reported that parents believe family video gaming is pleasurable and beneficial to families (Microsoft 2009; Nielsen 2008). According to global marketing company, TNS (2008), 60 per cent of parents who played games stated that social games, such as the Wii, were being enjoyed by the entire family, rising to 68 per cent for parents with 10–15-year-olds. In the evolving multi-screen home, the positioning of the video game console transformed the living room into a communal space with interaction characterised by a complex interplay between computer gaming, social chat and work-related activities within the living room space.

Home-based digital forms of learning and play by children are challenging prevailing notions of school-based learning (Hull and Kenney 2008). Independent reports on technology's role and impact on education recommend that families take on greater responsibility in guiding young people in their learning. A report by Becta (2008) encourages the use of communication and entertainment technology in informal settings such as the home. The demand by government and independent reports to place responsibility on parents to guide the development of young people's gaming skills is generated by assumptions about the social and educational value of family gaming. Yet such advice fails to take into consideration the kinds of household pressures that limit effective parental monitoring of children's gaming. However, lack of parental knowledge about family gaming is now being addressed by governments.[4] For example, the British Government requires changes to be made to the classification of video games in the UK, as set out in the Digital Economy Act 2010[5] in order to place age ratings of computer games on a statutory footing for ratings of 12 years and above. The UK Council for Child Internet Safety, which makes recommendation about video game ratings, identifies families as mainly responsible despite the lack of effective monitoring of children's gaming by parents (Byron 2008). Nevertheless, parents either do not have the time or the resources to investigate these monitoring issues.

On the one hand, parents are worried about the impact of home-based information and communication technologies (ICTs) entertainment on children's social and educational abilities, the cost of games and associated equipment, the safety of their children, levels of violence in games, and the duration and location of play (Livingstone 2009; Livingstone and Bober 2003; Nikken et al. 2007; Ofcom

2009b). On the other hand, both parents and children (aged 5–15 years) perceive that there are benefits to learning and playing video games as a family (Grant 2009; Ulicsak and Cranmer 2010). For example, parents have encouraged the use of Nintendo Wii while constraining the use of other gaming systems because Wii is 'about exercise' (Ames et al. 2010). Studies conducted on parent–child interaction in video games report that gaming promotes positive interactions between parents and children (Aarsand 2007; Coyne et al. 2011; Ito et al. 2010; Siyahhan et al. 2010). Interestingly, Ulicsak and Cranmer (2010) found that over a third of parents had played video games with a 3–16-year-old in the last six months. Parents highlight benefits from playing video games together as a family when the games selected emphasise parental monitoring or guidance roles and skills teaching. Co-play ensures that children play age-appropriate games and that parents can moderate games so that children learn social skills such as collaboration, turn taking and sporting behaviour. Family gaming claims to offer parents opportunities for both family bonding and control of children's use of new media (Ulicsak and Cranmer 2010). This mode of home-based gaming appears to offer positive ways of recuperating 'youth' within a familial entertainment discourse by promoting the idea that parents can supervise and participate in their children's use of new media. However, research findings also confirm that parent–child bonding through gaming is largely with primary school-aged children. Adolescents continue to be mainly solitary players (BBC 2005; Ulicsak et al. 2009). Young people in general continue to play alone much more than with their parents (Ulicsak and Cranmer 2010). Teenagers desire the freedom to be able to play games away from parental supervision (Horst 2010), representing a major challenge for family gaming.

How the family interacts around the gaming activities appears to depend on pre-existing family relationships with marked gender distinctions between parents in terms of types of play with children. Mothers are more likely than fathers to play active technology and fitness games, educational games and dance/music/singing games with a child. Conversely, fathers are more likely than mothers to play fighting games and strategy games with a child (Ulicsak and Cranmer 2010). These gender differences reflect divisions in families and wider society, indicating that gaming may be reinforcing rather than blurring traditional gender and age distinctions (Berker et al. 2006). While family togetherness is parents' main aim, with video gaming itself a secondary aim, family gaming is not something that parents find easy. Competitive games are popular among parents and children where differences in physical ability are reduced. But if players consistently lose the game they are likely to lose interest and play less. Activities where young people are encouraged to tutor their parents are most popular, indicating that Nintendo Wii have developed a successful formula by designing games that allow young people to display their skills. However, this impetus may be a burden on children since they sometimes find it difficult to tutor family members despite their own greater gaming knowledge (Ulicsak and Cranmer 2010).

In a Swedish study, Aarsand and Aronsson (2009) found that computers and game consoles were usually located in communal rather than private places in the home and used by several family members. However, gaming activities were recurrently a child-specific activity. Communal gaming spaces often involved territorial disputes between children and adults concerning who, when and for how long a specific space could be used for gaming. Children were more likely than parents to appropriate communal spaces, turning them into a private gaming space and ignoring bystanders and parental attempts at controlling their gaming. Meanwhile, parents attempted to restrict the children's gaming by limiting the scheduling, timing and duration of gaming; by interrupting gaming while the children positioned themselves as solo players; and by excluding the participation of others (Aarsand and Aronsson 2009). A Dutch study by Nikken and Jansz (2006) found that gaming parents were more likely to co-play with their children and used other active or restrictive mediation strategies. Gaming parents tended to have a positive view of the effects of gaming on children while those with little experience of gaming had strong views about its negative effects.

Further Swedish research by Eklund and Bergmark (2013) on children aged 9–16 years revealed that children usually gamed in the company of peers rather than parents even though gaming was conducted mainly in the home. Mothers used restrictive mediation strategies more than fathers. Importantly, they also found that parents tend to have quite negative views about gaming, which is likely to deter a more active parental role in mediating children's gaming. However, Swedish research also shows that parents who do use active mediation tools often talked to their children about usage or co-played with them and used less restrictive mediation than other parents. This indicates potentially greater parental trust of their children's activities (Nikken et al. 2007; Eklund and Bergmark 2013). Thus, active and participative involvement by parents is likely to generate more mediation (Yee 2008). Nonetheless, digital games continue to be viewed with scepticism by many parents who believe that online gaming is addictive and this affects how they view their children's gaming activities (Bergmark and Bergmark 2009; Bergmark et al. 2011). Although digital gaming can comprise a family leisure activity, parents continue to be less engaged and are therefore less likely to use gaming as a positive way to mediate children's domestic media uses (Eklund and Bergmark 2013).

The migration of digital gaming to mobile devices also presents further complications for parental monitoring. Recent UK data indicates that, in 2014, boys are more likely to use a fixed game player than girls at all ages from 5 to 15 years (Ofcom 2014). Among 8–11-year-olds and 12–15-year-olds, boys are more likely to use a handheld portable games player than girls. There is little gender difference for the use of fixed games consoles among 3–4-year-olds, but boys aged 3–4 years are more likely to use a handheld portable games player than girls (30 per cent vs. 21 per cent). As mentioned, parental monitoring of video gaming is challenged by those children who travel between two homes. Parents may find they have less control if the child moves to their ex-partners household and experiences more freedom to play video games that have more violent content. Relationships of power are enacted in family circles, particularly those in which children identified with two different households due to separation, divorce or remarriage.

In one-parent households, older children tend to have a stronger negotiating role in household rules (Haddon and Silverstone 1995; Hoover and Clark 2008). Yet costly video games may be beyond the reach of many single-parent families on low budgets even though home-based entertainment becomes paramount as a cheap way of accessing leisure for low-income families. The households of poorer parents may seem technologically deprived to children who have access to a wealthier and media-rich parent, usually the father, which may lead to expressions of dissatisfaction (Haddon 2006). The demand on space in poorer and/or smaller households for the kind of family gaming that requires sweeping body movements is also significant, within the moral economy of the household.

Conclusion

The chapter demonstrates that the recent practice of social gaming signifies a new accent on family reciprocity performed and displayed through familial 'social gaming' as entertainment. The notion of a *moral economy* developed by domestic media researchers (Silverstone et al. 1992) to understand the practices and meanings of ICT's use within late modern family life enables the identification of emerging family dynamics surrounding gaming practices. The chapter confirms that the pre-existing moral economy of the household was disrupted when the video game console initially migrated from the fairground and arcade into the living room. For video gaming to enter the home as a stable, regulated space and to be integrated as a family-centred domestic device, its earlier public and masculine connotations had to be erased. Gaming therefore highlights the contested and conditional nature of mediated domestic leisure space.

Underpinned by a history of arcade imagery, video gaming went through several stages before it was successfully redesigned and remarketed in 2006 as inherently multigenerational family entertainment to drive up sales. This transformation of the technology coincided with social aspirations of mediated family togetherness. For the previous two decades, parental and public concern centred on children's media-generated anti-social behaviour. However, the complexities involved in the moral economy of today's households influences the way games are played as much as the transformative design of new forms of gaming (Randall 2011). Parental wishes to control or monitor their children's home-based leisure conflict with young peoples' desires for independence and are exacerbated in single-parent and post-divorce families where children move between two households.

Nonetheless, today's family-centred video gaming is being embraced as having beneficial sociable and educational effects on children's social and coordination skills. The new accent on family reciprocity being displayed through social gaming reflects the late modern process of de-traditionalisation (Giddens 1992). Today's 'democratic', negotiating family expresses reciprocity, recognition and role flexibility through leisure. Social gaming seems to convey and embody these less hierarchical familial associations, which chime with the publicity generated by giant consumer electronic corporations that family gaming is inevitably 'good' for families. Representations of family interaction in the commercials after Nintendo Wii's launch convey a powerful and appealing recuperation of traditional family values in the fast-moving context of new media. The video game is tamed and domesticated as family-oriented leisure. The perceived separateness of parent–child, male–female and inter-generational leisure seems to be eroded by the Wii's apparent ability to foster the 'companionable family' (Chambers 2012). However, the disjunction between imagery and practice is confirmed in preliminary findings on the use of domestic spaces for gaming which suggest that both children and parents 'privatise' communal space to exclude the other party from gaming (Aarsand and Aronsson 2009).

The chapter indicates that computer gaming reflects and confirms the power relations of the living room in the sense that gender and generational relations correspond with the ways that the console is integrated into the domestic routines of the home. It also demonstrates that attempts, via video gaming, to foster relationships of trust between parents and children and give parents opportunities to provide guidance to young people though have had mixed outcomes. Important matters for future research include whether and how family-centred video gaming enhances social and educational skills and how far it may intensify or reduce differences in family and household types, age, social class, gender and ethnicity.

More recent advancements in technology are generating further changes to the social dynamics and contexts of gaming, thereby intensifying the policy concerns about parental, school and government monitoring. For example, the rise in popularity of touch-based technologies such as smartphones, computer tablets with haptic devices and via social network sites coincides with a drop in the age at which children start to play games. Issues of parental mediation will now extend to younger and younger children. Social network gaming is now a daily online activity for many individuals. By 2010, Facebook became a major site for gameplay with 40 per cent of all Facebook visits involving gameplay (Siegler 2010). To compete with Microsoft's Xbox live and Sony's PlayStation Network, Nintendo absorbed Nintendo Wi-Fi Connection from the Wii in 2012 to create Nintendo Network with the aim of supporting the Wii U's online multiplayer gaming and Internet facilities. Computer tablet technology is likely to change parental responses to children's digital activities such as gaming (Ekland and Bergmark 2013; Boudreau and Consalvo 2014). These technological developments raise questions about whether the longer-term trend will be towards increasingly individualised and personalised home-based media or towards communal activities. The following chapter addresses these issues.

Notes

1 Atari commercial, circa 1982, is available at: *http://www.tv-ark.org.uk/mivana/mediaplayer.php?id=a85b0ca62fe71228137dc7ac5d403d9a&media=atari_morecambewise&type=mp4*, accessed 10 November 2010.
2 *Super Mario Wii* commercial is available at: *http://uk.wii.com/wii/en_GB/tv/new_super_mario_bros_wii_-_tv_commercial_2510.html*, accessed 11 July 2010.

3 See *http://www.johnlewis.com/Electricals/Gaming/Nintendo+Wii_2c+DS+and+DSi/SubCate gory.aspx*, accessed 21/07/10.
4 See, for example, Pan European Game Information, available at: *http://videostandards.org. uk/VSC/games_ratings.html*, 'New Rules to Better Protect Children from Inappropriate Video Game Content', Gov.UK, available at: *https://www.gov.uk/government/news/ new-rules-to-better-protect-children-from-inappropriate-video-game-content* and Advice on Child Internet safety by UK Council for Child Internet Safety, available at: *https://www.gov. uk/government/uploads/system/uploads/attachment_data/file/251455/advice_on_child_inter net_safety.pdf*, all accessed 5 December 2015.
5 See *http://webarchive.nationalarchives.gov.uk/20100511084737/http://interactive.bis.gov.uk/ digitalbritain/author/admin/*, accessed 2 July 2010.

References

Aarsand, P.A. (2007) 'Computer and Video Games in Family Life: The Digital Divide as a Resource in Intergenerational Interactions', *Childhood* 14, pp. 235–256.

Aarsand, P.A. and Aronsson, K. (2009) 'Gaming and Territorial Negotiations in Family Life', *Childhood* 16 (4), pp. 497–517.

Baer, R. (2005) *Video Games in the Beginning*, Springfield, NJ: Rolenta Press.

BBC (2005) 'Gamers in the UK: Digital Play, Digital Lifestyles', available at: *http://crystaltips. typepad.com/wonderland/files/bbc_uk_games_research_2005.pdf*, accessed 6 December 2015.

Becta (2008) 'Harnessing Technology Review 2008: The Role of Technology and its Impact on Education – Full Report', available at: *http://dera.ioe.ac.uk/1423/*, accessed 6 December 2015.

Bergmark, K.H. and Bergmark, A. (2009) 'The Diffusion of Addiction to the Field of MMORPGs', *Nordisk Alkohol- och Narkotikatidskrift* 26 (4), pp. 415–426.

Bergmark, K.H., Bergmark, A. and Findahl, O. (2011) 'Extensive Internet Involvement – Addiction or Emerging Lifestyle?', *International Journal of Environmental Research and Public Health* 8 (12), pp. 4488–4501, *http://www.mdpi.com/1660-4601/8/12/4488/*, accessed 6 December 2015.

Berker, T., Hartmann, M., Punie, Y. and Ward, K.J. (eds) (2006) *The Domestication of Media Technology*, Maidenhead: Open University.

Boddy, W. (1994) 'Archaeologies of Electronic Vision and the Gendered Spectator', *Screen* 35, pp. 105–122.

Boudreau, K. and Consalvo, M. (2014) 'Families and Social Network Games', *Information, Communication & Society* 17 (9), pp. 1118–1130.

Bovill, M. and Livingstone, S. (2001) 'Bedroom Culture and the Privatization of Media Use', in Sonia Livingstone and Moira Bovill (eds) *Children and their Changing Media Environment. A European Comparative Study*, Mahwah, NJ: Lawrence Erlbaum Associates, pp. 179–200.

Bryce, J. and Rutter, J. (2003) 'Gender Dynamics and the Social and Spatial Organization of Computer Gaming', *Leisure Studies* 22 (1), pp. 1–15.

Bryce, J. and Rutter, J. (2006) 'Digital Games and Gender', in Jason Rutter and Jo Bryce (eds) *Understanding Digital Games*, London: Sage, pp. 186–204.

Carr, D. (2005) 'Context, Gaming Pleasures and Gendered Preferences', *Simulation and Gaming* 36 (4), pp. 464–482.

Chambers, D. (2001) *Representing the Family*, London: Sage.

Chambers, D. (2012) '"Wii Play as Family": The Rise in Family-centred Video Gaming', *Leisure Studies* 31 (1), pp. 69–82.

ChildWise (2009) *The Monitor Report 2008-9: Children's Media Use and Purchasing*, Norwich: ChildWise.

Clark, L.S. (2013) *The Parent App: Understanding Families in the Digital Age*, Oxford: Oxford University Press.

Courtois, C., Mechant, P., Paulussen, S. and De Marez, L. (2012) 'The Triple Articulation of Media Technologies in Teenage Media Consumption', *New Media and Society* 14 (3), pp. 401–420.

Coyne, S.M., Padilla-Walker, L.M., Stockdale, L. and Day, R.D. (2011) 'Game on . . . Girls: Associations between Co-playing Video Games and Adolescent Behavioral and Family Outcomes', *Journal of Adolescent Health* 49 (2), pp. 160–165.

Dietz, T.L. (1998) 'An Examination of Violence and Gender Role Portrayals in Video Games: Implications for Gender Socialization and Aggressive Behavior', *Sex Roles* 38 (5–6), pp. 425–442.

Dillon, R. (2011) *The Golden Age of Video Games: The Birth of a Multibillion Dollar Industry*, Boca Raton, FL: A K Peters/CRC Press.

Eklund, L. and Bergmark, H.K. (2013) 'Parental Mediation of Digital Gaming and Internet Use', FDG 2013: The 8th International Conference on the Foundations of Digital Games, pp. 63–70.

Fisher, S. (1994) 'Identifying Video Game Addiction in Children and Adolescents', *Addictive Behaviours* 19(5), pp. 545–553.

Finn, M. (2002) 'Console Games in the Age of Convergence', in Frans Mayra (ed.) *Computer Games and Digital Cultures Conference Proceedings*, Tampere, Finland: Tampere University Press, pp. 45–58.

Flynn, B. (2001) 'Video Games and the New Look Domesticity', *Document Actions*, no. 57, available at: *http://bad.eserver.org/issues/2001/57/flynn.html*, accessed 31 July 2013.

Flynn, B. (2003) 'Geography of the Digital Hearth', *Information, Communication and Society* 6 (4), pp. 551–576.

Forester, T. (1993) 'Consuming Electronics: Japan's Strategy for Control', *Media Information Australia*, 67, pp. 4–16.

Furlong, R. (1995) 'There's No Place Like Home', in Martin Lister (ed.) *The Photographic Image in Digital Culture*, London and New York: Routledge, pp. 170–186.

Gagnon, J.H. and Simon, W. (1973) *Sexual Conduct: The Social Sources of Human Sexuality*, Chicago, IL: Aldine Publishing Co.

Gauntlett, D. and Hill, A. (1999) *TV Living: Television Culture and Everyday Life*, London: Routledge.

Giddens, A. (1992) *The Transformation of Intimacy: Sexuality, Love and Eroticism in Modern Societies*, Cambridge: Polity Press.

Graner-Ray, S. (2004) *Gender Inclusive Game Design: Expanding the Market*, Wilmington, MT: Charles River Media.

Grant, L. (2009) 'Learning in Families: A Review of Research Evidence and the Current Landscape of Learning in Families with Digital Technologies (General Educators Report), available at: *http://www2.futurelab.org.uk/resources/documents/project_reports/becta/Learning_in_Families_educators_report.pdf*, accessed 6 December 2015.

Haddon, L. (1992) 'Explaining ICT Consumption: The Case of the Home Computer', in Roger Silverstone and Eric Hirsch (eds) *Consuming Technologies: Media and Information in Domestic Spaces*, London: Routledge, pp. 82–96.

Haddon, L. (2006) 'The Contribution of Domestication Research to Home Computing and Media Consumption', *The Information Society* 22 (4), pp. 195–203.

Haddon, L. and Silverstone, R. (1995) 'Lone Parents and Their Information and Communication Technologies', *SPRU/CICT Report Series*, No. 12, University of Sussex, Falmer.

Hoover, S. and Clark, L.S. (2008) 'Children and Media in the Context of the Home and Family', in Kirsten Drotner and Sonia Livingstone (eds) *International Handbook of Children, Media and Culture*, London: Sage, pp. 105–120.

Hoover, S.M., Clark, L.S. and Alters, D. (with Joseph G. Champ and Lee Hood) (2004) *Media, Home, and Family*, New York: Routledge.

Horst, H.A. (2010) 'Families', in M. Ito, S. Baumer, M. Bittanti, D. Boyd, R. Cody, B. Herr-Stevenson, et al. (eds) *Hanging Out, Messing Around, Geeking Out: Kids Living and Learning with New Media*, Cambridge, MT: The MIT Press, pp. 149–194.

Hull, G.A. and Kenney, N.L. (2008) 'Hopeful Children, Hybrid Spaces: Learning with Media after School', in Kirsten Drotner, Hans Siggaard Jensen and Kim Christian Schroder (eds) *Informal Learning and Digital Media*, Cambridge: Cambridge Scholars Publishing, pp. 70–101.

Ito, M., Baumer, S., Bittanti, M., Boyd, D., Cody, R., Herr-Stephenson, B., et al. (2010) *Hanging Out, Messing Around, and Geeking Out: Kids Living and Learning with New Media*, Cambridge, MT: MIT Press.

Ivory, J.D. (2006) 'Still a Man's Game: Gender Representation in Online Reviews of Video Games', *Mass Communication and Society* 9 (1), pp. 103–114.

Jansz, J., Avis, C. and Vosmeer, M. (2010) 'Playing The Sims 2: An Exploration of Gender Differences in Players' Motivations and Patterns of Play', *New Media & Society* 12 (2), pp. 335–351.

Jansz, J. and Martis, R.G. (2007) 'The Lara Phenomenon: Powerful Female Characters in Video Games', *Sex Roles* 56 (3), pp. 141–148.

Jenkins, E. (2008) 'My iPod, My iCon: How and Why Do Images Become Icons?', *Critical Studies in Media Communication* 25 (5), pp. 466–489.

Jenkins, H. (1998) 'Complete Freedom of Movement: Video Games as Gendered Play Spaces', in Justine Cassell and Henry Jenkins (eds) *From Barbie to Mortal Kombat: Gender and Computer Games*, Cambridge, MA: MIT Press, pp. 262–297.

Jenson, J. and De Castell, S. (2005) 'Her Own Boss: Gender and the Pursuit of Incompetent Play', in *Changing Views: Worlds in Play: Proceedings of the 2005 Digital Games Research Association Conference*, Vancouver, Canada, available at: *http://www.researchgate.net/publication/221217295_Her_Own_Boss_Gender_and_the_Pursuit_of_Incompetent_Play*, accessed 6 December 2015.

Jenson, J. and De Castell, S. (2010) 'Gender, Simulation, and Gaming: Research Review and Redirections', *Simulation and Gaming* 41(1), pp. 51–71.

Jenson, J. and De Castell, S. (2011) 'Girls@Play', *Feminist Media Studies* 11 (2), pp. 167–179.

Kafai, Y.B., Heeter, C., Denner, J. and Sun, J.Y. (eds) (2008) *Beyond Barbie and Mortal Kombat: New Perspectives on Gender and Gaming*, Cambridge, MA: MIT Press.

Krotoski, A. (2004) *Chicks and Joysticks: An Exploration of Women and Gaming*, London: Entertainment and Leisure Software Publishers Association.

Lally, E. (2002) *At Home with Computers*, Berg: Oxford.

Laurel, B. (1993) *Computers as Theatre*, Reading, MA: Addison-Wesley.

Livingstone, S. (2009) *Children and the Internet*, Cambridge: Polity Press.

Livingstone, S. and Bober, M. (2003) *UK Children Go Online: Listening to Young People and Their Parents*, London: London School of Economics and Political Science, available at: *http://eprints.lse.ac.uk/399/1/UKCGO_Final_report.pdf*, accessed 6 December 2015.

Livingstone, S., Marsh, J., Plowman, L., Ottovordemgentschenfelde, S. and Fletcher-Watson, B. (2014) 'Young Children (0–8) and Digital Technology: A Qualitative Exploratory Study – National Report – UK', Luxembourg: Joint Research Centre, European Commission.

Lubar, S. (1993) *Info Culture, the Smithsonian Book of Information Age Inventions*, Boston, MA: Houghton Mifflin Company.

Marsh, J., Brooks, G., Hughes, J., Ritchie, L., Roberts, S. and Wright, K. (2005) 'Digital Beginnings: Young Children's Use of Popular Culture, Media and New Technologies', University of Sheffield, available at: *www.digitalbeginnings.shef.ac.uk/ DigitalBeginningsReportColor.pdf*, accessed 3 August 2010.

Martins, N., Williams, D., Harrison, K. and Ratan, R.A. (2009) 'A Content Analysis of Female Body Imagery in Video Games', *Sex Roles* 61 (11–12), pp. 824–836.

Microsoft (2007) 'Play Smart, Play Safe', available at: *http://www.thinkuknow.co.uk/Safer InternetDay/downloads/Microsoft%20Play%20Safe%20Guide.pdf*, accessed 6 December 2015.

Mitchell, E. (1985) 'The Dynamics of Family Interaction around Home Video Games', *Marriage & Family Review* 8 (1–2), pp. 121–135.

Morley, D. (1986) *Family Television: Cultural Power and Domestic Leisure*, London: Comedia.

Morley, D. (2002) *Home Territories: Media, Mobility and Identity*, London: Routledge.

Nielsen (2008) 'Video Gamers in Europe – 2008. Nielsen Games: Prepared for the Interactive Software Federation of Europe (ISFE), available at: *http://www.pegi.info/es/ index/id/media/pdf/221.pdf*, accessed 6 December 2015.

Nikken, P. and Jansz, J. (2006) 'Parental Mediation of Children's Videogame Playing: A Comparison of the Reports by Parents and Children', *Learning, Media and Technology* 31 (2), pp. 181–202.

Nikken, P., Jansz, J. and Schouwstra, S. (2007) 'Parents' Interest in Video Game Ratings and Content Descriptors in Relation to Game Mediation', *European Journal of Communication* 22 (3), pp. 315–336.

Ofcom (2009) 'UK Children's Media Literacy 2009 Interim Report', October 2009, available at: *http://stakeholders.ofcom.org.uk/binaries/research/media-literacy/ annex.pdf*.

Ofcom (2014) 'Children Parents: Media Use and Attitudes Report', October 2014, available at: *http://stakeholders.ofcom.org.uk/binaries/research/media-literacy/media-use-attitudes-14/Childrens_2014_Report.pdf*, accessed 6 December 2015.

Quandt, T. and von Pape, T. (2010) 'Living in the Mediatope: A Multimethod Study on the Evolution of Media Technologies in the Domestic Environment', *The Information Society* 26, pp. 330–345.

Randall, D. (2011) 'All in the Game: Families, Peer Groups and Game Playing', in Richard Harper (ed.) *The Connected Home: The Future of Domestic Life*, London: Springer, pp. 111–132.

Riley, D. (2008) 'Video Game Software Sales across Top Global Markets Experience Double-Digit Growth', NPD Group. available at: *www.npd.com/press/releases/press_090202.html*, accessed 6 December 2015.

Rogers, E.M. and Larsen, J.K. (1984) *Silicon Valley Fever: Growth of High-technology Culture*, New York: Basic Books.

Schott, G. and Horrell, K. (2000) 'Girl Gamers and Their Relationship with the Gaming Culture', *Convergence* 6 (4), pp. 36–53.

Shinkle, E. (2008) 'Video Games, Emotion and the Six Senses', *Media Culture Society* 30 (6), pp. 907–915.

Siegler, M.G. (2010) 'Half of All Facebook Users Play Social Games – It's 40% of Total Usage Time', *TechCrunch*, available at: *http://techcrunch.com/2010/07/30/half-of-all face book-users-play-socialgames-its-40-of-total-usage-time/*, accessed 6 December 2015.

Silverstone, R. (1994) *Television and Everyday Life*, London: Routledge.

Silverstone, R. (1997) 'New Media in European Households', in *Exploring the Limits: Europe's Changing Communication Environment*, European Communication Council Report, Berlin: Springer-Verlag, pp. 113–134.

Silverstone, R., Hirsch, E. and Morley, D. (1992) 'Information and Communication Technologies and the Moral Economy of the Household', in Roger Silverstone and Eric Hirsch (eds) *Consuming Technology: Media and Information in Domestic Spaces*, London: Routledge, pp. 115–131.

Siyahhan, S., Barab, S.A. and Downton, M.P. (2010) 'Using Activity Theory to Understand Intergenerational Play: The Case of Family Quest', *Computer-Supported Collaborative Learning* 5 (4), pp. 415–432.

Spigel, L. (1988) 'Popular Discourses of Television and Domestic Space 1948–1955', *Installing the Television Set: Camera Obscura*, 16, pp. 11–47.

Spigel, L. (1990) 'Television in the Family Circle, the Popular Reception of a New Medium', in P. Mellencamp (ed.) *Logics of Television: Television, Essays in Cultural Criticism*, London: BFI Publishing, pp. 73–97.

Spigel, L. (1992) 'The Suburban Home Companion: Television and the Neighbourhood Ideal in Postwar America', in Beatriz Colomina (ed.) *Sexuality and Space*, New York: Princeton Architectural Press, pp. 185–217.

Thornham, H. (2008) '"It's a Boy Thing": Gaming, Gender and Geeks', *Feminist Media Studies* 8 (2), pp. 127–142.

TNS (2008) 'Wii are Family – Two Thirds of Parents Say Social Gaming Has a Positive Impact on Family Life', London: TNS Technology. Available at: *http://www.saferin ternet.pl/pl/raporty-i-badania/104-eng/about/eng-news/1988-Wii-Are-Family-two-thirds-of-parents-say-social-gaming-has-a-positive-impact-on-family-life*, accessed 6 December 2015.

Ulicsak, M. and Cranmer, S. (2010) 'Gaming in Families: Final Report', Bristol: Futurelab, Innovation in Education, available at: *http://archive.futurelab.org.uk/resources/documents/project_reports/Games_Families_Final_Report.pdf*, accessed 6 December 2015.

Ulicsak, M., Wright, M. and Cranmer, S. (2009) 'Gaming in Families: A Literature Review', Bristol: Futurelab, Innovation in Education, available at: *http://archive.futurelab.org.uk/resources/documents/lit_reviews/Gaming_Families.pdf*, accessed 6 December 2015.

Walkerdine, V. (2006) 'Playing the Game: Young Girls Performing Femininity in Videogame Play', *Feminist Media Studies* 6 (4), pp. 519–537.

Walkerdine, V. (2007) *Children, Gender, Video Games: Towards a Relational Approach to Multimedia*, Basingstoke: Palgrave Macmillan.

Wheelock, J. (1992) 'Personal Computers: Gender and Institutional Model of the Households', in Roger Silverstone and Eric Hirsch (eds) *Consuming Technology: Media and Information in Domestic Spaces*, London: Routledge, pp. 97–116.

Williams, D., Martins, N., Consalvo, M. and Ivory, J.D. (2009) 'The Virtual Census: Representations of Gender, Race and Age in Video Games', *New Media & Society* 11 (5), pp. 815–834.

Wolf, M.J. (2008) 'Arcade Games of the 1970s', in Mark J. Wolf (ed.) *The Video Game Explosion: A History from Pong to Playstation and Beyond*, Westport, CT: Greenwood press, pp. 35–44.

Yee, N. (2008) 'Maps of Digital Desires: Exploring the Topography of Gender and Play in Online Games', in Yasmin B. Kafai, Carrie Heeter, Jill Denner and Jennifer Y. Sun (eds) *Beyond Barbie and Mortal Kombat: New Perspectives on Gender and Gaming*, Cambridge, MA: MIT Press, pp. 83–96.

6

TOUCHSCREEN HOMES AND THE DOMESTICATION OF THE COMPUTER TABLET

Introduction

The introduction of mobile and personalised media technologies in the home raises issues about changes in the dynamics of domestic social interactions. Until recently, it was commonly assumed that the long-term trend in home media engagement was away from traditional communal media activities such as watching television (TV) as a family or household group to more personalised uses of media generated by cheaper and more personalised media devices (Livingstone and Das 2010). We hear of households in which people text each other from the sofa to the armchair to attract each other's attention. The adoption of mobile media technologies has generated academic debates about changing social interactions, movement and meanings of public space. However, less attention has been paid to changing family dynamics and meanings of domestic space associated with the growing presence of touchscreen mobile technology in the home. Computer tablets now form part of a range of mobile devices in the evolution of domestic mobile practices including gaming, e-book readers, laptops, netbooks and smartphones. This chapter's aim is to advance debates about mobile touchscreen technologies and evolving dynamics of home life.

Earlier chapters confirm that the marketing and advertising of media technologies form part of powerful media imaginaries that play a key role during the early stages of a technology's evolution, diffusion, adoption and domestication. These processes are examined in relation to multi-screen use in the home, underpinned by recent data on computer tablet adoption and a textual analysis of computer tablet advertisements to offer insights into expectations and norms of media use within family routines. The first section assesses data on the take-up of mobile touchscreen technology. The second section comprises a textual analysis of computer tablet advertisements between 2010 and 2014 to explain emerging popular media discourses and meanings about the new 'touchscreen' multi-screen home. It asks: how do advertisements of touchscreen technologies such as the computer tablet signify the 'mobile' as 'domestic'?

The third section focuses on the changing technology and uses of TV as an example of the tablet's relationship to other domestic media. The aim in this section is to identify emerging trends concerning householders' evolving engagement with the tablet in the context of touchscreen media in family-centred households. This section speculates about changing family dynamics in 'touchscreen homes', suggesting that a form of 'ambient domestic connectivity' emerges through the use of the computer tablet in the shared setting of the living room. The advertising of the tablet computer and its subsequent adoption in the home raises important questions about the role of advertising in the domestication process. In this chapter, I suggest that the link between the two is symptomatic of the mediatisation of the home. The concept of media imaginaries, developed in the first two chapters, is relevant here. It highlights the imaginative work involved in the discursive construction of new media use including the positive and negative public debates and possible social consequences of media advancement in institutional and everyday life.

The growth in touchscreen media

Mobile technologies such as laptops, computer tablets and smartphones offer users access to a wider range of communication tools not only while 'on the go' but also in the home. Marketed as personalised gadgets, the apparent geographical liberation and spatial dislocation associated with these portable technologies raises questions about the changing nature of today's home. Mobile technology's affordances of surmounting distances have prompted contradictory claims: that place has become less relevant as a result of the transcendence of the immobile, localised context of media reception (Castells 1996) and, conversely, that place become a more significant condition of everyday life (Morley 2007: 223). Clearly, digitised mobile technologies accelerate the mediatisation process including the blurring of boundaries between home and the public sphere as highlighted by the domestication approach (Peil and Röser 2014: 238). However, this chapter explains that through their incorporation into the home, mobile media gadgets are being adopted into new household and family dynamics. In the era of personalised mobile gadgetry, the home is being reimagined as a key context of mobile media use. As such, mobile media coincide with an intensified permeation of the boundaries around the home and the rise of new household dynamics involving both the sharing and personalisation of media.

The multi-touchscreen mobile computer tablet featuring a 9.7-inch display was made available in April 2010 with Apple's iPad. Thinner and lighter than any laptop or netbook, Apple's then CEO, Steve Jobs, described iPad as: 'our most advanced technology in a *magical* and *revolutionary* device at an unbelievable price' when it was unveiled (Apple 2010). Described as a touchscreen, pinch/zoom, 'surf from the sofa' device, this mobile media technology quickly moved beyond early adopters to enter the public imagination. In the UK, the household adoption of tablet computers almost doubled between 2013 and 2014 supported by the accelerated advent of wireless internet, with 44 per cent of UK households possessing at least one tablet by 2014 (Ofcom 2014a). This growth is mirrored in other western countries. Tablet ownership among adults in the US rocketed from 3 per cent in May 2010 to 34 per cent in May 2013 (Zickuhr 2013). The fast diffusion of tablet computers was triggered by an extensive range of apps made available through the device to facilitate tasks such as playing games; reading books; accessing films, TV programmes, music, news, sport and other information. For example, Apple reported that by July 2011 more than 15 billion apps for use on iPad, iPhone and iPod Touch were downloaded worldwide from its app store (Apple 2011).

During the same period that the tablet has caught on, the take-up of smartphones accelerated. As Ofcom observed in its Communications Market Report, 'We're now spending more time using media or communications than sleeping. The convenience and simplicity of smartphones and tablets are helping us cram more activities into our daily lives' (Ofcom 2014b). In 2014, UK adults typically spent eight hours and 41 minutes a day engaging with media such as texting, talking, typing, gaming, listening, or watching. During the same period that the tablet has caught on, the take-up of smartphones accelerated. In 2015, computer tablets in households increased to over half of all households at 54 per cent and smart phones were present in two-thirds of households at 66 per cent (Ofcom 2015). Children are interrupting their sleep to access their mobile phones, tablets and TV throughout the night. This embedded quality of mobile technology use in daily life is echoed in other countries such as the US (Pew Research Internet Project 2014). Previous studies reveal that the diffusion of a new technology tends to be related to age, with younger people adopting the technology earlier than older ages (Dutta-Bergman 2004; Greer and Ferguson 2015). However, today's increase in use of mobile touchscreen technologies intersects all age groups. Simplicity of use and mobility make these devices attractive to users across generations with more than a quarter (28 per cent) of over-55-year-olds in the UK owning a tablet in 2014, often using it as the main computing device (Ofcom 2014a).

Paralleling the rise in mobile media use, TV content is shifting from traditional delivery via a TV set and internet streaming to portable devices (Greer and Ferguson 2015). The growth in broadband use means that internet-connected devices are now used to view TV and film content: notably tablets, smartphones, laptops and game consoles. Mobile viewing is enabled by streaming and downloading technologies involving a mobile screen device. Smart TVs with inbuilt internet functionality and desktop computers can be used in combinations for viewing catch-up content. National media organisations - such as the UK's BBC and, in the US, Home Box Office (HBO) and – Cable News Network (CNN) – have developed their own apps. However, live TV viewing remains resilient with 69 per cent of viewing in the UK involving live TV in 2014, and recorded TV accounting for a further 16 per cent. Viewing online content represents 10 per cent of viewing, consisting of 5 per cent on on-demand catch-up services such as BBC iPlayer or 4oD, 3 per cent on other downloaded or streamed services such as Amazon Prime Video or Netflix, and 2 per cent on short video clips (Ofcom 2014c). Significantly, research suggests that tablet use tends to overlap with other media rather than being used on its own to the exclusion of other media (Google 2013; Greer and Ferguson 2015). A 2011 Nielsen survey indicated that 45 per cent of tablet owners in the US use their device while watching TV on a daily basis, with 26 per cent reporting simultaneous TV and tablet use several times a day. This was rivalled in the UK with 80 per cent use of tablets and 78 per cent use of smartphones while watching TV (Nielson 2012a). In the UK, adults were spending an average of 4 hours and 17 minutes per day viewing audio visual content in 2014 but, by now, through multiple mediums (Ofcom 2014c).

Among younger children, the tablet has become the most popular media device (Ofcom 2014d). Many own handheld game devices themselves, but children generally borrow devices from their parents or share family tablets or smartphones. While young children who cannot yet read or write are unable to interact with computer keyboards, the touchscreen interface of the tablet allows them to be used unaided at an earlier age. Young children typically use computer tablets for watching films, videos and TV programmes. This includes catch-up as well as streaming and on-demand services. In a study of 6–7-year-olds' uses of digital technology by Livingstone et al. (2014), it was found that parents emphasise the purposeful and focused way children use digital devices for learning, entertainment and communication. Parents highlight the value and usefulness of the devices for children while downplaying the more distracted types of use at times of the day when children need to be diverted or kept amused, such as when parents are shopping, cooking, driving or sleeping. Among this age group, children can identify the YouTube icon and know how to navigate the recommended links. Yet, until a problem occurs, parents appear to be unaware how much 'screen time' this amounts to, and of the limitations of children's online skills. Livingstone (2014) indicates, in a highly informative blog, that the tablet has replaced the TV as an electronic babysitter: 'As technology changes, families' attention has surely shifted away from one big screen towards multiple small screens and we've discussed various strategies for parents to manage their kids.'

At the time of writing, relatively little is known either about how these mobile touchscreen technologies are being incorporated into family-oriented households or how they relate to family relations and viewing practices in the home. Resonating with media imaginaries associated with the earlier establishment of TV technology (see Chapter 2), popular media discourses, commentaries in news, magazines and advertisements conjure up ideas about how mobile touchscreen technologies are to be used and interpreted. Public commentary about tablet computers is often pessimistic with speculations about the extent to which children and family relations may be at risk from the technology. For instance, in 2011 a *New York Times* article titled 'Quality Time Redefined' enquired about the changing nature of family togetherness. Recounting the incorporation of mobile media gadgets in an episode of the highest-rated new TV comedy, *Modern Family*, Alex Williams (2011) describes an episode in which Claire Dunphy attempts to serve breakfast to her family, only to be ignored by all. The husband is engrossed with football fixtures on his iPad, the son is gaming on his Nintendo DS and the two daughters are communicating with one another by email across the table. Eventually Claire loses her temper, declaring: 'OK, now that's it, everybody, gadgets down, now! You're all so involved in your little gizmos, nobody is even talking. Families are supposed to talk!' Williams remarks on this new kind of interaction with four screens in one room by one family: 'everyone huddled in a cyber-cocoon'. Is this a fair reflection of family dynamics in today's touchscreen home?

Negative news reports about computer tablets reveal public anxieties about the potential erosion of face-to-face family interaction and the harmful effects of parents using these devices as childminders. For example, an article in the *Daily Mail* titled 'WORRYING RISE OF THE IPAD CHILDMINDER: MORE AND MORE PARENTS ADMIT USING TABLETS TO KEEP THEIR CHILDREN QUIET' refers to 'the quick-fix rewards of a tablet' and notes that 'the royals have admitted Prince George [then aged 2] knows what to do with an iPad' (Carey and Hoyle 2015). Similarly, *Wired* magazine confirms that by 2014 nearly two-thirds of American 2–10-year-olds have access to a tablet or e-reader, and asks: 'ARE TOUCHSCREENS MELTING YOUR KID'S BRAIN?' (Honan 2014).

To place mobile touchscreen viewing practices in a historical context, it is worth recalling key issues relating to family togetherness and mediated household interaction raised by earlier studies of families and TV viewing (Lull 1990; Morley 1986; Silverstone 1994). Mediatised interpersonal communication builds on an earlier tradition of domestic mobilisation thanks to the popularity of portable TV in the late 1950s and 1960s as well as the cordless telephone since the 1990s (Peil and Röser 2014: 238). Studies of twentieth-century TV highlight the contradictory dynamics through which communications technologies were 'domesticated' from the late 1950s onwards (Morley 1992; Spigel 1992). As Chapter 2 recounts, these technologies were integrated into domestic routines during the same period that traditional notions of 'domesticity' were challenged: not only by TV content but also by design, marketing and advertising discourses that conveyed these objects through a futuristic, space-age aesthetic (Spigel 2001; Chambers 2011; Kosareff 2005). The growing diversity of information and communication technologies (ICTs) equipping the home from the 1970s and 1980s supported more personalised tastes and lifestyles. Corresponding with new household ties such as single-parent, post-divorce and blended families, domestic media offered householders opportunities to live together but separately under one roof through by compartmentalising family life (van Rompaey and Roe 2001). The individualising potential of domestic media technologies fuelled public concerns about fragmenting families. And the privatised space of teenagers' media-rich bedrooms highlighted the problems presented by multiple media affordances (see Chapter 4). Recent anxieties about the entrance of personalised mobile media into the home echo these earlier public debates about media's effects on family life.

The personalisation and mobility of devices changes the moral economy of the household. As mentioned in Chapter 2, media's dual capacity to draw the family together and separate it was demonstrated by research in the 1980s and 1990s (Livingstone and Das 2010; Gillespie 1995; Livingstone 2002). Confirming that TV supported family subgroups and subsystems, James Lull (1982; 1990) identified the ways families and householders manage separation and togetherness. He argued that, within its relational uses, TV can act as both a mode of 'affiliation' or 'avoidance'. It can act as a 'communication facilitator' by bringing the family together and opening up conversation yet may also create conflict (1990: 36). Householders build up an intimate understanding of each others' domestic routines and home-based uses of media technologies. This facilitates householders' coordination of habitual family life to circumvent tensions associated with using different media content in the same rooms. Various strategies are developed by households to generate a sense of collective identities by compartmentalising and individualising media engagement in the home. Lally (2002:136) refers to these as the 'techniques of managing their living together'. Parental strategies for monitoring children's media uses and more general strategies among adult householders also form part of this moral economy of the household (see Chapters 3 and 4). These earlier accounts of privatised and individuated familial media use relate, then, to questions about the domestic uses of today's mobile multi-screen technologies: whether for affiliation or avoidance of company in shared spaces.

The entrance of touchscreen technologies in the home comes at a time of growing public unease about changing family forms and household dynamics, and related fears about the fragmentation of families and challenges involved in parental monitoring of young people's immersion in media outlined in Chapter 4. These concerns prompt questions about how touchscreen mobile devices are marketed for home use and how family households are signified in the process of popularising these gadgets. The personalised nature and mobile quality of mobile screen-based devices may function as resources not only for connecting home with the outside world but also for organising new kinds of domestic interactions.

Tablet advertisements: from cosmopolitan mobility to familial and domestic imagery

To investigate evolving representations of the technology, I conducted a textual analysis of computer tablet advertisements from inception of the device in 2010 to 2014. Focusing mainly on British and US adverts, just over 30 commercials from leading global electronic and telecommunications corporations were examined. The year 2010 is a useful starting point for historical contextualisation, marking the onset of the mass production and adoption of tablets. Occurring within powerful media imaginaries, this technological development stage is referred to as a period of 'interpretive flexibility': when the technology's uses and meanings are contested, negotiated and shaped by social norms and practices as well as design (Natale and Balbi 2014: 207; Vickery 2014; see Pinch and Bijker 1984). Advertisements set parameters for the use of media devices; conjure up the ideal user experience and validate codes of behaviour and consumer choices by associating the technology with powerful values and meanings (Leiss et al. 1990; Lillie 2011). As such, they can evoke strong generational and gendered expectations and tensions relating to the domestication of technology. During the critical introductory phase of a new technology, this evocation of the ideal user contributes to the shaping of imaginary and anticipated social relations and practices (see Boddy 2004; du Gay et al. 1997).

Tablet advertisements representing subjects staged in 'public spaces' were compared with those in 'domestic settings'. Significantly, in an earlier content analysis of 288 images of men and women in mobile phone advertisements up to 2003, Nicola Döring and Sandra Pöschl (2006) found no household settings in their data. This absence of the 'domestic' in earlier adverts for mobile devices is striking, given well-established preceding research about the role of ICTs in sustaining networked households and the critical role of mobile phones for mothers in managing domestic tasks (see Silverstone and Hirsch 1992; Haddon 2003). This absence suggests something more than the disjunctions between imagery and everyday uses of mobile technologies. The tablet was not imagined or conveyed as a domestic item but as an item to be used 'in transit'. This signification of the technology changed over time.

The early phase of 'cosmopolitan' tablet imagery

The first phase of advertisements for computer tablets between 2010 and 2011 naturalised and aestheticised the image of a mobile male and on-the-go use of tablets by showing predominantly out-of-home, public settings with only fleeting segments of domestic settings. Yet even by 2011, research demonstrated that mobile out-of-home viewing via tablet or other mobile device was 'by far the least popular mode of viewing'. Almost 70 per cent of users had never used their mobile device for this purpose (Bury and Li 2013). This suggests the power of advertising. Although it tends to be used mostly in the home, the gadget was commonly assumed to be designed for use mostly beyond the home as an on-the-go technology.

These earlier 2010–2011 commercials employed a dramatic realist technique to depict subjects in a series of mainly public, urban settings to indicate how the object can enhance active, everyday life on the move. The realist type of advert involved four contextual themes: the intense 'how-to-use-it' advertisement; the 'active on-the-go' context; the 'mobile connective work context'; and a 'mobile domestic context'. The 'how-to-use' advert type was dominated by Apple iPad, exemplified by the 'April 3' (2010) advert. However, several adverts contained all four of these themes consecutively through a series of fast clips (for example, 'Time to tab' Samsung 2011). Most commercials figured young, urban cosmopolitans under the age of 35 to convey a dynamic, active and aspirational ambience. Subjects typically formed two types: an individual user signifying the personalised character of the device and sense of personal control; and a group of users conveying the interactive quality of the device and users. The personalised advertisement involved an image of a single 'networked' subject. Resonating with the idea of the masculinised active user, a mobile individual male user typically figured in a series of fast-moving public settings away from home with a particular emphasis on creativity and management of business and professional networks. This is exemplified by the 'make.believe' Sony (2011) commercial.

Advertisements staged in outdoor, on-the-move settings often involved young people engaged in youthful physical activities followed by images of groups sitting in outdoor cafés and city streets. Computer tablet symbolism drew on 'youth' as a trope to convey a sense of adventure, speed and immediacy. The Microsoft Surface 'click' advert of October 2012 features students, secondary school teenagers and business men dancing in a modern outdoor college campus setting. While most of the earlier adverts contained urban environments, a minority began to portray individuals in domestic settings. The subjects were mainly women and generally located in ultramodern, urban apartments. Highrise, glass-panelled apartments with spectacular views over city skylines convey the idea of luxury urban living. These indoor settings do not evoke 'domesticity' but rather a 'mobile urban living' fused with cosmopolitan on-the-go multitasking to convey the sophisticated, city lifestyle. Indeed, city skylines at night predominated throughout these advertisements set in urban spaces, as exemplified in the 'Time to Tab' Samsung Tab 10.1 commercial. These adverts typically guide viewers through creative tablet uses extending to contrasting, spectacular wilderness settings to form part of a wider genus of adverts for mobile devices as pioneering technology.

Yet the lack of imagery associated with the intersecting uses of tablets in households at this stage was conspicuous. The avoidance of domestic settings in promotions of mobile technologies corresponds with traditionally negative meanings associated with 'domesticity' despite the significant role of tablets in domestic convergence technology. Linking mobile devices with masculinity provides a contrast from post-war notions of TV as feminine (Parks 2004; Spigel 1992). Likewise, adverts for mobile gadgets convey masculine ideals of dynamism and freedom of public space, which are antithetical to domestic values and meanings. The literature on technology adoption represents the early adopter of digital and mobile technologies as young, male with higher socio-economic status (Dawson 2007; see Chapter 3). As Bury and Li (2013) explain, when TV is signified as a form of 'new' media, the notion of the 'passive viewer' transforms into an active user and, in the process, is masculinised (Parks 2004: 138). Similarly, Michael Newman (2012: 4) suggests that file sharing tends to be associated with 'youth, technological sophistication, and masculinity'.

The second phase of domestic and familial tablet imagery

How, then, do manufacturers overcome domesticity's negative connotations when signifying the tablet as a mobile device designed for home use? A striking contrast from the cosmopolitan adverts was noticeable in 2012. A domestic category of adverts emerged where the home and family comprise dominant themes. The cool, cosmopolitan flâneur was replaced by parents and children in domestic settings with humour and sentimentality employed as part of the process of domestication. Samsung invested heavily in this marketing approach to distinguish its brand from the ideal urban Apple user. The tablet was now domesticated and routinised to appeal to wider groups of consumers. A key characteristic of these commercials is the stereotyping of gender and generational roles through a domestic frame.

In this second phase of adverts, the accent is on family togetherness. With Samsung specialising in family-centred commercials, the Samsung Galaxy Note series of Android-based high-end tablets and smartphones were one of the first successful examples of 'phablets': smartphones with large screens that combine the functions of a tablet and phone. A 2013 advertisement, 'Day in the Life' shows a family of children and two parents using the phablet for multiple tasks. The setting is a large, modern house with the open-plan style emphasising the family's unity, to avoid notions of compartmentalisation. A series of images begin by showing mother and daughter bonding through tablet use, then father sitting on the sofa using the tablet for work purposes by video link. The male voice-over message is to men: 'MULTITASK TO STAY AHEAD OF THE GAME'. Switching to the kitchen, the tablet is used by the whole family to access recipes while cooking; then switches to show the family dancing in the living room while being recorded via tablet by the mother, with a voice-over offering ideas for use. The commercial ends with the family seated together in the living room with father selecting a movie via tablet then settling back to watch it on the big TV screen. The advert confirms the tablet's right to be in the living room by showing Dad performing the tablet movie connection. With the emphasis on family bonding and enhancement of the home environment through entertainment, the embedded nature of the technology is signified.

Expanding on this theme, Samsung released a further series of commercials for the Note 4, 'Do You Note?', screened on US TV in November 2014, the adverts featured individual members of an American family whose muddled lives in the run-up to Christmas are transformed by the Note 4. The family members are observed through the eyes of the precocious pre-teen son as narrator, thereby sanctioning the gender typecasting of family members. First, a frustrated older brother learns how to multitask. Then a vain teen sister who 'needs' to take more selfies is shown. A stressed 'Mom' learns to 'smart shop' for Christmas family gifts. The work-distracted 'Dad' can now charge his device to connect with the family while on-the-go, invoking the idea of the networked male. In the final video, the pre-teen male narrator, 'me', sends a Galaxy note message to Santa with his

Christmas wish list and a hyperlink to the desired skateboard. With the home as the organising backdrop, family members are gender stereotyped to convey ways to overcome personal deficiencies and enhance familial connectivity through the use of Note 4.

The 'What You Really Need' Galaxy Tab S commercial of 2014 featured celebrity husband and wife duo, Dax Shepard and Kristen Bell, who co-starred in romantic comedy movie, *When in Rome* (2010). The celebrity couple occupy a spacious, modern luxury home while depicted as 'just your normal average couple', using their tablets to negotiate Kristen's second pregnancy. The tablet is displayed multiple times around the house and beyond. The couple lie in bed and check the weather via tablet; Kristen listens to music via tablet in the bathroom; Dax watches sport on tablet in the kitchen and is contacted by Kristen from the bathroom via tablet to ask him what he is doing; they then sit on the veranda using tablets; Kristen then sits on the sofa playing a racing game on tablet while Dax is in the same room using his tablet; Dax then goes out to buy frozen yoghurt to help with his wife's cravings and keeps in continuous contact with Kristen while he negotiates the purchase. They end up missing a night out by watching a film on tablet together, snuggled up on the sofa to demonstrate the gadget's versatility.

A second advertisement with the celebrity duo in 2014, leading up to Christmas, 'Kristen and Dax at Home for the Holidays' features the tablet as part of a range of mobile devices for home use. The domestic setting is now scripted as a legitimate context for promoting today's integrated mobile technologies. The home comprises a metaphorical space in which intimate, familial connectivity is played out. Yet these advertisements continue to portray men and women in conventional gender roles. Kristen is now almost immobilised through pregnancy ('Hun, I can't even tie my shoes at this point'), invoking feminine passivity vs. male activity. Meanwhile, Dax bounds around freely: using a different mobile device for each communication, he is in the attic, on the roof (assembling fairy lights), out shopping. The mobile gadget becomes a tool for organising and upholding highly traditional family values. As Morley (2002, 2003) and Spigel (1992, 2001) remind us, 'hi-tech' discourse is often carefully framed and domesticated by a rather nostalgic vision of 'family values'.

Producers of mobile communication and media devices have a major commercial incentive to shape discourses about young people and mobile gadgets. They must both acknowledge and then allay fears at the same time as offering parents a line of reasoning for purchasing mobile devices (Vickery 2014: 388). Adverts for tablets aimed at toddlers showed pre-school education tablets with chunky designs in bright primary colours. The bright green Leapfrog Leappad 2 Explorer was marketed as a 'learning tablet' in 2013. The marketing strategy to attract parents was also expressed through gendered blue and pink tablet frames and through tablet images of cartoon and racing games to categorise the tablet as a toy.

The 'Kid Connect' tablet by VTech was marketed at mums as a learning toy. A female voice-over in the 2013 commercial states:

Nothing takes the place of the time you and your child spend together. But there is a way to stay connected with each other, Sharing feelings, intimacies and laughter, even when you are away. With kid-safe wifi, you and your child can stay in touch anywhere anytime – send each other a special message – you get the comfort of hearing each others' voice – 'I love you Mum'. Stay close together even when you are far apart.

While the advert depicted a series of domestic settings, the child is the one confined at home while the mother is presented as mobile, beyond the home. The key parenting responsibility of staying connected is designated to mothers. The tablet toy is marketed unequivocally as a babysitter device, as a normal part of family life. Representing mothers as the ones charged with responsibility for managing the safety of their children, parents are offered an array of new gadgets and services to monitor the child (Shade 2011). This later group of adverts signifies the tablet as a family management tool to organise the family's demanding schedules (Vickery 2014). No longer just a gadget for young urban cosmopolitans or adventurers, by 2014 the tablet is now a domesticated tool: a technology and toy that can bring the family closer together while in the home, as well as beyond.

Touchscreen technologies, family dynamics and multi-screen homes

How, then, is the domestication of tablets in the second stage of advertisements being played out in the domestic lives of households and families? Multi-platform, connected media content is identified as a central aspect of growth by media companies. Digitalisation is facilitating the circulation of TV content on multiple technological platforms and devices. At the same time, it enables the presence of different media content on a single platform. TV audiences are increasingly active in content curation and distribution. Digitalisation is also enabling TV content to be viewed in spaces other than the traditional setting of the living room, thanks to mobile devices. Yet in discussions with companies such as BT, Red Bee, Ofcom and Thinkbox, Martindale et al. (2013) found that the media industry is struggling to understand how households are incorporating the technological changes into their lives, including how the status of the TV set is changing in relation to the introduction of mobile media in the home. This is illustrated by the conflicting views about live TV by Tim Cook (Apple Inc's CEO) and Lindsey Clay (CEO, TV industry body Thinkbox). In a US chat show interview, Tim Cook stated:

> TV is the one we continue to have great interest in . . . TV, its one of those things, if we're really honest, it's stuck back in the 70s. Think about how much your life has changed, and all the things around you that has changed. Yet when you go in your living room to watch or wherever it might be it almost feels like you're rewinding the clock and you've entered a time capsule and you're going backwards. The interface is terrible! I mean it's awful.[1]

Lindsey Clay disagreed, emphasising the importance of liveness:

> Live television has never been more important. And particularly to teenagers because they need stuff to be able to talk about and they need to watch it live because it is only if you watch it live that you can talk about it at the same time as other people. They want to talk about it in the room with other people but also on social media: that's what teenagers are doing . . . TV is fundamentally a social and communal experience. People like to bond over it, they like to watch it at the same time, they like to talk about it. So live TV is here for good.[2]

Despite the appeal of laptops, tablets, mobile phones, games systems and e-books, the large TV screen remains the centrepiece of the home both technologically and in terms of composition and layout of the living room. In the same way as the video cassette recorder (VCR) led to a radical change in the ways people structured their daily TV schedules (Gauntlet and Hill 1999), the personal video recorder (PVR) such as Tivo offers a range of ways to collect, record and share TV. A US study of PVR households by Brown and Barkhuus (2011) revealed that in multi-screen homes, the communal, family TV set does compete with other screens. However, they also found that since this is the largest screen in the house, it becomes the default equipment around which family members continue to gather to watch TV together. It becomes the destination for event TV watching. Even when house-holders are not watching, they can occupy themselves with other activities in the same space, allowing them to be co-present. This contradicts the idea of the TV as inherently anti-social. It remains a media device that facilitates TV viewing as a shared experience. The importance of the household set was also reflected among students who were interviewed.

Research evidence about the integration of tablets in daily routines from a large cross-nation study by Bury and Li (2013) concurs with Brown and Barkhuus that most viewing continues to occur in front of a TV screen. Growing numbers of people transnationally are using digital recording devices and services to time-shift viewing and also for watching TV content on their computers as well as their mobile devices (Madden 2009; Nielsen Company 2011, 2012a, 2012b, 2012c; Purcell 2010). In a 4-year study of multiple media use, Greer and Ferguson (2015) found an increase in total media use in that time. Time spent watching TV on an iPad did not appear to replace time spent watching a TV set. Instead, tablet use for TV denotes a convergence of portable media, TV viewing, and online content. This synchronised use of social media and TV viewing via tablets and smartphones in the home gener-ates new media practices in shared domestic spaces. The styles of interaction made possible by the new touchscreen technology and social TV appear to conform to the tendency highlighted by Sherry Turkle (2011) that people in the same space use technologies to connect with people from a distance: 'alone together'. This creates a distinctive form of 'ambient domestic connectedness' involving new moods and atmospheres in the home. In a qualitative Flemish study, D'heer et al. (2012; D'heer and Courtois 2014) found that secondary screens now form part of the daily TV viewing routine while household members are seated together in the living room around the TV. Tablets were regarded as easier to use and to offer a better viewing and interactive experience than laptops or smartphones. Tablets were typically used for games, browsing, email checking and other small tasks, to facilitate the switching between TV and other screens. These mobile devices tend to be placed in easy reach and accessed repeatedly throughout the evening, whether when alone or with other household members.

As Peil and Röser (2014) argue, the rise of mobile gadgets such as tablet personal computers in the home demonstrates that 'mobilization should not be considered as the opposite of domesticity'. They refer to the concept of domestic mobilisation of media practices to understand various uses of mobile media in the home. In their study of 25 couples in Germany between 2008 and 2011, Peil and Röser examined the co-existence of old and new media and how householders manage them. They confirm that while mediatisation, digitalisation and mobilisation seem to have placed an emphasis on flows and networks rather than on locality and domesticity, the home continues to represent a significant environment for people to negotiate the meaning and uses of media technologies. They argue that the domestic mobilisation of media practices can be linked to new socio-spatial routines and new ways of negotiating interactions at home. Mobile media are permeating more and more domestic localities, giving rise to a variety of new situations and contexts of mediatised communication in which media uses overlap and intersect in a complex way with daily life (Peil and Röser 2014).

Peil and Röser found that couples mostly relied on mobile media such as smartphones and laptop computers when they wanted to share a physical space in the home with their partners without having to share involvement in the same media content. Some form of community was enabled even with diverging media preferences. For example, one partner would watch TV while the other was surfing on the internet. Peil and Röser's household studies showed that these social situations were clearly connected to the content and kind of online activity that was performed. Demonstrating the breaching of public/private boundaries through mobile media use, some respondents reported that they would answer emails or administer their social networking profiles in the living room in order to be in the company of their partner or other household members. For work-related internet users, however, they would rather retreat to a separate room. This is a good example of how domestic media are used to adjust communal and individuated uses within the home (Peil and Röser 2014: 245)

TV is not only a facilitator of conversation. It also lessens the demand for talk or social interaction, a quality of TV that Lull (1990) refers to as 'avoidance'. Diminishing the demand for conversation, TV and related screens can act as 'social distractors' (Lull, 1990: 39). Likewise, the use of second mobile screens enables avoidance of the communal screen while remaining in the same room and therefore facilitates consumption of preferred content and the avoidance of disputes over programme selection. This new practice signifies what Evelien D'heer et al. (2012) refer to as a 'parallel' viewing process. Although multitasking reduces the prospects of conversation, communication between co-present household-ers tends to be tolerated and sustained while watching TV and using mobile screen devices (D'heer et al. 2012). Household members remain accessible to one another even while using screens individually. Drawing on Lull's typology of social uses, we can suggest that TV viewing combined with mobile screen use sustains interpersonal communication or 'affiliation' (Lull 1990) as features of family togetherness. However, D'heer and Courtois (2014: 13) explain that while TV remains a communal activity when watched in the living room, the presence of multi-screens changes family dynamics. Interaction becomes more distracted while online connection fosters dialogue and discussions about TV while watch-ing TV, as Lindsey Clay asserts above.

TV viewing triggers social media interaction with computer technologies allow-ing online sociability that bypasses co-present family members. Users of mobile technologies pass on comments about TV programmes via Twitter or Facebook to networked publics (Boyd 2011) beyond the home. D'heer and Courtois (2014: 13) call this 'outbound affiliation', a form of outbound social connection that entails mul-titasked TV viewing. Yet the non-immersive quality of the small screen allows it to be interrupted easily, facilitating albeit distracted offline interaction. It seems then that mobile devices such as computer tablets used in relation to TV are triggering a new mode of interaction which might be called 'ambient domestic connectivity'. By this I mean that these devices are generating new intimate registers and rescripting family togetherness. In these ways, multi-screen media facilitate uses through social media channels that entail a resocialisation of the living room (D'heer et al. 2012).

The living room turns into a space where multiple screen-based devices are accessed 'alone together'. Of course, this multiple media use occurs through tradi-tional media engagement such as reading the newspaper, books and watching TV as well. But what makes multi-screen use distinctive is the ease with which family members can interact with the outside world from the heart of the living room in a continuous flow by blending traditional audience activities (watching films, catch-up TV and so on) with social media engagement. Underpinned by the work of Lull (1900), D'heer et al. (2012; D'heer and Courtois 2014) assert that 'the audi-ence' is constituted through these new social practices of TV viewing. They argue that this new multi-screen environment gives rise to a participatory digital culture which tends towards 'privatisation' through individual domestic consumption. At the same time, it gives rise to a process of 'socialisation' through online social inter-action. The mobile device and social TV converge to facilitate domestication of the technology and social media-networked practices from the living room. This entails domestic-based public networking with the outside world.

Despite these dramatic changes in home-based communication, the multi-screen technology's presence is taken for granted and rarely registered by users according to D'heer et al. (2012). This indicates the inconspicuous and discreet nature of the multi-screen environment. This mental connective disconnection or 'dislocation' of family members while in each others' company in the living room signifies increased privatisation and individualisation of media use in the home, yet D'heer and his colleagues also argue that this new multi-screen environment fosters new forms of socialisation. While the living room continues to be the social hub of the family, it is now transformed into a highly mediatised environment. Social media engagement on a computer tablet while watching TV generates a new mode of non-immersive engagement with household members and spirit of sharing with public networks beyond the home, which D'heer et al. (2012) call 'outbound affiliation'.

Users of mobile devices in the home are learning new social norms, new protocols of abstracted connectedness which may complicate and challenge former domestic media routines. The touchscreen home may well present new challenges for household harmony. Yet, through a new kind of ambient domestic connectivity, they may also provide solutions for managing generational separateness in homes where affiliation and avoidance are essential for family harmony, such as in post-nuclear family households made up of reconstituted or 'blended' families and those containing the extended youth or 'boomerang' generation of adult children living with parents. Rather than undermining family dynamics in the home, it is possible that mobile multi-screens and social TV match the multiple, complex needs of household forms in late modernity.

Conclusion

The introduction of the tablet computer in the home brings into focus the conflict of values associated with domestic space. At the same time, it raises questions about the management of family connectedness in the context of personalised mobile media and multi-screen homes during a phase of domestic media convergence. The home remains an ambiguous setting for mobile technologies, which have, for so long, been saturated with associations of flight from home and urban adventure (Morley 2002; Spigel 2001; see Chapter 2). Media engagement is evolving into a new set of experiences in multi-screen households involving a juggling of householders' differing media demands. While the domestication approach explains the processes of adoption and assimilation of new technologies in the home at the level of practices, the marketing and advertising of media technologies pre-figure and intersect this process through attempts to shape public meanings and encode uses. However, the preceding and framing stage of 'media imaginary' involves a key phase of 'imagination' which resonates with Ward's sixth prior stage of domestication addressed in Chapter 3. During this stage, the technology goes through a process of enculturation within the wider social imagination. This involves sparking a fascination with and desire for the media object through advertising. This stage of imaginative work can be viewed as part of a process of 'discursive domestication' (Hartman 2009). It forms part of the process of mediatisation which fosters consumption by stimulating and channelling desires for domestic media gadgets.

The touchscreen mobile computer has come of age in the public imagination: it has progressed into a 'domesticated' item. Yet, importantly, initial public representations of the computer tablet within advertisements did not signal the birth of the newly imagined touchscreen home. Instead, they negated the tablet's link to the home. Over a 4-year time span, tablet commercials reveal two distinct stages and scripts. Both sets of imaginaries relied on gendered and generational stereotypes and expectations, confirming the gendered nature of contested values surrounding public and domestic space. When tablets were more expensive, they were advertised to professional groups, largely men, with a strong emphasis on out-of-home use. With the emphasis on networking outside the home, tablet advertisements between 2010 and 2012 celebrated the personalisation of technology through the presentation of mobile, young, cosmopolitan professionals. Images of business, creativity, entertainment and adventure evoked personal agency mainly beyond the home.

As prices lowered, the tablet was designed and targeted, through marketing, at children and family home use. Coinciding with changing family dynamics and the convergence of TV and mobile devices, this second advertising phase entails a validation of the domestic family setting. Family-oriented tablet commercials no longer focus on the networked individual. Individuals are portrayed as family members connecting with one another in and around the home. These family household adverts invoke and reflect key shifts in adoption by establishing the tablet as a routine, personalised but also 'communal' tool. The marketing objective of this later stage of advertisements is to revalidate tablets as devices for fostering family togetherness.

Humour and sentimentality are used in adverts as strategies to deal with this lingering ambiguity of 'the domestic', thereby offsetting the lack of 'urban cool'. Comical, romantic, interpersonal communication narratives convey the potential ease of use and pleasures associated with tablet devices. These lifestyle advertisements invoke traditional values about gender and family togetherness to allay public anxieties about the negative impact of digital mobile media on family life. Tablet advertisements figuring domestic spaces necessarily depend on gendered and generational typecasting to accentuate togetherness. The tension between masculine mobile and feminine domestic is resolved by heteronormative domestic narratives involving family bonding between mother/daughter and father/son; and confined but connected pregnant wife contrasted with mobile, work-connected husbands. The figure of the absent mother seems, at first glance, to be an intriguing departure from the stereotype to convey the babysitting role of the toddler tablet. Meanwhile, fathers tend to be portrayed as flexible 'networking' figures rather than targeted as 'problem parents' grappling with dilemmas of absence and distant emotional bonding. In these ways, generational and gendered cultural boundaries are preserved.

However, these are early days in the imagery and life of touchscreen technology. At this juncture, media scholars and the media industry continue to grapple with the emerging data on patterns of use to understand how touchscreen technologies are integrating into or disrupting conventional TV viewing habits and household interactions. The tablet is so flexible in terms of affordances that manufacturers are still searching for ways to fix the meanings and practices associated with the gadget. Nevertheless, we can speculate about the evidence so far which suggests that the tablet's integration into household practices is challenging past predications about the evolution of media technology uses in the home. The tablet is prompting a dramatic re-evaluation of domestic interaction. Until the rise of touchscreen technologies, the predicted long-term trend for TV viewing in the home was away from collective viewing towards an individualisation of activities. In the early 1980s, Lull (1982) claimed that the more TVs present in the home, the more scattered family members will be. With an emphasis on personalisation, this prediction coincided with the apparent individualisation of other spheres of our lives. Yet the entrance of smart TV and mobile screen-based technology in the home indicates a reorganisation of domestic space by creating new practices and meanings of connectedness in communal spaces of the home. In addition to sustaining traditional family relations invoked in family tablet adverts, new modes of communality are emerging through social media and TV that the media industry find difficult to promote through domestic advertising narratives.

The emerging evidence assessed in this chapter suggests that these dynamics may be marshalling new modes of family interactivity. Multiple mobile media appear to be providing householders with opportunities to stay together in one room by avoiding the tensions traditionally associated with media engagement such as TV. The paradox is that 'personalised' devices are operating in intimate yet communal domestic settings to create new kinds of interactivity beyond as well as within the home. Computer tablet devices enable a resocialisation of the living room through a new kind of outside contact, 'outbound affiliation', via social media channels, at the same time as a non-immersive interaction with other household members (D'heer et al. 2012). This new form of ambient domestic connectedness involves new moods and atmospheres in the home. It seems, then, that users of mobile devices in the home are learning new social norms, new protocols of abstracted connectedness, which may complicate and challenge past domestic media routines.

Notes

1 Charlie Rose Show, 12 September 2014, available at: *http://www.theguardian.com/technol ogy/2014/sep/15/apple-tim-cook-tv-beats*, accessed 18 February 2014.
2 Interview with Lindsey Clay on BBC Radio 4's *Today* programme 15 September 2014.

References

Apple (2010) 'Apple Launches iPad' (Press release), 27 January, available at: *www.apple.com/ pr/library/2010/01/27Apple-Launches-iPad.html*, accessed 13 February 2015.
Apple (2011) 'Apple's App Store Downloads Top 15 billion' (Press release), 7 July, available at: *https://www.apple.com/uk/pr/library/2011/07/07Apples-App-Store-Downloads-Top-15-Billion.html*, accessed 13 February 2015.
Boddy, W. (2004) *New Media and Popular Imagination: Launching Radio, Television and Digital Media in the United States*, Oxford: Oxford University Press.

Boyd, D. (2011) 'Social Network Sites as Networked Publics: Affordances, Dynamics, and Implications', in Zizi Papacharissi (ed.) *A Networked Self: Identity, Community, and Culture on Social Network Sites*, New York: Routledge, pp. 39–58.

Brown, B. and Barkhuus, L. (2011) 'Changing Practices of Family Television Watching', in Richard Harper (ed.) *Connected Home*, London: Springer, pp. 93–110.

Bury, R. and Li, J. (2013) 'Is It Live or Is It Timeshifted, Streamed or Downloaded? Watching Television in the Era of Multiple Screens', *New Media and Society* 6 (0), pp. 1–19.

Carey, T. and Hoyle, A. (2015) 'Worrying Rise of the iPad Childminder: More and More Parents Admit Using Tablets to Keep Their Children Quiet', *MailOnline*, 8 January, available at: *http://www.dailymail.co.uk/femail/article-2901261/Worrying-rise-iPad-childminder-parents-admit-using-tablets-children-quiet.html*, accessed 6 December 2015.

Castells, M. (1996) *The Rise of the Network Society*, Oxford: Blackwell.

Chambers, D. (2011) 'The Material Form of the TV Set: A Cultural History', *Media History* 17 (4), pp. 359–375.

Dawson, M. (2007) 'Little Players, Big Shows: Format, Narration, and Style on Television's New Smaller Screens', *Convergence* 13 (3), pp. 231–250.

D'heer, E. and Courtois, C. (2014) 'The Changing Dynamics of Television Consumption in the Multimedia Living Room', *Convergence* 24 July, pp. 1–16.

D'heer, E., Courtois, C. and Paulussen, S. (2012) 'Everyday Life in Front of the Screen: The Consumption of Multiple Screen Technologies in the Living Room Context', *Proceedings of the 10th European Conference on Interactive TV and Video*, pp. 195–198.

Döring, N. and Pöschl, S. (2006) 'Images of Men and Women in Mobile Phone Advertisements: A Content Analysis of Advertisements for Mobile Communication Systems in Selected Popular Magazines', *Sex Roles* 55, pp. 173–185.

Du Gay, P., Hall, S., Janes, L., McKay, H. and Negus, K. (1997) *Doing Cultural Studies: The Story of the Sony Walkman*, London: Sage.

Dutta-Bergman, M.J. (2004) 'Complementarity in Consumption of News Types across Tradition and New Media', *Journal of Broadcasting & Electronic Media* 48 (1), pp. 41–60.

Gauntlett, D. and Hill, A. (1999) *TV Living: Television Culture and Everyday Life*, London: Routledge.

Gillespie, M. (1995) *Television, Ethnicity and Cultural Change*, London: Routledge.

Google (2013) 'The World Has Gone Multi-screen: How the Mobile Internet Changed Our Lives', available at: *http://www.google.co.uk/think/research-studies/the-world-has-gone-multi-screen.html*, accessed 15 January 2015.

Greer, C.F. and Ferguson, D.A. (2015) 'Tablet Computers and Traditional Television Viewing: Is the iPad Replacing TV? *Convergence: The International Journal of Research into New Media Technologies*, 21 (2), pp. 244–256.

Haddon, L. (2003) 'Domestication and Mobile Telephony', in James Katz, (ed.) *Machines that Become Us: The Social Context of Personal Communication Technology*, New Brunswick, Canada: Transaction Publishers, pp. 43–56.

Hartmann, M. (2009) 'Everyday: Domestication of Mediatisation or Mediatized Domestication?', in Knut Lundby (ed.) *Mediatization: Concept, Changes, Consequences*, New York: Peter Lang Publishing, pp. 225–242.

Honan, M. (2014) 'Are Touchscreens Melting Your Kid's Brain?', Wired.com, available at: *http://www.wired.com/2014/04/children-and-touch-screens/*, accessed 15 January 2015.

Kosareff, S. (2005) *Window to the Future: The Golden Age of Television Marketing and Advertising*, San Fransisco, CA: Chronicle Books.

Lally, E. (2002) *At Home with Computers*, Berg: Oxford.

Leiss, W., Kline, S. and Jhally, S. (1990) *Social Communication in Advertising*, New York: Routledge.

Lillie, J. (2011) 'Nokia's MMS: A Cultural Analysis of Mobile Picture Messaging', *New Media and Society* 14 (1), pp. 80–97.

Livingstone, S. (2002) *Young People and New Media: Childhood and the Changing Media Environment*, London: Sage Publications.

Livingstone, S. (2014) 'As Ever Younger Kids Go Online, How is the Family Responding?' Parenting for a Digital Future Blog (LSE), available at: *http://blogs.lse.ac.uk/parenting 4digitalfuture/2015/06/12/as-ever-younger-kids-go-online-how-is-the-family-responding/*, accessed 6 December 2015.

Livingstone, S. and Das, R. (with contributions from Georgiou, M., Haddon, L., Helsper, E. and Wang, Y.) (2010) *Media, Communication and Information Technologies in the European Family Working Report* (April 2010). Family Platform, Existential Field 8, available at: *http://eprints.lse.ac.uk/29788/1/EF8_LSE_MediaFamily_Education.pdf*, accessed 5 December 2015.

Livingstone, S., Marsh, J., Plowman, L., Ottovordemgentschenfelde, S. and Fletcher-Watson, B. (2014) 'Young Children (0–8) and Digital Technology: A Qualitative Exploratory Study – National Report – UK', LSE Rsearch Online, available at: *http:// eprints.lse.ac.uk/60799/1/__lse.ac.uk_storage_LIBRARY_Secondary_libfile_shared_reposi tory_Content_Livingstone,%20S_Young%20children%200-8_Livingstone_Young%20chil dren%200-8_2015.pdf*, accessed 6 December 2015.

Lull, J. (1982) 'How Families Select Television Programs: A Mass Observational Study', *Journal of Broadcasting and Electronic Media* 26 (4), pp. 801–811.

Lull, J. (1990) *Inside Family Viewing: Ethnographic Research on Television's Audiences*, London: Routledge.

Madden, M. (2009) 'The Audience for Online Video-sharing Sites Shoots Up', available at: *http://fe01.pewinternet.org/Reports/2009/13–The-Audience-for-Online-VideoSharing-Sites-Shoots-Up.aspx*, accessed 6 December 2015.

Martindale, S., Coughlan, T., Evans, L. and Reeves, S. (2013) 'Understanding the Multi-screen Household: An Interdisciplinary Approach', *Methods for Studying Technology in the Home Workshop*, CHI'13, April 27–May 2 2013, Paris, France.

Morley, D. (1986) *Family Television: Cultural Power and Domestic Leisure*, London: Routledge.

Morley, D. (1992) *Television, Audiences and Cultural Studies*, London: Routledge.

Morley, D. (2002) *Home Territories: Media, Mobility and Identity*, London: Routledge.

Morley, D. (2003) 'What's 'Home' Got to Do With It? Contradictory Dynamics in the Domestication of Technology and the Dislocation of Domesticity', *European Journal of Cultural Studies* 6 (4), p. 435.

Morley, D. (2007) *Media, Modernity and the Geography of the New*, London: Routledge.

Natale, S. and Balbi, G. (2014) 'Media and the Imaginary in History', *Media History* 20 (2), pp. 203–218.

Nielsen Company (2011) 'Time Shift Viewing: Setting the Scene for 2012', pp. 1–22, available at: *http://www.thinktv.co.nz/wp-content/uploads/TSV-Charts2_Part11.pdf*, accessed 6 December 2015.

Nielson (2012a) 'Double Vision – Global Trends in Tablet and Smartphone Use While Watching TV', available at: *http://www.nielsen.com/us/en/insights/news/2012/double-vision-global-trends-in-tablet-and-smartphone-use-while-watching-tv.html*, accessed 13 February 2015.

Nielsen (2012b) 'The Cross-platform Report: Quarter 4', 2011, pp. 1–12', available at: *http://www.nielsen.com/us/en/reports/2012/the-cross-platform-report-q4-2011.html*, accessed 18 February 2015

Nielsen (2012c) 'Global Online Consumers and Multi-screen Media: Today and Tomorrow', 15 May, pp. 1–9, available at: *http://www.nielsen.com/us/en/search.html? tag=Article%3AReport&q=Global+Online+Consumers+and+Multi-Screen+Media%3A&sor tbyScore=false*, accessed 18 February 2015)

Newman, M.Z. (2012) 'Free TV: File-sharing and the Value of Television', *Television and New Media* 13 (6), pp. 463–479.

Ofcom (2014a) 'Adults' Media Use and Attitudes Report April 2014', available at: *http:// stakeholders.ofcom.org.uk/binaries/research/media-literacy/adults-2014/2014_Adults_report. pdf*, accessed 13 February 2015.

Ofcom (2014b) 'The Communications Market Report', available at: *http://stakeholders. ofcom.org.uk/market-data-research/market-data/communications-market-reports/cmr14/uk/*, accessed 13 February 2015.

Ofcom (2014c) 'TV and Audio-visual: Industry Metrics and Summary', available at: *http:// stakeholders.ofcom.org.uk/market-data-research/market-data/communications-market-reports/ cmr14/uk/uk-2.01*, accessed 13 February 2015.

Ofcom (2014d) 'Children and Parents: Media Use and Attitudes Report', available at: *http://stakeholders.ofcom.org.uk/market-data-research/other/research-publications/childrens/ children-parents-oct-14/*, accessed 6 December 2015.

Ofcom (2015) 'The Communications Market Report', available at: *http://stakeholders.ofcom. org.uk/binaries/research/cmr/cmr15/CMR_UK_2015.pdf*, accessed 6 December 2015.

Parks, L. (2004) 'Flexible Microcasting: Gender, Generation and Television-internet Convergence', in Lyn Spigel and Jan Olsson (eds) *Television after TV: Essays on a Medium in Transition*, Durham, NC: Duke University Press, pp. 133–156.

Peil, C. and Röser, J. (2014) 'The Meaning of Home in the Context of Digital Mediatisation, Mobilization and Mediatisation', in Andreas Hepp and Friedrich Krotz (eds) *Mediatized Worlds: Culture and Society in a Media Age*, Basingstoke, Palgrave Macmillan, pp. 233–252.

Pew Research Internet Project (2014) 'Device Ownership over Time', January 2014 available at: *http://www.pewinternet.org/data-trend/mobile/device-ownership/*, accessed 24 December 2014.

Pinch, T.J. and Bijker, W.E. (1984) 'The Social Construction of Facts and Artefacts: Or How the Sociology of Science and the Sociology of Technology Might Benefit Each Other', *Social Studies of Science*, 14, pp. 399–441.

Purcell, K. (2010) 'The State of Online Video', available at: *http://pewinternet.org/ Reports/2010/State-of-Online-Video.aspx*, accessed 6 December 2015.

Shade, L.R. (2011) 'Surveilling the Girl Via the Third and Networked Screen', in Mary Celeste Kearney (ed.), *Mediated Girlhoods: New Explorations of Girls' Media Culture*, New York: Peter Lang, pp. 261–275.

Silverstone, R. (1994) *Television and Everyday Life*, London: Routledge.

Silverstone, R. and Hirsch, E. (eds) (1992) *Consuming Technologies: Media and Information in Domestic Spaces*, London: Routledge.

Spigel, L. (1992) *Make Room for TV: Television and the Family Ideal in Postwar America*, Chicago, IL: University of Chicago Press.

Spigel, L. (2001) *Welcome to the Dreamhouse: Popular Media and Postwar Suburbia*, Durham, NC: Duke University Press.

Turkle, S. (2011) *Alone Together: Why We Expect More from Technology and Less from Each Other*, New York: Basic Books.

Van Rompaey, V. and Roe, K. (2001) 'The Home as a Multimedia Environment: Families' Conception of Space and the Introduction of Information and Communication Technologies in the Home', *Communications* 26 (4), pp. 351–369.

Vickery, J.R. (2014) 'Talk Whenever, Wherever: How the US Mobile Phone Industry Commodifies Talk, Genders Youth Mobile Practices, and Domesticates Surveillance', *Journal of Children and Media* 8 (4), pp. 387–403.

Williams, A. (2011) 'Quality Time, Redefined', *New York Times*, 29 April 2011, available at: *http://www.nytimes.com/2011/05/01/fashion/01FAMILY.html?pagewanted=all&_r=0*, accessed 13 February 2015.

Zickuhr, K. (2013) 'Tablet Ownership 2013, Pew Internet & American Life Project', 10 June, available at: *http://pewinternet.org/Reports/2013/Tablet-Ownership-2013.aspx*, accessed 13 February 2015.

Appendix: advertisements included for analysis

These links were accessed on 16 February 2015.

1. 'April 3', Apple iPad (2010) retrieved from *https://www.youtube.com/watch?v=R41NNPBqRCk*.
2. 'Time to Tab', Samsung Galaxy Tab 10.1 (2011) retrieved from *https://www.youtube.com/watch?v=QL8ePbYsdc8*.
3. 'make.believe', Sony (2011) retrieved from *https://www.youtube.com/watch?v=UqATFLwp0uE*.
4. 'Click in at Microsoft.com' Microsoft Surface (2012) retrieved from *https://www.youtube.com/watch?v=uBg9-X1gHM4*.
5. 'Time to Tab', Samsung Tab 10.1 (2011) retrieved from *https://www.youtube.com/watch?v=QL8ePbYsdc8*.
6. 'Day in the Life', Samsung Galaxy Note (2013) retrieved from *https://www.youtube.com/watch?v=MI7P7leMono&index=10&list=PLI0vqcScB7gzYbFcuYnczNvwG5D2z9c69*.
7. 'Do You Note?', Galaxy Note 4 (2014), retrieved from
   a) 'Brother' *https://www.youtube.com/watch?v=GFgwTxaU0CY&list=PLI0vqcScB7gzYbFcuYnczNvwG5D2z9c69&index=15*.
   b) 'Sister' *https://www.youtube.com/watch?v=EvLE7JWiDt8&index=16&list=PLI0vqcScB7gzYbFcuYnczNvwG5D2z9c69*.
   c) 'Mom' *https://www.youtube.com/watch?v=zwXPEIJd474&list=PLI0vqcScB7gzYbFcuYnczNvwG5D2z9c69&index=17*.
   d) 'Dad' *https://www.youtube.com/watch?v=o85Y4XfBUuQ&list=PLI0vqcScB7gzYbFcuYnczNvwG5D2z9c69&index=13*.
   e) 'Me' *https://www.youtube.com/watch?v=NYMaF76LWlg*.
8. 'What You Really Need', Galaxy Tab S (2014) retrieved from *https://www.youtube.com/watch?v=g3Kjj2ca4oQ*.
9. 'Kristen and Dax: Home for the Holidays', Samsung Mobile USA (2014) retrieved from *https://www.youtube.com/watch?v=LqAxBL5wStc*.
10. 'Leapfrog Leappad 2 Explorer Learning Tablet' (2012) retrieved from *https://www.youtube.com/watch?v=Hv0278fTkN0*.
11. 'Inno Tab 3 S "Kid Connect"', VTech (2013) retrieved from *https://www.youtube.com/watch?v=aq3qR7onqi8*.

7

HOME, MEDIA AND MIGRATION

Introduction

The previous chapters emphasise some of the major ways in which media create and sustain permeable boundaries around the home. This chapter provides insights into the changing meanings of home involving media and communication technologies in the context of migration and diasporic cultures. Intimate, personal lives associated with family, home life and the parochial are deeply affected by global processes of migration, colonialism and other global processes. In the context of migratory experiences of interruption, travel and settlement, media and communication technologies play a central role in shaping meanings of home, domesticity, and our sense of belonging to national and transnational communities, as Morley (2007) emphasises. Families and extended kinship networks can no longer simply be perceived as distinct households or institutions detached from other locations and structures, particularly for migrant families where parents and children may be hundreds of miles apart. Research on migration indicates that the process of relocation challenges traditional meanings of home (Levitt and Waters 2006). In the context of migration, 'home' can have many connotations, stretching beyond domestic space to encompass a transnational range. Within studies of diaspora and transnational families, the home is therefore now a key unit of research involving home-making activities, material culture, mediated communication and the sense of belonging to and inhabiting the world.

The emphasis on home as an intimate, symbolic, private space has been complicated by the use of technologies of communication from Skype to mobile phones for maintaining transnational intimate contact (see Bachelard 1957). Demonstrating the vital role of media in connecting people across distances, migrants are among the most advanced users of communications technology (Broadbent 2011; Metykova 2010). Research undertaken in Australia, Canada and Europe confirms that rates of computer and internet access and use tend to be higher among international migrants than among those who are native born, to keep in contact with family and friends (Madianou and Miller 2012). With a reduction in the costs and accessibility of media technologies, services such as voice-over-internet, instant messaging (IM) and webcams are cheap or even free after the initial outlay on equipment.

While transnational families are maintaining connections through multiple media platforms, coinciding with new meanings of 'home', migrant families are regularly marginalised within media imaginings and public debates about the role of media in the home. This chapter therefore examines the use of old and new media across households to determine how households and families interconnect across distances. It assesses the impact of media globalisation on familial connections and tensions, and on individuals' sense of rootedness and belonging. The importance of understanding the ways in which race/ethnicity and migration may affect children's media worlds and relationships to communication technologies is also emphasised. The chapter begins by exploring the negotiation of 'home' from a distance and the reconfiguration of 'home' and 'belonging' among transnational communities involving media technologies such as Skype, mobile phone, social media and email.

Forming part of a wider set of issues concerning the 'politics of dislocation' (Grossberg 1996: 185–186), the chapter asks: what does 'home' mean in a media globalised world? In the first section, the chapter identifies the range of media and communication technologies used by migrants to keep in touch, drawing attention to the polymediated nature of today's transnational communication. The second section addresses ways in which media content are used. It also highlights both positive and negative experiences of transnational migrant communication in relation to ideas of home and belonging. The third section discusses the uses of media and communication technologies by migrant children in facilitating migrant families' engagement with media in their adopted home and by migrant parents in maintaining children's links with their home country. Finally, the chapter considers the role of digitally produced family albums in facilitating family narratives of migration and enabling an intimate connection with a new country and new neighbourhood.

Transnational uses of communication technologies

People and communities are connected to place through ideas of belonging, generated by emotions of attachment and expressions of identity (Mee and Wright 2009). Our ideas of home relate not only to our possessions, material environment, household structure and type of home but also to our sense of belonging. Feeling at home is an emotional state that can be experienced anywhere, not just in the geographical place that people are born into or reside in. Studies of transnational migrants' identities confirm that home is a key signifier within individuals' experiences of their migratory passage, affecting how they envisage their future (Blunt and Bonnerjee 2013; Blunt 2005; Ho 2006). Migrants often associate a sense of home with a place of origin far from their place of residence (Ahmed 1999; Basu 2004; Butcher 2003; Haller and Landolt 2005; Pratt 2004; Wiles 2008; Wise 2011). Moreover, for migrants, home can be a site of inclusion and exclusion. Thus, complex emotions of loss and gain are often involved in migrants' imagining of home as a place of belonging.

These complexities are exemplified in a study of Chinese migrants to New Zealand by Liangni Sally Liu (2014) who explains that transnational migration is a rational decision for Chinese migrants hoping to take advantage of the economic opportunities while balancing family members' different needs. However, their feelings of home become increasingly fluid and ambivalent. 'Home is often hard to define or re-define, and migrants continue to load new meanings onto it centered on family, social relations, and emotional attachment and investment' (Lui 2014). As Lefebvre (1974/1991) emphasises, our everyday experiences and feelings about home are mediated through representations of space involving material, affective and aesthetic dimensions of media. Within critical approaches to geographies of home, transnational migrants' identification with their cultural origins can be explained as a 'diasporic imagination' of home (Brah 1996: 192). Blunt and Dowling (2006) refer to 'spatial imaginary' to describe the intersecting and variable ideas and feelings related to context that construct places, extend across spaces and scales, and connect places. They argue that as well as addressing 'the lived experience of home on a domestic scale', we need to consider the interconnections between 'material and imaginative geographies of the home' generated at all levels: locally, regionally, nationally and transnationally (Blunt and Dowling 2006: 198).

Decisions about moving from one country to another are frequently made at the level of family rather than individuals. Families are therefore addressed as a pivotal category in studies of migration and diaspora. Paradoxically, migration disrupts family life yet simultaneously reinforces and intensifies family relations (Georgiou 2010). Within the diaspora, the family is re-established as a system of support that can provide a sense of security and stability for those experiencing interruption and relocation. Myria Georgiou (2010) explains that, in terms of media consumption, this simultaneous disruption and intensification of family relationships is characterised in three ways. First, it entails the advanced use of transnational media and communications such as the mobile phone, internet and television (TV). Second, close connections with families, which are often strengthened in the diaspora, coincide with everyday-shared familial media consumption of certain genres and media, particularly TV. Certain TV programmes can foster a sense of 'back home'. A third characteristic is that, as media consumers of national and transnational media, family members select media according to their identity and status in terms of migration, generation and age.

Today's digital technologies are providing opportunities for migrant and other users to 'experience' two places simultaneously and to move between them both. A vital feature of such multiple habitations is the use of media and communication technologies as resources to bridge the gaps between different places and ideas of home. Among transnational families separated by migration, relatives regularly text each other to arrange Skype or FaceTime exchanges, send photos by email and follow family members' day-to-day activities on social network sites. In these ways, families and friends who keep in touch across distances benefit from a converged media experience. Research confirms that these new modes of communication become the infrastructure of family life (Madiannou and Miller 2012).

Addressing the home as a mediated space and media as a domesticated space, Tiziano Bonini (2011) argues that the existential condition of the migrant can be alleviated and eventually 'domesticated', at least temporarily, through the use of mobile media and communication technologies. By presenting the case study of a Filipino family living in Milan, Bonini identifies the role of the media not only in temporarily connecting migrants to their private homes or their public sphere of origin, but also in recreating the 'warmth' of domesticity, that is, in 'making them feel at home'. He speaks of media as 'home-making tools' for transnational migrants and argues that media are used by migrants 'to return home', emphasising the value of media technologies as 'home-making tools' that shape a desire for home among 'away-from-home' people. As Bonini points out, this conception of media as home-tools resonates with research by Mizuko Ito and colleagues (2008) on young urban people who use mobile phones to 'inhabit' space. Urban *flâneurs*, metropolitan nomads and tribes of teenagers renegotiate spatial boundaries to manage their social networks through the use of this mobile communication technology. However, for migrants, the mobile phone is likely to be the most essential tool available to them. Bonini states: 'A migrant may have no place to sleep, but he cannot afford not to have a mobile phone. His telephone is his office and his home: that is where he can be reached by his boss, or by his wife' (Bonini 2011: 871).

Bonni (2011) explains that, for migrants living on the margins of society, the mobile phone confers a sense of familiarity and routine by lowering experiences of isolation. The accelerated take-up of mobile phones in Africa and other parts of the developing world enables migrants who travel to Europe to participate in the lives of children and other relatives back home. Research by Heather Horst (2006) also confirms that the widespread adoption of cellphones among Jamaicans has facilitated connections with their migrant relatives. At a personal and private level, mobile phones comprise part of a range of mediums, such as emails, social media and Skype, that facilitate communication to retain familial and intimate connections. Through the mobile phone, global diasporic communities are able to keep up with news, current affairs and social trends associated with the public dimension of 'back home' (Bonini 2011). These examples indicate, then, that under certain circumstances, such as processes of migration, the smartphone involves a mobile domestication of technology.

Raelene Wilding's (2006) Australian study of the appropriation of information and communication technologies (ICTs) in transnational exchanges demonstrates that the appearance of a new technology does not necessarily lead to the replacement of an old one. Rather, families tend to increase the regularity of use through the addition of further levels of communication as part of the adaptation of their communication strategies to the technological possibilities made available. Although ICTs have replaced slow mail systems such as letters, new communication systems such as mobile phones, texting, satellite, the internet and social media are used in overlapping ways. These are incorporated with newer media by acting as multipliers of a sense of nearness (Wilding 2006). As Bonini (2011) states: 'The immediacy of email communications has generated a deeper feeling of attachment of migrants to their home' (Bonini 2011: 874). Among many cultures, individuals have adapted to media and communication technologies to be in 'two places at once'. Wilding (2006) points out that technology such as email and phone engender a sense of shared space and time during the exchange for families divided from one another. The more frequent use of Skype also fosters this sensation. But this kind of contact is precarious as Wilding points out. The sense of distance swiftly returns if, for example, a parent on the other side of the world becomes ill and is no longer able to stay in immediate contact. Cheap telecommunications enhance migrant parents' engagement in the lives of their spouses and children. They can offer support and encouragement, and participate in their children's educational and emotional development while being involved in the decision-making routine in the household back home (Horst 2006: 149).

Taking the time to converse with remote grandparents and other relatives allows families to articulate and strengthen their values and bonds (Ames et al. 2010; Kaye 2011: 186). In the last few years software packages such as Skype and iChat and hardware configurations such as built-in cameras or cheap external webcams have made videoconferencing feasible for families and other casual users. Broadbent (2011) refers to a family of immigrant workers from Kosovo who live in Switzerland and have installed a large computer screen in their lounge. Nearly every morning they breakfast with their grandmother back in Kosovo via a webcam. Indeed, Broadbent argues that migrants emerge as some of the 'most aggressive' adopters of new communication tools. In a Spanish family who live in Switzerland, the daughter often conducts her homework with her aunt who lives in Spain over a free Skype video link. The sense of immediacy offered by conversational media is viewed as an ideal quality for families that communicate across great geographical distances.

These kinds of connected relationships can modify the distinctions between 'absence and presence' and offer a feeling of being 'at home' while away from home (Wilding 2006: 132). Similarly, a study of day-to-day use on 3G mobile phones by O'Hara et al. found that their 21 UK-based early adopters of mobile videochat successfully used video calling once every two weeks (O'Hara et al. 2006). The home was the most common setting for making a call (30 per cent), and the main reason for the call was 'small talk' (50 per cent). Dedicated-use videoconferencing units helped elderly users feel more connected to their community in a study by Gregg (2001). Research on divorced families by Yarosh (2008) showed that a third of the families occasionally used videoconferencing as a significant way of sustaining bonds with relatives to overcome problems of isolation and provide an important avenue of moral support.

Joseph Kaye (2011) examined the bonding connections generated between grandparents and grandchildren and the role of love in the family. His findings on the use of Skype and iChat among 23 families on the west coast of USA confirm that these technologies are commonplace in many homes and that their use by families to communicate at a distance is accelerating. Reminding us that 'love is work', in the sense that the sustaining of intimacy requires the investment of time and effort, Kaye explains that videochat is the work that brings grandparents and kids, mums and dads together. For example, he observed that French-speaking grandparents in France used a combination of text chat and videochat to communicate with their 9-year-old, non-French-speaking granddaughter living in California. Another pair of grandparents used iChat to watch their grandson play the trumpet from hundreds of miles away. Over Skype, grandparents witnessed their 2-year-old granddaughter, who insisted she did not need a nap, start crying and fall asleep on her father's lap. Such interactions are now mundane and everyday. Ames et al. (2010) identified non-technical challenges involved in videochat including difficulties in staying in frame to be seen by the person at other end of connection and in coordinating schedules so that both parties are available at same time. They point out that these technical issues are easier to deal with at work where there are often better network connections than those servicing the home and with meetings easier to schedule at work through meeting requests. Yet videochat use is far more popular in the home where it has become the major medium for intimate, family affairs.

However, video calls have two important affordances that match this technology effectively to intimate, domestic use in a way that would seem incongruous in the more formal work setting. They involve connections in real time, between people in the 'here and now', and the appeal of 'seeing' which allows visual displays of physical tenderness associated with initiating family interactions. Videochat involves quality time by the giving of focused, undivided attention to the person connected with. The giving of undivided attention is an increasingly scarce resource (Turkle 2011). For some, videochat is the main channel through which people express or feel love. Skyping can, then, be conceived as a gift like a greeting cards or an act of service. Kaye (2011) refers to *Farmville*, Facebook, *Second Life* and other online environments, particularly those in South Korea, which show how digital gifts can be given and exhibited to express affection and love.

The escalation of global migration, coupled with the feminisation of migration, has generated a new 'transnational family' characterised by a woman from the global south who migrates for employment to the global north and who leaves behind her children. This leads to a new category of transnational motherhood (Hondagneu-Sotelo and Avila 1997) that entails the management of the relationship through long-distance communication. Studies conducted on such long-distance relations maintained between parents and children separated by migration show that these transnational families have distinct communication experiences. For example, within research on Filipina transnational families, Rhacel Parreñas (2005) describes the fervent exchange of phone calls and text messages between migrant mothers and their children who are left behind in the Philippines. Similarly, Madianou and Miller (2012) studied distant mothering by interviewing migrant mothers in the UK and their children left behind in the Philippines. Like Wilding (2006), they found that 'old' forms of contact such as letter writing, long-distance phone calls and the recording of voice messages on cassette recorders overlap with, but are gradually overtaken by, more 'modern' modes of contact such as texting, email, social network sites and blogs. They also discovered that each medium generates and conveys a distinctive set of practices, functions and values for communicating and sustaining interpersonal and familial ties. The immediacy of synchronous, conversational mediums is highly valued by migrant families. Madianou and Miller therefore developed the term 'polymedia' to address the diverse resources for connecting and sustaining relationships. They explain that the multiple uses of communication technologies by these transnational families exemplify the 'poly-mediated' nature of today's digital media engagement (Madianou and Miller 2012). This quality associated with today's digital media affordances is a manifestation of the mediatisation of intimate life. Under spatial conditions marked by convergence of old and new media, social subjects move with ease between different channels and sources (Jansson 2013).

Research also demonstrates that cultural traditions and social norms can affect the ways in which communication technologies are used to keep in intimate contact, leading to negative as well as positive experiences. For example, Francis Leo Collins (2009) examines the use of personal homepages among seven South Korean international students in Auckland, New Zealand, to understand how this communication technology facilitates a connection between idealised notions of 'home' (South Korea) with the physical realities of 'here' (in this case, in Auckland). A range of different technologies are used by the students to connect with South Korea, from older media such as letters and telephone through to a variety of internet tools. With a focus on internet use through a discussion of personal homepages on the Cyworld domain, Collins explains that personal homepage systems like Cyworld play a key role in facilitating the extended reach of interpersonal relationships between families and friends and therefore also in the production of this sense of co-nationality.

However, this link with 'home' can also have a negative effect on students' everyday transnational lives by inhibiting, as well as facilitating, their activities. Whether personal, familial or national, Cyworld is also a form of surveillance that enables the extension of Korean social norms to lives in Auckland through subtle (and not-so-subtle) disciplining of students' actions and behaviour. Students were tracked down, through the search function, by users from Korea who sent abusive messages. For example, a student who uploaded photos of herself in bars in Auckland with non-Korean men received several abusive messages which prompted her to censor the photos she posted and the discussions she had on her online diary (known as 'minihompy'). Collins explains that her actions recorded on her minihompy were condemned through a form of patriarchal nationalism that aims to discipline the Korean female body. Her decision to close her minihompy and then reopen a new one was prompted by the realisation that she could be watched by anyone at any time.

Social network sites such as Cyworld therefore play a role in emphasising the sense of distance that students experience between themselves, 'home' and 'here'. Even in the case of a student who was the most embedded in local networks in Auckland, Cyworld was used only for including her relationships with other Koreans in Auckland. The social medium was very unlikely to assist in the building of friendships and the establishment of networks with non-Korean individuals. Collins concludes that internet activities are likely to play a significant role in students' feelings of estrangement in Auckland. First, these practices only connect students to 'home' through their personal online diary, emphasising the fact that they are not at home but are a great distance away both physically and culturally. Second, the comfort that students may receive from Cyworld makes it more difficult for them to engage with individuals who are not Korean and to learn English which, paradoxically, is the main reason why so many choose to study overseas in the first place. Thus, while communication technologies such as social media can bridge the gap between 'home' and 'here' to the extent that the medium itself represents the security and comfort of 'home', the same technology can also become an alienating force that harbours meanings oppositional to ideas of the homeland as 'home', as a secure space.

A study of the ways in which migrants use the internet to maintain transnational family relationships by Tingyu Kang (2012) also exemplifies the negative experiences that can arise from using the internet for transnational family communication. Kang examined transborder households among 53 Chinese migrants in London and their ageing parents in China. She encountered major differences in digital knowledge and skills between men and women. The families' high socioeconomic status meant that the parents in China had effective access to computers and internet apparatus so inequalities were not based on access. However, Kang found other forms of digital inequality within these transborder households relating to age and gender. The majority of the informants' mothers and other female elderly relatives in China experienced difficulties in communicating with family members overseas because the internet had replaced the telephone as the main mode of transnational communication. This shift in the type of technology used led to a change in the power dynamics in the family sphere, at a transnational level.

The traditionally feminine role of care and intimacy was increasingly reassigned to male family members within this transnational process. This is because engagement with internet technology was perceived to be a male responsibility in a context where the man is deferred to as the one who develops the competencies required to operate new technologies. He is therefore responsible for exchanges within this new mode of communication. 'Women in transnational families are thus silenced' (Kang 2012: 146). In one group, women were unable to convey intimate feelings towards their families or support their mothers' wellbeing. A second group of women gained help from their families to facilitate their online contact from spouses and other younger family members. But this was constrained by the time frame of those assisting, and was under the constant surveillance of the male group member and the young. A third group of mothers sought out ways to advance their digital skills, indicating the potential for resistance and agency within the parameters of technology adoption. This study confirms that the power dynamics of age and gender are as important factors as digital inequalities in attempts to maintain communication in transborder households.

The role of media content within transnational identities

Media content also play a key role in expressing a distant homeland and domestic spaces at one and the same time. A range of studies exemplify the significance of age, gender and generational identities within patterns of diasporic media consumption (see Gillespie 1995; Georgiou 2006; Bailey et al. 2007). Studies of migrant transnationalism have examined the ways in which certain individuals and families are able to conduct their lives in more than one locale. Among many cultures, people have adapted to media technologies to be in 'two places at once', as mentioned above. The content of media such as TV and films comprise major resources among migrants and diasporic communities for maintaining ethnic, religious and transnational identities (Brinkerhoff 2009; Adoni et al. 2006). For example, a seminal study of migrant media engagement by Kevin Robins and Asu Aksoy (2001) chronicled the ways in which distant media affects everyday domestic cultures among Turkish migrants in London. They found that migrants regularly 'travel' back and forth from the UK to Turkey at various points of the day. Able to watch Turkish national TV live via satellite, they sustain synchronised contact with life in Turkey, moving between British and Turkish TV channels and between local communication and long-distance phone calls (Aksoy and Robins 2002).

Despite geographical separation from Turkey, Turkish TV provided migrants the chance to encounter daily life in Turkey through their home life in London. At the same time, the mediated relationship sustained with Turkey changed the London Turks' relationship with London as a home. Turkish TV was seemingly detached from their surroundings in London, creating a form of media engagement that Aksoy and Robins (2002: 18) refer to as a 'dislocated kind of viewing'. While many more channels of communication are available today, such as Skype and social media, the point made by Robins and Aksoy (2001) is that, for many migrants, the local and domestic consumption of transnational culture is now an 'ordinary' rather than exceptional experience forming a central feature of everyday life. However, although migrants may use transnational media to sustain a close cultural connection to their 'homeland', their media practices are situated and framed within a lived experience of locality (Ahmed 1999: 34). This corresponds with Lebfevre's (1974/1991) concept of 'perceived' and 'lived space' addressed in Chapter 1, by reminding us of the socially constructed nature of space involved in our experiences of home.

Migrants and minority ethnic groups take advantage of the wide choices of media content available through digital global networks in order to watch news and films about their own communities and diasporas. In these ways, they bypass national and regional broadcasting that generate transnational and diasporic public spheres (Morley 2002: 125). Indian, Pakistani and Chinese communities across the world reinforce their identities and make connections with their homelands though their choice of media content. Transnational modes of identification and community are practised through tangible and lived spaces, as Morley points out. At the same time as fragmenting national media audiences, Morley (2002) emphasises that domestic media technologies are being used to generate multifarious networks between the domestic and local, on the one hand, and the national and global on the other.

Children, migration and media

Children perform a pivotal role in the process of migration involving the use of mass media. Children are usually the impetus for families' migration in search of economic prospects and, thereafter, children regularly act as mediators between their parents and the new community by helping their parents negotiate their settlement within the adoptive country. Parents are keen for children to nurture cultural ties with the home country. Mass media is a means through which migrants search for ways to sustain intimate ties with their home countries and gain an understanding of their new homes. Likewise, children's media-making forms a resource for the articulation of families' experiences and ideas about their new environment. Through their use of media and communication technologies, children in diaspora tend to be active agents who develop identities and meanings through their media use. By more readily consuming local, regional and global media, migrant children generally develop an interest in diverse media within the home. This tendency highlights the generational viewing distinctions between the adoptive country's culture and the traditions of the home country, yet these media habits also influence and often broaden the parents' experiences. Young people shape cultural spaces that are both separate from and overlap the adult world (de Leeuw and Rydin 2007). As de Block and Buckingham (2007: 23) explain, children often act as the family's 'front line' by absorbing the language more quickly at school, making new school friends and through their exposure to popular media content. This can often lead to changes in the power relations between parents and children.

Children are often adept at using new gadgets yet lack wider knowledge of the media environment and the crucial competences required for decoding and evaluating media content (Strasburger and Wilson 2002). Performing important connections between the family home and the local community, children's brokering activities involve the use of traditional as well as new media technologies, from landline phones and letters to mobile phones and the internet, to integrate their families into their new local vicinities (Katz 2010; Orellana et al. 2003; Tseng and Fuligni 2000). Media engagement by young people can be eclectic and cosmopolitan, with studies of diasporic media use revealing inter-generational frictions in the home associated with children's activities such as TV viewing and video gaming. To some extent, this relates to the challenges faced by all families with children within the moral economy of the household as indicated in Chapter 4. But in the case of migrant families, it is also complicated by the shift in parental–child power relations in situations where parents are unfamiliar with the language, the technology or both. Children learn new languages very rapidly, and while at school they are in constant contact with new cultural norms through the kinds of immersive experiences that are unavailable to parents.

Nevertheless, domestic media also offer important resources for enhancing family bonding through regular viewing of films and TV as a family group (de Block and Buckingham 2007). Domestic media are used as a valuable tool for cross-generational communication among diasporic families (Livingstone and Das 2010). For example, TV programmes can provide a medium through which common or new values are discussed. Children's viewing of national TV such as national soap operas can offer a cultural space in which they can share values associated with the host culture. Young people's diverse media engagement can provide opportunities for older members of the household to encounter new programmes or films and share certain new cultures and languages. Similarly, parents can introduce their children to traditional values from 'back home'. Parents often play a part in brokering activities in the home by providing their adult knowledge of the world and teaching their children to decode media messages. A form of cultural exchange is facilitated with parents translating and conveying diasporic language and values to their children. In these ways, media consumption can form a space of cultural cohesion for diasporic families and cross-generational communication.

Although global and ethnic media can broaden the media environments of ethnic/racial minority children, they are likely to be hampered by restricted access to new communication technologies. For example, in the US, 78 per cent of white school-age children have a computer at home, compared with 48 per cent of Latino and 46 per cent of African-American students (Katz 2010). Across the globe, many migrant families and communities have low incomes, limited knowledge of the language of the host country and do not trust formal institutions. A study of Spanish parents and their children in an immigrant Latino community in Los Angeles by Katz (2010) found that children's media brokering practices can be either hampered or facilitated by the unique domestic infrastructures specific to their family households. The invisibility of children's brokering activities means that families often fail to recognise the pressures of brokering placed on the children's personal development. Often putting their families' needs ahead of their own, these children were identified as their family's helpers and often did not perform well in school. They sometimes miss homework or after school extra-curricular activities to help their families. And teachers are frequently unaware of the vital role played by these children for their families.

For diasporic families, TV viewing forms a cultural context of cohesion and cross-generational communication (Gillespie 1995; Georgiou 2006; de Block et al. 2005). A study of the way video was used among members of a South Asian diaspora in Southall, West London by Marie Gillespie (1989) demonstrates how domestic media are used by families to navigate modes of domestic culture that sustain links to migrants' homelands. Gillespie found that times were set aside at the weekend for the whole family to watch 'Asian' films on video to generate a sense of family togetherness. The films' content provided an occasion for parents to experience a sense of nostalgia for their homeland and, at the same time, an opportunity to socialise children into their cultural, religious and linguistic heritage. Video watching offered a way of engaging children with a distant regional culture in the context of their home in London. Watching 'Indian' films at home in the UK provided a means through which new British–Asian identities could be articulated. This custom also facilitated multifaceted understandings of 'home' that conveyed aspects of global, national and local cultures in a home-based context. Likewise, Shaun Moores and Karen Qureshi (2000: 132–133) have explored the use of Asian cable and satellite channels by parents in Pakistani–Scottish families to facilitate their children's connection with their 'cultural heritage'. These studies confirm significant age differences in the use of media facilities at home. However, Gillespie's study showed that children used the video films as strategies for understanding their own Asian and British identities, while the study by Moores and Qureshi reveal that the children often ignored Asian channels, preferring to identify with British terrestrial TV programmes.

With young people's media interests steered by their peer group as well as home viewing, migrant children are more likely to engage with media which either have a global compass or are produced in the adoptive country rather than from their home country. The 'VideoCulture' project by de Block and Buckingham (2007) confirms that global media content such as Disney, Harry Potter and Pokemon are specifically aimed at children transnationally. This lends weight to the idea that childhood is now a universal category and that 'young people might have more in common with other young people who live in other parts of the world and who speak different languages than they do with the adults in their own country, and even their own homes' (de Block and Buckingham 2007: 150).

Diasporic families regularly criticise mainstream national and transnational media for misrepresenting minority ethnic groups. This is likely to affect their media engagement and viewing choices. Diasporic audiences draw attention to the policy need for fair media representation of ethnic and diasporic minorities in the mainstream media and the need for more diversified mediascapes. As Myria Georgiou states:

> Young people might not fit within a singular national imaginary; this area presents a challenge in developing social cohesion policies that are inclusive and reflexive'. Some minority groups develop a sense of exclusion and alienation in relation to (mediated) dominant narratives of identity and citizenship.
>
> *(Georgiou 2010: 67)*

Family albums, the migrant gaze and domestication of public places

Families communicate online to gain immediate news or to download photos and music from home. Despite geographical distance, this immediacy and combination of visual and audio communication brings families and friends together to celebrate group events and give a stronger sense of occasion to the interaction. Videos of family-centred rituals such as graduations, weddings and funerals are regularly sent to family members living abroad via email, social media or image and video-hosting websites (Horst 2006; Panagakos and Horst 2006; Wilding 2006; Horst 2010). Family albums have traditionally comprised important media objects for migrant families as ways of projecting home as an ideal place (Tolia-Kelly 2004: 285; Chambers 2006; Aguirre and Davies 2014). Photographic snapshots of migrants' adopted homes and of special public spaces during family travels can now be sent directly to relatives via digital media. Posting photos on social media such as Facebook and archiving digital photos facilitate an experience of 'the family as a whole group in constant interaction with each other' (Miller 2011: 194). Offering a site of convergence of production and consumption of family images, photos are archived and manipulated to compile digital albums of family life, to express powerful narratives of family togetherness.

Haldrup and Larsen (2003) use the term 'family gaze' to explain the cultural, semiotic and reflexive performance of family photography that enables a memorialising and expression of desired familial identities and settings. The notion of the 'family gaze' indicates that family photography functions to perform sociality within intimate social worlds (Haldrup and Larsen 2003). In the case of migrant families and through interaction with social media, everyday family photography enables the recording of memories of lives in a new land. Photography facilitates a family narrative of migration by providing a means through which to make an intimate connection with a new country and new neighbourhood. As I have said elsewhere: 'The ritual of taking family photographs in national monuments and events reveals the family's desire to, essentially, produce evidence of taking part in constructing meanings of the nation' (Chambers 2006: 105). Images of public space can be approached as pictorial spectacles and visual memories of the ownership and domestication of unfamiliar, alien space.

In terms of the migrant experience, Aguirre and Davies (2014) use the term 'migrant gaze' to explain the role of family photography in inhabiting a new country, domesticating unfamiliar spaces and inscribing them with familiar meanings in the process of settling into that country. Family photography facilitates a reconfiguration of public and domestic spaces. Through an in-depth case study of the Facebook activities of Amy, a Filipina immigrant to New Zealand, Aguirre and Davies analyse the construction of place and the discourse of the 'good life' which forms part of Amy's audio-visual commemoration of her family's second year as New Zealanders. Amy's 'migrant gaze' makes an audio-visual claim to national belonging articulated through everyday family photography by interrogating the boundaries of private and public spaces. While the locations of the images are predominantly outdoors, in public parks and among national monuments, there is a shot of 'our first home in New Zealand' after the 'first few days in New Zealand' and of the family posing in the garden of the home and then of their second home in Wellington.

Among Amy's audio-visual images, Aguirre and Davies (2014: 8) found only three sets that were explicitly identified as domestic spaces (through the captions). In these instances, the space is specifically labelled as 'home' or 'house', signalling permanence in the family's placement. 'It is interesting to note that the first set of images that bears the label "home" only appears after the first nine images. Pictures of their domestic life were preceded by pictures of playgrounds, parks, the museum, and the beach that go under the label *First few Days in NZ*' (Aguirre and Davies 2014: 10). They had no home for the first few days, as they had to stay with friends. Aguirre and Davies (2014) explain that treating the material dwelling in the new country as home depends on developing a sense of belonging. They moved three times in two years. 'Every move is indexed by a declaration of having a place they could invest in – materially and emotionally – to be able to establish a recognised domiciliary status. Every home, in turn, becomes a marker of a foray outside the private space and into the public sphere' (Aguirre and Davies 2014: 8). Acquiring a home frames the stages of the settling in as migrants. Once a base is secured, the world outside is actively explored. Thus, the ways in which the public and private spheres are interconnected through the photographic depiction of the family's life and new home is crucial in achieving a successful migration story.

Research highlights the importance of ordinariness, the everyday and the mundane as indicators of successfully navigating settlement in the new country and gaining a sense of belonging there as home (Aksoy and Robins 2002; Aguirre and Davies 2014). Media play a central role in achieving a sense of this ordinariness by facilitating a feeling of agency and control over the technology. As Aguirre and Davies (2014: 12) state: 'If being pictured in national public spaces creates an impression of national belonging, being photographed in the domestic sphere and depicting the domestication of public places create an image of *natural* belonging.' The strangeness of place is dissipated and the immigrants' sense of strangeness is erased through the visualisation of an imbedded presence in difference sites. Aguirre and Davies go on to say that the entire photographic collection can be understood as 'migrant place-making'. It celebrates the place to build an ideal home that conforms to the hegemonic discourses and dominant myths of a gentrified, middle-class, nuclear immigrant family life. Research confirms, then, that a new country and new home can be tamed and rendered familiar by controlling spaces through new imaginings of that space. By presenting an idea of life in a new country and new home, migrants generate a sense of belonging to a new space as 'place'. Taking photos and uploading them to a social network site offers a way of handling the challenges of creating a new life as a migrant by developing an identity of place.

Conclusion

The normalising role of media communication involves new types of interaction and new ideas of belonging across distances as features of mediatisation. In answering the question, 'What does "home" mean in a media globalised world?', this chapter concurs that 'home' can be experienced at different scales: the household residence, local neighbourhoods or homeland (Blunt and Dowling 2006). It outlines research indicating that conceptions of home often involve a transnational sense of belonging: transnational migrants often consider 'home' to be their place of origin, far from their current place of residence. The chapter provides examples of the central role played by media and communication technologies in generating fluid and dynamic meanings of home for migrants and diasporic communities. In a mediatised world, the stabilising role of media and communication technologies entails new social interactions and new ideas of belonging.

Unsurprisingly, migrants are among the most advanced users of communications technology. Transnational families make use of multiple communication technologies to sustain intimate relationships across distance. Madianou and Miller (2012) confirm the 'polymediated' nature of today's digital media engagement. The importance of mobile technology in creating a sense of belonging to national and transnational communities is also confirmed by migrants' personalised uses of the cellphone. For newly arrived migrants, this device is indicative of a process of 'mobile domestication' in the sense that it plays a key role in fostering a sense of normality by combating feelings of loneliness and separation (see Chapter 3). And video calls sustain intimate contact in real time, enabling visual displays of physical tenderness.

The chapter identifies both positive and negative experiences of long-distance communication among migrants and transnational families. Studies of migrant transnationalism allow individuals and families to straddle more than one locale, demonstrating the positive role of media content in creating and communicating powerful ideas of distant 'homelands'. Global media technology facilitates the circumvention of national and regional broadcasting borders within the aim of generating transnational and diasporic public spheres. Individual migrants and global diasporic communities have adapted to media and communication technologies to be in 'two places at once'. Certain TV programmes can foster a sense of 'back home'. Importantly, this ability to be in two places at once has become a central and normalised feature of everyday life, as a manifestation of the transnational aspects of today's 'mediatised home'.

While internet technology can foster idealised notions of 'home' it can also have a negative effect on migrants' everyday transnational lives by constraining as well as enabling their activities. Social network sites can operate as forms of surveillance by extending social norms from 'back home' to migrants' lives in the west through various strategies of disciplining students' actions and behaviour. Other studies highlight the ways in which new technologies can complicate or act as a barrier to traditional modes of intimacy within attempts to sustain transborder households.

In the transnational process of mediating transborder households, the supposedly feminine role of care and intimacy is often reassigned to male family members, preventing women from conveying intimate feelings towards their families or support their mothers' wellbeing. These findings draw attention to the clash between traditional and mediatised cultures involved in sustaining transnational intimacies.

The chapter confirms that migrant children tend to develop an interest in diverse media within the home by more willingly engaging with local, regional and global media, drawing attention to film and TV viewing differences between parents and children. Children are more inclined to engage with the adoptive country's culture while parents often engage with the traditions of the home country. In addition, children's media habits play a key role in influencing parents' experiences of the new home. Children create important connections between the family home and the local community through their brokering activities, involving the use of traditional as well as new media technologies from landline phones and letters to mobile phones. Research also indicates that domestic media act as major resources for augmenting familial bonding through habitual viewing of films and TV as a family group. For diasporic families, TV viewing can comprise a cultural context of cohesion and cross-generational communication. The term 'migrant gaze' used by Aguirre and Davies (2014) illustrates the ways family photography is used to connect emotionally with a new country by domesticating unfamiliar spaces and inscribing them with familiar meanings within the process of settling into the new country. 'Public' and 'private' spheres are interlinked through the photographic depiction of the family's life and new home as vital features of a successful migration narrative. Photographic collections can, then, be understood as 'migrant place-making'.

After identifying some of the key ways in which 'home' is conceptualised, perceived and lived through engagement with diverse media and communication technologies by migrants and transnational families, the following chapter examines 'home' imaginaries through a contrasting lens by addressing 'smart home' designs of the past and the digitally automated 'connected homes' of today.

References

Adoni, H., Caspi, D. and Cohen, A.A. (2006) *Media, Minorities and Hybrid Identities*, Cresskil, NJ: Hampton Press.

Aguirre, A.C. and Davies, S.G. (2014) 'Imperfect Strangers: Picturing Place, Family, and Migrant Identity on Facebook', *Discourse, Context and Media*, pp. 1–15.

Ahmed, S. (1999) 'Home and Away: Narratives of Migration and Estrangement', *International Journal of Cultural Studies* 2 (3), pp. 329–347.

Aksoy, A. and Robins, K. (2002) 'Banal Transnationalism: The Difference Television Makes', *Working Papers Series*, available at: *http://www.transcomm.ox.ac.uk/working%20 papers/WPTC-02-08%20Robins.pdf*, accessed 6 December 2015.

Ames, M., Go., J. Kaye, J. and Spasojevic, M. (2010) 'Making Love in the Network Closet: The Benefits and Work of Family Videochat', *Proceedings of the CSCW 2010*, New York: ACM, pp. 145–154.

Bachelard, G. (1957) *La Poétique de l'espace* (The Poetics of Space), Paris: Presses Universitaire de France.

Bailey, O.G., Georgiou, M. and Harindranath, R. (2007) *Transnational Lives and the Media: Re-imagining Diasporas*, London: Palgrave Macmillan.

Basu, P. (2004) 'My Own Island Home: The Orkney Coming', *Journal of Material Culture* 9 (1) pp. 27–42.

Blunt, A. (2005) *Domicile and Diaspora: Anglo-Indian Women and the Spatial Politics of Home*, Oxford: Blackwell.

Blunt, A. and Bonnerjee, J. (2013) 'Home, City and Diaspora: Anglo–Indian and Chinese Attachments to Calcutta', *Global Networks* 13 (2), pp. 220–240.

Blunt, A. and Dowling, R. (2006) *Home*, London: Routledge.

Bonini, T. (2011) 'The Media as 'Home-making' Tools: Life Story of a Filipino Migrant in Milan', *Media, Culture & Society* 33(6), pp. 869–883.

Brah, A. (1996) *Cartographies of Diaspora: Contesting Identities*, London: Routledge.

Brinkerhoff, J. (2009) *Digital Diasporas: Identity and Transnational Engagement*, Cambridge and New York: Cambridge University Press.

Broadbent, S. (2011) *L'intimite' au Travail*. Paris: Fyp Editions.

Butcher, A. (2003) 'No Place Like Home? The Experiences of South-East Asian International Students in New Zealand and Their Re-entry into Their Countries of Origin', PhD dissertation, Department of Sociology, Massey University.

Chambers, D. (2006) 'Family as Place: Family Photograph Albums and the Domestication of Public and Private Space', in Joan M. Schwartz and James R. Ryan (eds) *Picturing Place: Photography and the Geographical Imagination*, London: IB Tauris, pp. 96–114.

Collins, F.L. (2009) Connecting 'Home' with 'Here': Personal Homepages in Everyday Transnational Lives', *Journal of Ethnic and Migration Studies* 35 (6), pp. 839–859.

de Block, L. and Buckingham, D. (2007) *Global Children, Global Media: Migration, Media and Childhood*, London: Palgrave Macmillan.

de Block, L., Buckingham, D. and Banaji, S. (2005) *Children in Communication about Migration: Final Report*, London: Institute of Education, University of London.

de Leeuw, S. and Rydin, I. (2007) 'Migrant Children's Digital Stories: Identity Formation and Self-representation through Media Production', *European Journal of Cultural Studies* 10 (4), pp. 447–464.

Georgiou, M. (2006) 'Cities of Difference: Cultural Juxtapositions and Urban Politics of Representation', *International Journal of Cultural and Media Politics* 2 (3), pp. 283–298.

Georgiou, M. (2010) 'Special Focus: Diasporic Families and Media Consumption', in Sonia Livingstone and Ranjana Das (eds) *Media, Communication and Information Technologies in the European Family, Existential Field 8 Working Report*, April 2010, pp. 65–68, available at: *http://eprints.lse.ac.uk/29788/1/EF8_LSE_MediaFamily_Education.pdf*, accessed 6 December 2015.

Gillespie, M. (1989) 'Technology and Tradition: Audio-visual Culture among South Asian Families in West London, *Cultural Studies* 3 (2), pp. 226–239.

Gillespie, M. (1995) *Television, Ethnicity and Cultural Change*, London: Routledge.

Gregg, J.L. (2001) 'Tearing Down Walls for the Homebound Elderly', in *CHI '01 Extended Abstracts on Human Factors in Computing Systems*, Seattle, Washington DC, pp. 469–470

Grossberg, L. (1996) 'The Space of Culture, the Power of Space', in Iain Chambers and Lidia Curti (eds) *The Post-Colonial Question; Common Skies, Divided Horizons*, London: Routledge, pp. 169–188.

Haldrup, M. and Larsen, J. (2003) 'The Family Gaze', *Tourist Studies* 3 (1), pp. 23–46.

Haller, W. and Landolt, P. (2005) 'The Transnational Dimensions of Identity Formation: Adult Children of Immigrants in Miami', *Ethnic and Racial Studies* 28 (4), pp. 1182–1214.

Ho, E. (2006) 'Negotiating Belonging and Perceptions of Citizenship in a Transnational World: Singapore, a Cosmopolis?', *Social and Cultural Geography* 7(3), pp. 385–401.

Hondagneu-Sotelo, P. and Avila, E. (1997) 'I'm Here, But I'm There': The Meanings of Latina Transnational Motherhood', *Gender & Society* 11 (5), pp. 548–571.

Horst, H.A. (2006) 'The Blessings and Burdens of Communication: Cell Phones in Jamaican Transnational Social Fields', *Global Networks* 6 (2), pp. 143–159.

Horst, H. (2010) 'Families', in Mitzuko Ito, Sonja Baumer, Matteo Bittanti, Danah Boyd, Rachel Cody, Becky Herr-Stevenson, et al. (2010) *Hanging out, Messing Around, Geeking Out: Kids Living and Learning with New Media*, Cambridge, MT: The MIT Press, pp. 149–194.

Ito, M. Okabe, D. and Anderson, K. (2008) 'Portable Objects in Three Global Cities: The Personalization of Urban Places', in Rich Ling and Scott Campbell (eds) *The Mobile Communication Research Annual, Vol. 1: The Reconstruction of Space and Time through Mobile Communication Practices*, New Brunswick, NJ: Transaction Books.

Jansson, A. (2013) 'Mediatisation and Social Space: Reconstructing Mediatisation for the Transmedia Age', *Communication Theory* 23 (3), pp. 279–296.

Kang, T. (2012) 'Gendered Media, Changing Intimacy: Internet-mediated Transnational Communication in the Family Sphere', *Media, Culture and Society* 34 (2), pp. 146–161.

Katz, V. (2010) 'How Children of Immigrants Use Media to Connect Their Families to the Community: The Case of Latinos in South Los Angeles', *Journal of Children and Media* 4 (3), pp. 298–315.

Kaye, J. (2011) 'Love, Ritual and Videochat', in Richard Harper (ed.) *The Connected Home: The Future of Domestic Life*, London: Springer, pp. 185–202.

Lefebvre, H. (1974/1991) *The Production of Space*, Oxford and New York: Blackwell.

Levitt, P. and Waters, M. (2006) 'Introduction', in Peggy Levitt and Mary C. Waters (eds) *The Changing Face of Home: The Transnational Lives of the Second Generation*, New York: Russell Sae Foundation Publications, pp. 1–32.

Livingstone, S. and Das, R. (with contributions from Georgiou, M., Haddon, L., Helsper, E. and Wang, Y.) (2010) 'Media, Communication and Information Technologies in the European Family', Family Platform, *Existential Field 8 Working Report* (April), available at: *http://eprints.lse.ac.uk/29788/1/EF8_LSE_MediaFamily_Education.pdf*.

Liu, L.S. (2014) 'A Search for a Place to Call Home: Negotiation of Home, Identity and Senses of Belonging among New Migrants from the People's Republic of China (PRC) to New Zealand', *Emotion, Space and Society* 10 (4), pp. 18–26.

Madianou, M. and Miller, D. (2012) *Migration and New Media: Transnational Families and Polymedia*, London: Routledge.

Mee, K. and Wright, S. (2009) 'Geographies of Belonging', *Environment and Planning A* 41 (4), pp. 772–779.

Metykova, M. (2010) 'Only a Mouse Click Away from Home: Transnational Practices of Eastern European Migrants in the United Kingdom', *Social Identities: Journal for the Study of Race, Nation and Culture* 16 (3), pp. 325–338.

Miller, D. (2011) *Tales from Facebook*, Cambridge: Polity Press.

Moores, S. and Qureshi, K. (2000) 'Identity, Tradition and Translation', in Shaun Moores (ed.) *Media and Everyday Life in Modern Society*, Edinburgh: Edinburgh University Press, pp. 117–134.

Morley, D. (1992) *Television, Audiences and Cultural Studies*, London: Routledge.

Morley, D. (2002) *Home Territories: Media, Mobility and Identity*, London: Routledge.

Morley, D. (2007) *Media, Modernity and Technology: The Geography of the New*, London: Routledge.

O'Hara, K., Black, A. and Lipton, M. (2006) 'Everyday Practices with Mobile Telephony', in *Proceedings of the SIGCHI Conference on Human Factors in Computing* Systems, pp. 871–880.

Orellana, M., Dorner, L. and Pulido, L. (2003) 'Accessing Assets: Immigrant Youth's Work as Family Translators or "Para-phrasers"', *Social Problems* 50(4), pp. 505–524.

Panagakos, A. and Horst, H. (2006) 'Return to Cyberia: Technology and the Social Worlds of Transnational Migrants', *Global Networks* 6 (2), pp. 109–124.

Parreñas, R. (2005) 'Long Distance Intimacy: Class, Gender and Intergenerational Relations between Mothers and Children in Filipino Transnational Families', *Global Networks* 5 (4), pp. 317–336.

Pratt, G. (2004) *Working Feminism*, Philadelphia, PA: Temple University Press.

Robins, K. and Aksoy, A. (2001) 'From Spaces of Identity to Mental Spaces: Lessons from Turkish–Cypriot Cultural Experience in Britain', *Journal of Ethnic and Migration Studies* 27 (4), pp. 685–711.

Strasburger, V.C. and Wilson, B. (2002) *Children, Adolescents and the Media*, London: Sage.

Tolia-Kelly, D.P. (2004) 'Landscape, Race and Memory: Biographical Mapping of the Routes of British Asian Landscape Values', *Landscape Research* 29 (3), pp. 277–292.

Tseng, V. and Fuligni, A.J. (2000) 'Parent–Adolescent Language Use and Relationships among Immigrant Families with East Asian, Filipino and Latino American backgrounds', *Journal of Marriage and the Family* 62 (2), pp. 465–476.

Turkle, S. (2011) *Alone Together: Why We Expect More from Technology and Less from Each Other*, New York: Basic Books.

Wilding, R. (2006) 'Virtual Intimacies? Families Communicating across Transnational Contexts', *Global Networks* 6 (2), pp. 125–142.

Wiles, J. (2008) 'Sense of Home in a Transnational Social Space: New Zealanders in London', *Global Networks* 8 (1), pp. 116–137.

Wise, A. (2011) '"You Wouldn't Know What's in There Would You?" Homeliness and "Foreign" Signs in Ashfield, Sydney', in Katharine Brickell and Ayona Datta (eds) *Translocal Geographies: Spaces, Places, Connections*, Burlington, VA: Ashgate, pp. 93–108.

Yarosh, S. (2008) 'Supporting Long-distance Parent–Child Interaction in Divorced Families', in *CHI '08 Extended Abstracts on Human Factors in Computing Systems*, Florence, Italy: ACM, pp. 3795–3800.

8

HOMES OF THE FUTURE

From smart homes to connected homes

Introduction

This chapter addresses 'homes of the future'. These are houses designed to express utopian visions of home living through an architectural and technologised lens. At a technical level, today's 'smart' or 'connected' home describes 'a residence equipped with computing and information technology which anticipates and responds to the needs of the occupants, working to promote their comfort, convenience, security and entertainment through the management of technology within the home and connections to the world beyond' (Aldrich 2003: 17). While most research on the 'smart' or 'connected home' has focused on its technical affordances, the concept is much more than a series of building experiments. At a cultural level, homes of the future signify the culmination of domestic technology. Yet the motives behind the idea, and the antecedents and consequences of smart home technology, have tended to be ignored. They involve utopian fantasies and dystopian uncertainties about the meaning of the modern home and the domestication of technology. As Morley (2003) argues, the 'smart' house is the outcome of a particular kind of discourse about 'home' in which the household itself becomes a fully technologised environment: a sphere circumscribed by the technologies that constitute it.

Several descriptors are used to convey this imagined future home: 'smart home', 'intelligent home', 'digital living', 'home automation', the 'networked home', the 'home of the future' and the 'connected home' (see Harper 2011). The term 'smart home' remains in use today to describe what is also called the digitally automated 'connected home', signifying intersecting intensions and aspirations. However to avoid confusion, in this chapter the term 'smart home' refers to past twentieth century electronic homes powered by electronic automated systems (including American 'homes of tomorrow') while 'connected home' refers to today's new digitally connected homes that comprise digitally integrated and automated systems.

Innovations such as media interactivity and technological convergence provoke deliberations about media progress in terms of social and spatial changes. Yet new domestic spaces shaped by digital connectivity depend on *pre-existing* ideas and socio-spatial arrangements. Today's digitally connected homes are underpinned by deep-rooted values relating to 'inside' and 'outside' space, private and public place, mobility and communication, work and leisure. This chapter examines the meanings, values and aspirations that underlie the inscription of home as a digital domestic space. It argues that these values often reflect commercial interests, gendered power relations and middle-class ideals. From the outset, global electronic corporations have been centrally involved in the pre-production phase and promotion of smart home and connected home designs.

The chapter examines the processes through which homes of the future are evoked via media technologies and architectural designs and how these processes are linked to wider cultural fantasies and social unease about changing gender and family relations, and changing ideas of private and public space. The approach taken towards the nature of contemporary connected homes is underpinned by noteworthy earlier debates about the smart home advanced in cultural history and media studies exemplified by the influential work of Lynn Spigel (2001, 2005, 2010), David Morley (2007) and Anne-Jorunn Berg (1992; 1994) among others. The motivations and meanings behind the idea of the connected home are examined through three strands. First, the aesthetic ideas and economic motives underpinning the 'smart home' are explored to understand the social processes involved in the imaginary home of the future shown by the 'houses for tomorrow' projects of the early twentieth century. The second strand focuses on the technological possibilities being offered today through cultural representations and material forms of the smart homes of the 1980s and 1990s. The third strand examines the meanings associated with more recent, digitally automated 'connected homes'. Addressing this new, digitally automated connected home agenda, this third section explores how the digitalised home is envisaged and promoted through marketing, advertising and popular imagery. The chapter pinpoints the changing relationships between modern domestic spaces and gendered subjectivities, demonstrating that domestic identities associated with homes of the future involve a shift from feminine to masculine associations.

Homes of tomorrow

In the late nineteenth century, the home environment was assumed to be the antithesis of the work setting. This notion of home as a place of non-work was an ideal reflected in the designs of domestic interiors. Major aesthetic strategies for separating the home from the public sphere of work involved the cultivation of special standards of taste and design for the home. For example, Victorian house decoration advice manuals of the nineteenth century offered particular choices in interior design, colour schemes and furniture styles to deny associations with the world of work (Forty 1986: 102). These interior designs and styles conveyed the home as a context for perfect domestic life. The role of the home as a source of moral wellbeing was gradually extended to a new role in the early twentieth century. It became a place for physical wellbeing propelled by the domestication of electricity followed by visions of the electronic home. This new role was expressed visually by transforming the home from a place of beauty and decorativeness to one of efficiency (Forty 1986; Sparke 2008). Modernist architecture set out to censure 'cosiness' through a kind of radical egalitarianism and emancipation from bourgeois individualism (van Herck 2005). Nevertheless, new ideas of home as a place of work as well as leisure continued to be framed by householders' intimate relationships with material things, with home décor continuing to be indicative of personal taste and wider social status (Bourdieu 1984).

The idea of the smart home accompanied dramatic twentieth-century transformations in architecture and domestic technology. First, the introduction of electricity in the early twentieth century fuelled the emergence of a range of appliances designed for the home, leading to the futuristic 'homes of tomorrow' from the 1960s. New ways of imagining the home as a symbol of progress in the twentieth century involved the erosion of earlier distinctions between leisure and work. A blurring of the boundaries between the domestic interior and public space allowed ideas about public space to move into the domestic arena and vice versa. This was expressed at aesthetic and technological levels through décor and media equipment that, in turn, reshaped meanings of domesticity as efficient, mediated spaces. These changes were motivated by ideas of technological progress, as Spigel states:

> . . . since the advent of modern communications media, domesticity has largely been defined by the transport of data in and out the home. From Edward Bellamy's pneumonic tubes in *Looking Backward* to Le Corbusier's 'machine for living' to Bill Gates's digitally powered Seattle fortress, the media-saturated 'home of tomorrow' is a constituent and recurring theme in modern ideals of progress. Whether for leisure, labour, or surveillance, the media home is 'a whole way of life' for privileged populations.
>
> *(Spigel 2001: 386)*

The second stage of the smart homes' evolution involved the growth in information technology in the 1980s and 1990s. Via computers, these changes provided the technological resources for homes to become information networks and systems. This prompted a further extension of the meaning of home from a place of sanctuary to a technologically efficient space for multiple leisure and work-related tasks. New technologies such as computing and the internet facilitated patterns of home-working, teleworking and flexible working. These trends are addressed in Chapter 3 in relation to the adoption and integration of media technology into household routines. As Haddon (1992) points out, the meanings and values associated with home computing were not confined to the domestic sphere. They were shaped by wider public cultures and gendered values. A third stage of the smart home, the 'connected home', involves the arrival of digital interactive technologies in the early twenty-first century, leading to home automation systems and to the development of the 'Internet of Things' (IoT), addressed below.

The smart home concept was first advanced in the US in the early twentieth century through 'homes of tomorrow'. These early smart homes were architectural imaginings of what home life might look like in the future. They were influenced by modernism of the 1920s and 1930s, represented by the designs of French/Swiss architect, Le Corbusier, who challenged conventional ideas of home by famously describing houses as 'machines for living in'. Le Corbusier designed them not for decorativeness but as unadorned structures that endorsed prefabrication, mass production, technological advancements, new materials and functional design. Le Corbusier also conceived of the home as a type of projection screen that could offer wide, window-framed and terraced views of the external landscape. The window frame acted as a massive display screen that dissolved inside/outside boundaries (Colomina 1996). These aesthetic principles were also developed by a group of architects that included Mies van der Rohe, Walter Gropius and Frank Lloyd Wright to form modernist architecture. Referred to as the International Style, modernist designs were characterised by the use of modern materials such as glass, concrete slabs and exposed steel to create a modernist aesthetic (Jencks 1973). Le Corbusier's Villa Savoye (1928–1931) and Mies van der Rohe's Barcelona Pavilion (1929) exemplified the advancement of modernist houses around the world.

Underpinned by these modernist experiments, the first stage of futuristic housing which took place in the US in the late 1920s was influenced by the modernist International Style. Designed specifically to embrace the principles of mass production, this was represented in the US by Buckminster Fuller who designed the 'Dymaxion Dwelling Machine', one of the first automated houses, exhibited in 1927 but not built until 1945. This design contained entertainment and office equipment as well as a service core of appliances (Spigel 2005). It was Fuller's answer to the need for affordable, mass-produced and environmentally efficient housing. Subsequent smart house styles were inspired by science fiction as well as by the principles of modernist architecture to embrace the design of entertainment and automation technologies (Spigel 2010). These aesthetic experiments challenged old ideas of outside–inside and triggered further technological imaginings such as the wired home; Archigram's automated house; geodesic dome of the 1930s to the 1960s; and Finland's flying saucer-shaped Futuro House of 1968. Several futuristic house designs remained only as architectural plans.

At the commercial level, the aim of these early visionary homes was to introduce and market new electronic appliances to the public. Large home appliance, electrical and communication corporations and institutes such as General Electric, Kelvinator and MIT sponsored 'homes of tomorrow' between the 1920s and 1940s. Model homes designed for public exhibition demonstrated the multiple ways that electronics could become part of domestic life (Horrigan 1986). Homes of tomorrow were displayed at trade fairs, exhibitions and department stores in the US and Europe. At the aesthetic level, these designs formed architectural utopias that tapped into a discourse of progress through visions of technological splendour and efficiency (Spigel 2001). In the US, a Disney-like architectural utopia was confirmed by the display of MIT's ultramodern Monsanto House, exhibited in the Tomorrowland in a section of Disneyland in 1957. Smart homes also entered the popular imagination through regular appearances in women's lifestyle magazines from the 1930s and 1940s (Spigel 2005). Later, in the 1960s, ideas of technological progress were propelled by corporations such as IBM, Panasonic and Philips that exhibited smart homes to stage their corporate vision by expounding ideas about the human–technology interface in a domestic setting.

Drawing on utopian discourses of future technology, these futuristic homes attracted groups of architects, designers and engineers who promoted values of liberation, environmentalism and democracy within futuristic visions (Spigel 2001). Yet, significantly, as Spigel explains, the electronic 'dreamhouse' was also framed by corporate marketing strategies and socially conformist schemes. Ironically, despite their highly conservative visions of home life, smart homes came to stand for ideals of freedom, progress and clean living as well as imaginaries of increased mobility through media and information technologies and telerobotics. Nevertheless, the public were unsure about these bizarre, machine-driven homes. Coinciding with ambivalent social responses to the presence of early domestic media technologies in the home, such as radio and TV, consumers were wary of these strange domestic futures. Indeed, the term 'domestic futures' conjured up contradictory meanings. Through the display of sophisticated home theatres and dream kitchens, these 'homes of tomorrow' were designed to uphold and preserve traditional domestic ideals associated with white, middle-class suburbia according to Spigel (2001).

Smart homes of the 1980s and 1990s

In the 1980s, the commercial pursuit of home automation evolved with manufacturers of consumer electronics and electrical equipment developing digital systems and components suitable for use in domestic buildings. Smart houses were designed and built in the US, Europe and Japan. In 1984, the National Association of Home Builders (NAHB) in the USA launched a Smart Home special interest group to advance the technology within home-building methods. Interest accelerated in the fields of building, electronics, architecture, energy conservation and telecommunications. Anne-Jorunn Berg (1992) documented the designs of three smart homes in USA during that decade: first, the Honeywell House, built by multinational corporation Honeywell which produced automation and control systems; second, a mobile demonstration house built from 1986 by the US NAHB; and third, the experimental Xanadu House of the early 1980s designed by a team that included Roy Mason.

Involving light and heat regulation, and alarm and security control, the Honeywell House included the company's thermostats, air cleaners, burglar alarms and fire alarms integrated through programmable communication networks inside the building. Remarkably, the house contained no technologies relating to housework. The NAHB mobile demonstration house contained a multi-cable system for integrating power. The smart house boasted a washing machine, home computer and telephone plugged into the same power point – something revolutionary at the time. The vacuum cleaner was programmed to stop if the doorbell or phone rang. Integration of in-house appliances also involved cooking dinner with a microwave oven that synchronised with the stove so that the soup could be warmed up at the same time. The in-house appliances were also integrated with the outside communication systems, designed for telework, telebanking and teleshopping. The experimental Xanadu Houses built in the early 1980s in the US replicated other smart houses but showcased more computer and automation systems in the homes. The first house built in Orlando, Florida, represented architectural innovations but also involved integrated information technology within the building's design structure.

Thus, these 1980s smart houses included prototypes of appliances and integrated systems that mainly entailed energy control, safety control and environmental control. In terms of their media systems they included communication such as messaging and information such as telephone or telematics; entertainment including television (TV), CD player, video cassette recorder (VCR) and computer games. Yet Berg was surprised to find that while energy-saving systems and better entertainment were highlighted in all these smart homes, housework-saving systems were ignored. According to Honeywell's R&D manager, the futuristic Honeywell House 'does more things for you, the way you would like to have them done, than today's houses' (Berg 1992: 11). The slogan, 'A HOUSE THAT WILL DO THE JOB FOR YOU' showed promise, generating expectations of technical solutions to ease the burden of housework. Yet domestic work was not even mentioned among the tasks of the smart house. Similarly, NAHB, who advertised their smart home as 'A HOUSE WHICH WILL TAKE CARE OF ME', provided a communication network but no housework tasks. NAHB stated that housework was not their concern; this was the responsibility of white goods manufacturers. It was explained that the infrastructure would need to be modernised to deal with such appliances. Xanadu demonstrated the same oversight, leading Berg to conclude: 'Housework has no place in the general idea of what a smart house is, even though the ideas are vague enough to include the actual work that is done in a home' (Berg 1992: 11). Likewise, the title page of the book on Xanadu contained a picture of a robot serving mother breakfast. The accompanying text read: 'We are not replacing Mommy with a robot. We are presenting ideas on how to design, build and use a home in new ways that can reduce drudgery while increasing comfort, convenience, and security' (Berg 1992: 1).

Berg draws attention to the double speak involved in the promotion of these smart homes. Xanadu's message about future family life displayed an ambiguity of language about the smart home and what it was capable of doing to alleviate 'work'. But the wording in their marketing masked the labour involved in housework, rendering invisible the gendered nature of household chores. In interviews with designers of these experimental smart homes, Berg discovered that they showed no interest in housework and a lack of concern about gender despite the home being women's traditional domain. The designers of Xanadu insisted that they had paid attention to some housework, giving the example of the automatic light switch. 'They saw it as a facilitation of housework, because it would enable a housewife to enter a room with her hands full of wet clothes without having to put them down to turn on the light' (Berg 1992). Similarly, the robutler was exemplified as a housework appliance. But it turned out that 'the glasses had to be filled before they could be served and placed in the right spot for the robutler to get them'. Significantly, technical solutions required advanced manual work, as Berg observes. A 'gourmet autochef' was nothing more than a computer programme capable only of suggesting dinner party menus. Someone had to plan, shop, cook and clean up after the dinner party. Xanadu described the contemporary home as 'often little more than a place to sleep, eat a meal or two, and store possessions' (Berg 1992: 16). Berg comments somewhat wryly, 'I suppose very few housewives would come up with such a description of a home' (1992: 13; see Cowan 1993).

Berg explains that, reminiscent of the computer hacker, the designers she interviewed were captivated by the technology rather than by consumer needs and saw men who are fascinated by information and communication technologies (ICTs) as their target market. This was a 'technology push' initiative with the typical smart house user imagined as a man with interests and aspirations relating to male-oriented professional and managerial work. Thus, the 'smart house' is a technology rendered masculine by the process of design and marketing and by the denial of the relevance of housework. It presents a technical construction that preserves gendered power relations. Propelled by computer connection to information and services, the new smart home of the following decade in the 1990s focused on the exchange of information, systems and networks within, between and beyond homes (Aldrich 2003). During the 1990s, ideas about the 'home of the future' were projected into postmodern architectural initiatives within postindustrial settings. By transcending functional and formalised modernist shapes, these homes involved eclectic and playful stylistic juxtapositions between nature and media (Spigel 2010: 67). Elizabeth Diller and Ricardo Scofidio's design of the Long Island, NY, vacation home, the Slow House (unbuilt, 1990) exemplified this ideal of blurring the interior with outside nature through the digital transmission of an image of the outside landscape via a large-screened monitor in front of a picture window. The Slow House also expresses, via digital telecommunications, the combining of a vacation home–work space to celebrate escape from the city with the ability to work from home through access to communication technology.

The late twentieth-century stage of transformations in domestic technology was, then, associated with the rise of information technology. Microsoft founder, Bill Gates, promoted his own idea of the house of the future in his 1995 best-selling book *The Road Ahead* (1995). Gates advanced a particular high-tech version of future domestic bliss based on a computer-operated dream house.

A chapter titled 'Plugged in at Home' highlighted the embrace of digital connectivity as the pinnacle of the ideal home. Gates then built a large mansion in a Pacific lodge style on the shore of Lake Washington near Seattle, based on this vision. The house has walls of glass, concrete and stone and is built into the hillside with windows on the lakefront boasting views towards Seattle to evoke the idea of the outside as an observable screen and a blurring of outside/inside boundaries (see Allon 2000).

Visitors to this lavish smart home are presented with an electronic pin to clip on their clothes to connect them to the electronic services of the house (Gates 1995: 250) which comprise a sophisticated media entertainment system, digitally controlled lighting, temperature control (called 'climate control') and security. Every room has information screens that offer digital archives of art, music and other cultural 'data'. As a supreme example of portability, the smart home's entertainment and information facilities pursue the occupants throughout the house. A reception hall that seats 150 people contains a 22-feet-wide video display made up of 24 rear-projected TV monitors, each with a 40-inch screen. A multi-purpose room also contains a video projector evoking the idea of a home theatre. And the 60-feet swimming pool boasts an underwater music system. The ability to mediate work and play through technological connectivity is revered. Spigel (2010: 72) states that the founding text was a 1996 issue of *Wired* magazine that portrayed Bill Gates on its cover, afloat in a swimming pool while connecting with work via his cellphone. Spigel describes a 2001 issue of *Broadcasting House* magazine, in which a family is displayed at work and play, again father in a pool using his cellphone with the mother and children engaged in digital work (Spigel 2010). From this period onwards, families are depicted regularly as multitasking across leisure and work activities in domestic settings, using an array of digital devices such as touchscreen computer tablets as described in Chapter 6.

Morley (2007) chronicles the domestication of digital systems leading to Bill Gates' 'fully-wired' domestic paradise. He reiterates the ongoing significance of Raymond Williams' concept of mobile privatisation, discussed in Chapter 2, to emphasise that media intercedes the apparently private realm of the home. Scrutinising the recurring discourses of futurology employed to describe media technologies of the home, Morley explains that Gates' smart home signifies visions of a future of domesticity derived from a mid twentieth-century suburban ideal. The type of family life that Gates cultivates and foresees in his fully-wired 'dreamhouse' is articulated in conventional suburban terms (Allon 2000). It confirms that, as Allon (1999) states: 'futurology is almost always as much "backward" as it is "forward looking"' (quoted in Morley 2007: 215).

Despite the design of lavish one-off smart homes, the smart home industry in Europe during the 1980s and 1990s lacked a common protocol and was largely confined to single application on–off switching systems such as remote control. Suppliers took little notice of users' needs. They were unable to convince women, who continue to take responsibility for most domestic tasks, of the advantages of the smart home (Meyer and Schulze 1996). This draws attention to the highly gendered as well as age-bound conceptualisation and dynamics of the smart home as a haven for able-bodied wealthy men and their nuclear families. Having undertaken little research to assess the practical usefulness and functionality of their products, most smart homes remained commercial showcases with limited research agendas (Aldrich 2003).

Yet the late twentieth-century conceptualisation of the smart home continued to be explored in popular culture in the 1990s and continued to fascinate the public in the same ways as earlier imaginings of 'homes of tomorrow' in the 1950s and 1960s described by Spigel. Extending beyond the realm of sci-fi fans and electronics hobbyists, smart home articles appeared in lifestyle magazines in the US such as *Boys' Life*, *Vanity Fair* and *House Beautiful* (Spigel 2010). 'Smart families' leading glamorous lives were presented in a manner that conveys their opulence not just via leisure but also via their control of work.

And in the UK, the BBC ran a TV documentary series entitled *Dream House* (1999), which documented a family that lived in an experimental smart home for six weeks. The popular media conveyed the anxieties expressed about problems of keeping control of the technology. These kinds of concerns had been explored earlier in films such as *Demon Seed* (1977) yet also persisted as a significant theme over a decade later. The dystopian visions of the smart home were explored in TV programmes and films that showed the failings of the technology and the ways it could cause accidents. For example, a 1998 film also called *Dream House* drew on the horror genre to depict a malicious smart home that confines its residents (Aldrich 2003). Deep anxieties surrounding smart home technology remain with us, extending to fears about surveillance and the undermining of physical communities by technology (Spigel 2010).

Today's digitally automated 'connected home'

Contemporary 'connected homes' perpetuate the relationships between modern domestic spaces and masculine subjectivities articulated through the design of earlier 'homes of tomorrow'. Advertisements for today's digitally automated 'connected homes' promote home automation systems, as exemplified by the online shopping website of the UK John Lewis department store which offers consumer goods across the categories of Fashion, Home and Electricals and Home Technology. Its website devotes a substantial section of its shopping pages to the 'Smart Home' and the 'Connected Home', using these terms interchangeably to promote automated systems. It contains a video called 'A Smarter Home' to explain the range of gadgets and services available under its umbrella. The website offers 'Inspiration and Advice', to guide potential consumers to 'The Connected Home'.[1] The section titled 'Connected Home' displays a diagram image of a home set out in the style of a geometric dolls house with no roof, reminiscent of a *Sims* video game. From above, viewers can look down into the rooms and corridors. Devoid of humans and clutter, the image conveys a virtual space of clean, sanitised, domestic fantasy that can be controlled and surveyed from anywhere via smartphone or tablet. The accompanying caption states: 'As more technology becomes wireless, *the dream of a connected, fully automated home is becoming a reality*. Here's how new products can save you time, energy and take the hassle out of chores' (my emphasis).

Under a section called 'Home Living', the website offers electronic products with a 'Smart Home' subsection containing smart TVs, wireless speakers, media streaming, connected lighting, home automation and net learning thermostats. This 'Smart Home' subsection is introduced with the announcement:

> From *streaming audio* to *multiple speakers* to *automated power and heating control* these gadgets make light work of creating the ideal environment for you to enjoy your free time. Bright ideas like *Connected Lighting* will let you set the mood, while Smart TVs and Media Streaming devices provide the entertainment so you can simply sit back and relax.[2]

Beneath this claim is a further segment about smart technologies for the garden and for security:

> If mowing the lawn is a chore you abhor, then a *robotic lawnmower* can do the hard work for you, while a *wireless plant sensor* will give you the best information to help you take care of your plantlife. If security is a worry, then our *home monitoring systems* bring advanced safeguards to your tablet.

John Lewis recommends technologies for home monitoring to be placed in the hallway in the forms of home automation, connected lighting and thermostats. For the utility room, it suggests buying connected lighting, a robotic vacuum cleaner, smart scales and a smart washing machine. For the bedroom, the website suggests:

> Bring your tablet to bed with you and keep everything running smoothly throughout the night. With *wireless baby monitors*, you can keep an eye on your young ones as they sleep and even receive alerts of any changes in their comfort on your tablet or phone. With *Connected Lighting*, your lights can gently wake you up in the morning or simulate a setting sun at night, while no modern bedroom is complete without a *wireless speaker* and *Smart TV*.

The promotion of these technologies is surprisingly prescriptive, signifying that consumers need a great deal of information and guidance in embarking on the design of a connected home, in much the same way as guidance was given to consumers of earlier new technologies by governments, manufacturers, designers and advertisers. On closer inspection, most of the 'hard work' done by the devices involves simply switching things on and off, echoing the exaggerated claims of earlier smart homes. A remote-controlled washing machine requires someone to fill it, empty it and do the ironing. The only housework-related chore conducted by a gadget is the robotic vacuum cleaner, referred to as follows:

A robotic cleaner is one of the most common science fiction depictions of future home inventions, but the LG *Hom-Bot* range of vacuum cleaners are practical powerful and completely automatic. Dual cameras snap the landscape of your home and the Hom-Bot navigates floors with ease, returning to a charge station when your room has been cleaned. A two-hour charge will give 100 minutes of cleaning time, and if it runs out of battery it will return to its base to charge and then pick up again where it left off. Also, low noise levels mean you can watch TV while it cleans, or you can programme it to do the vacuuming while you're at work.

The technology is represented less as a way of alleviating housework by freeing up time for mediated leisure and more as a way of enhancing the imagined agency of the home owner by offering the potential to 'take control of your home'. 'YOU take control of all your connected devices from the living room, bedroom or kitchen'. Yet, while offering the opportunity to access your computer files from all over your house, the home reveals the tension between work, relaxation and entertainment.

Similarly, a YouTube promotional video of *Smart Housing* by company Jung with KNX (2014)[3] features a complete multimedia range. From the music system to the TV, this multimedia range can be controlled in the living room using the KNX controller. The video presents a computer-generated geometric-styled simulated house, not a real house. This is a large, ultramodern, individually designed home reminiscent of the International Style: a long way from the traditional semi-detached or terraced housing stock that so many householders continue to inhabit today. Urgent, pulsing, futuristic music propels the geometric images as the camera travels through the interior and external spaces of the home. The home is typically sparsely furnished with hyper-minimalist interiors. This computer-generated home boasts network cameras, a security system, automatic lights and a ceiling detector in the bathroom that censors your movement, leaving messages (solar radiation summer, reduction of heat transmission in winter). The differing sections of the video are punctuated by architectural drawings to convey superior and exclusive design. This is the 'conceived space' of professionals ranging from architects to digital automation engineers (Lefebvre 1974/1991). Again, this image of 'home' is absent of humans. Ironically, the nearest image to a human is a shadow of a potential burglar lurking outside. This glimpse of outside human movement triggers digitally controlled surveillance to emphasise the level of security and privacy of this sealed environment. The film signifies safety and convenience yet also a sense of privacy and isolation: of being exclusive and disconnected from the community. Under the 'Comments section' of a 2012 version of the video, one person comments wryly: 'Since they do not show an actual home but only a simulation I am assuming that this is for simulated people.'

The PR information on a website about the Samsung Consumer Electronics Show claims that the Internet of Things (IoT) has arrived, 'connecting you not only with your devices but also with family, friends, colleagues and your lifestyle'.[4] The website goes on to declare:

For Samsung, these always on and always connected smart devices will offer better solutions and services, totally personalized to you. Naturally, the connected home will be at the heart of it all. By 2017, all Samsung TVs will be IoT enabled, as will all our devices be in just five years.

A YouTube video of the Samsung Consumer Electronics Show at Las Vegas in 2015 is titled 'Inside the Smart Things Smart Home'.[5] It shows a presentation for Samsung by US trade show presenter and TV host Madison Alexander and hones in on a sign stating 'Infinite Possibilities of IoT', with its stage set up in the 'Internet of Things zone'. Throughout the video, the emphasis is on the words 'smart', 'intelligent' – 'make your homes smarter'. The camera swings round to the audience to reveal an almost all-male audience, with a lone woman detectable in the crowd. Absent of decoration, these digital representations of home interiors are designed to appeal to men. Comprising geometric designs, they generate a high-tech ambience. As a branch of computational geometry, geometric modelling aims to address the core 'problem' of curves and surface modelling. This aesthetic style, which evokes computer-mediated communication, smoothes out curves, untidiness and disorder: no humans, no clutter, no housework, no problems. These imaginary homes are sterilised fantasy houses. The priority is the connections between things. A geometric, simulated world is presented as a life goal with the 'real world' of complex and messy life vanquished in a home with no human interaction, or maybe just a solitary, gender-neutral avatar (The theme of IoT is returned to below).

Advertisements and promotional pieces in magazines about the contemporary connected home follow a similar discourse. They typically contain 3D geometric images of the rooms of a house angled from above so that each room can be looked down into like a dolls house without the roof. For example, an article titled 'BACHELOR PAD OF TOMORROW' in the men's popular UK weekly lifestyle magazine *Shortlist* (9 July 2015, Issue 380) contains two double-page spreads about the digitally connected home. It is introduced with the following: 'THE FIFTIES VISION OF ROBOT BUTLERS AND VOICE-ACTIVATED EVERYTHING WASN'T ENTIRELY SCI-FI NONSENSE. *STUFF*[6] MAGAZINE'S TOM WIGGINS PICKS THE TECH THAT WILL TURN YOUR HOME INTO A GADGET HEAVEN' (page 42). Significantly, *Stuff* magazine is pitched towards a young, heterosexual male audience (confirmed by the fact that it often displays scantily clad women on its covers and additional photos of her figure inside the magazine). The article in *Shortlist* displays a large geometric diagram of a high-tech open-plan kitchen and living room containing a tiny computer-generated image of a human that resembles a cross between an avatar and a robot. Furnished with rectangular fittings, the kitchen and living room are packed with gadgets from lighting systems to smart coffee machines. The living room houses a large projector, Immersis, which transforms walls into screens. The TV's targeted 'surround sound' allows sound targeted at specific points so that while sitting on the sofa hearing the bullets whizzing past your ears, the person sitting next to you hears nothing.

A robo-wingman is also present in the living room: it can order take-away, remind the owner about events, turn lights on on entry into the room, and entertain the kids (jibo.com). A smart robo-vacuum cleaner by Dyson is poised in the middle of the room with the 360-degree camera to work out where it is and to cover the room. A digital houseplant waterer is undertaken by Parrot Pots. Aside from the entertainment devices, this list of gadgets conveys a toy-like triviality. As well as phone-activated mood lighting, the bedroom/bathroom boasts a window that generates solar power from Ubiquitous Energy, smart body analyser (translatable as 'bathroom scales') and toothbrush feedback system. Again, the 3D computer-generated geometric-shaped model of the interior space resembles a dolls house, redolent of *Sims* game imagery. This is no accident. This clean, hygienic space is presented as uncluttered and controllable. While the preferences, conduct and activities of the home dweller can be monitored, surveyed and regulated in precise detail as part of the monitoring of the technologised domestic sphere, 'he' is produced as an 'agent' invited to reimagine and to take responsibility for revolutionising experiences of domesticity. Men are now signified as architects of domestic space (Gorman-Murray 2008).

As Osgerby (2005: 100) observes, the bachelor pad of the 1950s in American films and magazines presented the spatial expression of 'a consuming masculine subject'. Through modern technologies and stylish fashions, bachelor masculinity signified virility and agency in relation to the seduction of women (Cohan 1996). Bachelor apartments offered a workable contrast to the suburban nuclear family home for men who defied hegemonic masculinity (Cohan 1996; Osgerby 2005; Gorman-Murray 2008). Challenging dominant domestic signifiers of femininity and family, bachelor domesticity forms a space that validates the project of men living alone. The nineteenth-century bachelor philosophy of domestic self-hood endorses the mid twentieth-century connection between men and domesticity, offering a link to the popular media assumptions of gay men's 'natural' domestic flair, characterised by the TV series *Queer Eye for the Straight Guy* which employs a queer sensibility to renovate straight men's homes (Gorman-Murray 2008; Cook 2014). However, in the case of digitally connected homes, more conventional hegemonic masculinities are invoked.

The transformation of home into a technologised, smart space is converted into a key site for the cultivation of masculine identity, indicating a departure from dominant associations of home with femininity and/or family. But this shift does not embrace the fluid and diverse styles of masculinity that contest normative imaginaries of home invoked through a queer sensibility (Gorman-Murray 2008). The geometric aesthetic offers a connection with the technology as a work-like rather than homely or aestheticised environment. The geometric structure of the connected home creates a digital metaphor of virtual space in which the only activities are digital. Domestic routines are eliminated. With all messy human activities smoothed away, the digitalised space endorses norms of masculine control rather than feminised norms of decorativeness, housework and childcare. Absent of traditional signifiers of feminine domesticity, this new domestic masculinity is, ironically, dissociated from domestic responsibilities and childcare.

Tensions between work, leisure and domestic responsibilities

This 'always on', connected-to-work home involves a contemporary renegotiation of home life. Yet by concealing deep contradictions concerning the tensions between work, leisure and domestic responsibilities it leaves gendered power imbalances intact. As Spigel (2005) argues, descriptions of women's conspicuous production are often accompanied by related images of conspicuous household chores. Spigel found many examples of US lifestyle magazines and advertisements depicting women multitasking while posing with their children and performing caretaking roles. The difficulties of combining a professional career with mothering or other caretaking roles are magically resolved through smart home devices. Traditional nuclear families are preserved through advertising images of families brought together and cemented through technologies of work and leisure. Past smart homes and contemporary connected homes are, then, classed and gendered by reproducing sexual differences. However, these popular images refer to new kinds of households comprised of dual-income families dependent on personalised technologies. A new term 'multitasking', associated particularly with women's paid and unpaid work, is embedded in the spirit of the futuristic home. Spigel (2005) argues that the promotion of the home office involves a subtext in which advertisers suggest that new technologies can undo the harm done to families by women's liberation and, in particular, their entrance into the workforce.

Promoters of smart homes persuade men that the home is now a quintessentially 'masculine' space. Home offices designed for men characteristically avoid the domestic décor associated with femininity. Instead, discreet modernism conveys masculinity. Accordingly, advertisements conventionally show men in 'macho' postures, aiming remote controls like guns at wide-screen TVs, monitoring surveillance systems, gaming and even, in the more fantastic versions, jumping into (virtual) sports matches they watch on TV. Although advertisements do portray domesticated family men, these are juxtaposed with images of men who have prestige jobs, mobile lifestyles and/or dominion over their professional careers. As Spigel explains, when men are depicted sharing space with their children, they are rarely presented performing traditional forms of housework associated with women such as cleaning or feeding children. Instead, fathers are either presented as in charge of technology such as installing the network, building home theatres, or engaged in mediated leisure such as watching TV or playing games with their children. And, unlike multitasking mothers, dads are typically presented as focused on the task, often alone in offices or dens away from the family (Spigel 2010).

It is no accident that the concept of smart homes and connected homes has evolved in the US, which, as Spigel states, has the longest long-hours culture. This excess of imaginaries centred on the work–play fusion comes at a time when individuals are pressured to work longer hours and work seamlessly across domestic and leisure contexts, 'in office' and on the go (Madden and Jones 2008). The transformation of families from the traditional male breadwinner and full-time housewife to dual-income families is part of this social change that gives rise to 'networked workers' (Madden and Jones 2008; Spigel 2010). For women as partners and mothers, the home is a place of domestic work and childcare. Its configuration into a place of paid work makes it even more difficult for women to establish clear boundaries between work and leisure. The erosion of these traditional boundaries is often expressed through a decrease in family time and rise in home-centred work (Shumate and Fulk 2004). As Chapter 3 points out, the teleworking studies of the 1990s reveal that it is consistently women who take on home-working with the main commitment being to their domestic responsibilities (Haddon and Silverstone 1992, 1994). Computers at home can generate family tensions, with members of families competing over screen time (Lally 2002). Likewise, research reveals that women who work from home on home computers feel guilty and worried about the irritation generated among partners and children (Burke 2003).

Addressing the incursion of work life into private spaces, Mellissa Gregg (2011) argues that the middle-class passion for work leads to 'presence creep' with affective side effects. Gregg interviewed 26 mainly white, middle-class professionals from the information, communication and academic spheres in Australia. While flexible home-based work conditions have been hailed as a successful way for mothers to have a work–life balance, many of Gregg's informants worked a third shift: first in the workplace, second undertaking domestic and emotional labour at home, and a third by catching up on emails and other work before going to bed. Even within creative industries, flexibility in paid employment does not extend to deadlines or ease domestic responsibilities. Workers log many hours catching up on email at home and fail to count them as a form of labour. In the UK, among those who work during their own personal time, the largest amount of work-related communications occur in the evening at home, with 59 per cent engaged in work-related emailing or texting in their personal time (Ofcom 2014). Earlier feminist studies showed that women use solitude to catch up on soap operas (Hobson 1982) or romance novels (Radway 1991). But Gregg found that today's middle-class women use their solitude for unacknowledged paid work rather than for leisure or relaxation. As she emphasises, neoliberal demands for productivity are invading the domestic realm.

Importantly, Gregg critiques the media's role in aestheticising mobile work styles, arguing that telecommunications companies naturalise and universalise the work styles of business executives through advertising. The facility of checking in from anywhere has transformed not only the hotel room but also the bedroom into a workplace, particularly for workers who are on the lower rungs of the organisational ladder. The glamorisation of mobile technology through smart home and connected home imaginaries obscures the degree to which professional life is being reshaped to meet the requirements of a networked information economy. Mobile devices are sold as markers of class distinction yet they have become necessary work tools. The urge by working mothers to remain connected from home while caring for a toddler, or connected to work while seated on the sofa in the living room during quality 'couple time' with a partner present, represents the decidedly unglamorous impact of middle-class work on contemporary self-identity (Gregg 2011: 33).

Since 2014, the IoT has evolved as part of the convergence of multiple technologies including the internet, embedded systems and micro-electromechanical systems. This digital innovation involves the extension of network connectivity to everyday objects by designing them to send and receive data. It includes embedded and wearable computing and is expected to have widespread and beneficial effects according to the Pew Research Internet Project (Anderson and Rainie 2014). Excepted to be the next stage of the information revolution, governments and commercial organisations are investing significant funds in the technology. For example, the UK Government allocated £40 million of its 2015 budget towards research on the IoT, to advance interconnectivity of a wide range of systems including medical devices, urban transport and household appliances.

Creative initiatives using the IoT are being developed for the home. A British example called the Family Rituals 2.0 project[7] is researching ways to incorporate the benefits of the IoT into home and family life by enhancing rituals and ritualised interaction that takes place in familial and domestic contexts. The project explores ways to help people working away from home to engage in family rituals while absent by examining how mobile workers manage their work and life commitments. The virtual connectivity provided by mobile ICTs allows individuals to 'be present' and communicate with home and family almost anywhere and anytime. Like the smart home agenda, the literature addressing mobile workers tends to refer to those who have a high status and are seen to embody the cosmopolitan experience of physical and technological mobility. These tend to be professionals from knowledge and service sectors whose work has become increasingly dislocated and mobile in contemporary 'hyper-mobile' and 'fluid' society (Bauman 2000).

To understand how simple technologies can support inclusion of absent workers in domestic rituals, a team of artists have produced 'ritual machines' for three different families whose work involves regular absence from home. These artefacts have been displayed as Ritual Machines in the 'Home\Sick' exhibition at the Science Gallery in Dublin.[8] In 'Anticipation of Time Together' a mechanical flip-flop display counts down the time to a family event. With the passage of time, the display gradually transforms like a sand timer. But as the moment of the event arrives, the pace changes to show a fast-moving animation as a celebration of the event. The display can be viewed and operated anywhere with a smartphone app. 'A Message for the Moment' sends a message when the lorry driver mother is held up in a traffic jam. In the home, an electronic jam jar can store spoken messages, which can then be sent to a speaker in the cab. Rather than representing 'solutions' to the 'problem' of absence, this experimental work with digital technologies allows a creative rethink about the nature of connectivity between household members and between the inside and outside of home by focusing on family rituals, intimacy and the emotions involved in absence and homesickness.

However, today's connected homes are based on integrated systems researched and designed by global corporations such as IBM, Microsoft and Intel. The problem is that the IoT creates an opportunity to measure, collect and analyse an ever-increasing variety of behavioural statistics. These technologies therefore trigger wider questions about surveillance (Spigel 2005). Big Data and the IoT work in conjunction. In the process of attempting to activate the body and track residents' habits and preferences, contemporary digital homes emulate internet search engines by involving the kind of invasive surveillance that allows market researchers to plug into the home through techniques of observation.

Conclusion

The early twentieth-century smart home underpins today's digitally 'connected home' imaginaries. By tracing the history behind the electronic smart home agenda, this chapter has identified the cultural values that shape visions of the future home. It reveals several contradictions inscribed in the intertwined smart and connected home agendas. The early concept of the smart home conveys notions of technology as the driving force of change. As Spigel argues, smart homes comprise architectural and technological fantasies through which a better world is imagined. Likewise, imageries of today's digitally connected home convey the idea that digital technologies provide technical solutions to everyday social problems.

We might assume futuristic home designs to have particular significance for the elderly, disabled persons and children. Yet these social groups have been demoted as secondary concerns within the commercially led connected home agenda (Aldrich 2003). The smart home agenda involves the domestication of increasingly complex forms of media and information technology as both an expression of and response to the dramatic restructuring of conventional work schedules occurring from the mid twentieth century. Working from home is now facilitated by an array of communication gadgets that aestheticise and popularise a particular kind of cosmopolitan 'work' associated with today's businessman: someone mobile yet also working from home. Redefinitions of the relationship between home and work give rise to an 'always on' networked home, triggering profound tensions about the home as a place of recuperation and a place of constant connectivity. Ironically, people's concerns about being alienated or displaced by the technological future are seemingly alleviated by invoking a sense of technical control over communication with outside work.

Paradoxically, the concept of the smart home, in both its early and later stages, was heavily promoted to women within popular discourses via women's magazines as well as on radio and TV, as Spigel (2001) points out. However, throughout its history, a central aim of the smart home and connected home agenda has also been to appeal to able-bodied men to validate the domestication of electronic and then digital technology. The chapter explains that the early period of smart home design involved corporate promotions of consumer technology, expensive architectural fantasies, science fiction and exhibitions, which spoke to an exclusive millionaire and electronic hobbyist audience. Yet remarkably, the futuristic designs of a labour and energy-saving smart home failed to address the thorny issue of housework. Popular images portray simulated geometric images of pristine connected homes entirely absent of people. These hyper-sanitised images continue to be aimed at men fascinated by digital technology, exemplified by the 'Bachelor Pad of Tomorrow' article addressed above.

Women remain a marginalised consumer group within the world of the automated connected home. This is despite the growing presence of women in the workplace, the acceleration of dual-career families and the fact that women form the largest group of home-workers, which highlights the challenges of work–life balance with household responsibilities and chidcare. Apart from glimpses of robo-vacuum cleaners, representations of smart and connected home gadgets and automated systems still barely address the physical labour of housework. Smart home designers have disregarded the important detail that the home is generally a place of work for women and discounted half the population as a potential group of consumers, demonstrating that smart homes were not designed to democratise gender relations (Berg 1994). The work that supports the smooth running of the smart home and connected home setting has been rendered invisible. Rather, these futuristic homes have been preoccupied with an alternative type of 'work': working from home facilitated by an array of communication gadgets. Smart and connected homes are gendered socio-technical constructions produced from the perspective of male designers (Berg 1994).

The futuristic home turns out to be an example of 'technology push', an aesthetic vision of technology driven by what is technically achievable rather than socially principled (Berg 1999). Designed with men in mind within a masculine discourse, the technologised home forms a 'niche market' that grants access to an exclusive group. The former smart home and the contemporary connected home invoke a new masculine domesticity. But rather than subverting hegemonic masculine identities, this new identity fixes a dominant technologised masculinity. The futuristic house presents and aestheticises a technical construction that preserves gendered power relations at the same time as generating new domestic gendered identities (see Chapter 9). Even though it is more likely to be women who work from home, the futuristic home presents a technical and aesthetic vision that maintains traditional gendered power relations. By celebrating a particular kind of domestic digital agency in which technology is controlled by male connectivity with the outside world of work, the smart home agenda shifts the identity of the home from feminine to masculine.

Notes

1 See John Lewis, 'The Connected Home', available at: *http://www.johnlewis.com/inspiration-and-advice/technology/connected-home-technology*, accessed 26 July 2015.
2 See John Lewis, 'Home Living', Smart Homes, available at: *http://www.johnlewis.com/electricals/smart-home/c7000070016?rdr=1*, accessed 26 July 2015.
3 Smart Housing by Jung with KNX, available at: *https://www.youtube.com/watch?v=bHvZukbLlo0*, accessed 17 July 2015.
4 'Samsung at the 2015 Consumer Electronics Show', available at: *http://www.samsung.com/uk/discover/news/samsung-at-ces-2015/*, accessed 17 July 2015.

5 Samsung CES 2015: 'Inside the Smart Things Smart Home', available at: *https://www. youtube.com/watch?v=FTiFt9mplCE*, accessed 17 July 2015.
6 *Stuff* is a popular British gadget and lifestyle men's magazine with editions in the USA and other countries that previews future technology and provides news, reviews and features on the latest gadgets, see *http://www.stuff.tv/*, accessed 6 December 2015.
7 Family Rituals 2.0 is an Engineering and Physical Sciences Research Council-funded project with partners from Newcastle University and the Royal College of Art, University of the West of England and Bournemouth University. Information about the Family Rituals 2.0 Project is available at: *http://familyrituals2-0.org.uk/about-2/*, accessed 7 December 2015.
8 Ritual Machines (installation 2014), Science Gallery, Dublin, details available at: *https:// dublin.sciencegallery.com/homesick/ritualmachines*, accessed 7 December 2015.

References

Aldrich, F.K. (2003) 'Smart Homes: Past, Present and Future', in Richard Harper (ed.) *Inside the Smart Home*, London: Springer, pp. 17–40.

Allon, F. (1999) 'Altitude Anxiety: Being at Home in a Globalised World', PhD thesis, University of Technology, Sydney.

Allon, F. (2000) 'Nostalgia Unbound', *Continuum* 14 (3), pp. 275–287.

Anderson, J. and Raine, L. (2014) 'The Internet of Things Will Thrive by 2025', Pew Research Centre, available at: *http://www.pewinternet.org/2014/05/14/internet-of-things/*, accessed 7 December 2015.

Bauman, Z. (2000) *Liquid Modernity: On the Frailty of Human Bonds*, Cambridge: Polity Press.

Berg, A.-J. (1992) 'The Smart House as a Gendered Socio-Technical Construction', *Working Paper 14/92*, Centre for Technology and Society, University of Trondheim, Norway, available at: *https://www.ntnu.no/c/document_library/get_file?uuid=b77e6da1-2511-4d43-a390-33d61b378e28&groupId=10265*, accessed 7 December 2015.

Berg, A.-J. (1994) 'A Gendered Socio-technical Construction: The Smart House', in Cynthia Cockburn and Ruza First-Dilic (eds) *Bringing Technology Home: Gender and Technology in a Changing Europe*, Maidenhead: Open University Press, pp. 165–180.

Bourdieu, P. (1984) *Distinction: A Social Critique of the Judgement of Taste*, London: Routledge.

Burke, C. (2003) 'Women, Guilt and Home Computers', in Joseph Turow and Andrea L. Kavanaugh (eds) *The Wired Homestead*, Cambridge, MA: MIT Press, pp. 332–333.

Cohan, S. (1996) 'So Functional for Its Purposes: The Bachelor Apartment in *Pillow Talk*', in Joel Sanders (ed.) *Stud: Architectures of Masculinity*, New York: Princeton Architectural Press, pp. 30–45.

Colomina, B. (1996) *Privacy and Publicity: Modern Architecture as Mass Media*, Cambridge, MA: MIT Press.

Cook, M. (2014) *Queer Domesticities: Homosexuality and Home Life in Twentieth-Century London*, Basingstoke: Palgrave Macmillan.

Cowan, R.S. (1983) *More Work for Mother: The Ironies of Household Technology from the Open Hearth to the Microwave*, New York: Basic Books.

Forty, A. (1986) *Objects of Desire: Design and Society Since 1750*, London: Thames and Hudson.

Gates, B. (1995) *The Road Ahead*, New York: Penguin.

Gorman-Murray (2008) 'Masculinity and the Home: A Critical Review and Conceptual Framework', *Australian Geographer* 9 (3), pp. 367–379.

Gregg, M. (2011) *Work's Intimacy*, Cambridge, MA: Polity Press.

Haddon, L. (1992) 'Explaining ICT Consumption: The Case of the Home Computer', in Roger Silverstone and Eric Hirsch (eds) *Consuming Technologies: Media and Information in Domestic Spaces,* London: Routledge, pp. 82–96.

Haddon, L. and Silverstone, R. (1992) 'Information and Communication Technologies in the Home: The Case of Teleworking', *Working Paper 17*, SPRU CICT, University of Sussex, Falmer.

Haddon, L. and Silverstone, R. (1994) 'Telework and the Changing Relationship of Home and Work', in Robin Mansell (ed.) *Management of Information and Communication Technologies: Emerging Patterns of Control*, London: Aslib, pp. 234–247.

Hardyment, C. (1988) *From Mangle to Microwave*, Cambridge, MA: Polity Press.

Harper, R. (ed.) (2011) *The Connected Home: The Future of Domestic Life*, London: Springer.

Hobson, D. (1982) *Crossroads: Drama of a Soap Opera*, London: Metheun.

Lally, E. (2002) *At Home with Computers*, Berg: Oxford.

Jencks, C. (1973) *Modern Movements in Architecture*, Garden City, NY: Anchor Books.

Lefebvre, H. (1974/1991) *The Production of Space*, Oxford and New York: Blackwell.

Madden, M. and Jones, S. (2008) 'Networked Workers', Pew Research Centre, available at: *http://www.pewinternet.org/2008/09/24/networked-workers/*, accessed 7 December 2015.

Meyer, S. and Schulze, E. (1996) 'The Smart Home in the 1990s: Acceptance and Future Usage in Private Households in Europe', in 'The Smart Home: Research Perspectives, The European Media Technology and Everyday Life Network (EMTEL)', *Working Paper No. 1*, University of Sussex, Brighton.

Morley, D. (2003) 'What's Home Got to Do With It? Contradictory Dynamics in the Domestication of Technology and the Dislocation of Domesticity', *European Journal of Cultural Studies* 6 (4), pp. 435–458.

Morley, D. (2007) *Media, Modernity and Technology: The Geography of the New*, London: Routledge.

Ofcom (2014) *The Communications Market Report*, available at: *http://stakeholders.ofcom.org.uk/binaries/research/cmr/cmr14/2014_UK_CMR.pdf*.

Osgerby, B. (2005) 'The Bachelor Pad as a Cultural Icon: Masculinity, Consumption and Interior Design in American Men's Magazines, 1930–65', *Journal of Design History* 18 (1), pp. 99–113.

Radway, J. (1991) *Reading the Romance: Women, Patriarchy and Popular Literature*, Chapel Hill, NC: The University of North Carolina Press.

Shumate, M. and Fulk, J. (2004) 'Boundaries and Role Conflict When Work and Family are Colocated: A Communication Network and Symbolic Interaction Approach', *Human Relations* 57 (1), pp. 55–74.

Sparke, P. (2008) 'The Modern Interior Revisited', *Journal of Interior Design* 34 (1), pp. v–xii.

Spigel, L. (2001) *Welcome to the Dreamhouse: Popular Media and Postwar Suburbs*, Durham, NC and London: Duke University Press.

Spigel, L. (2005) 'Designing the Smart House: Posthuman Domesticity and Conspicuous Production', *European Journal of Cultural Studies* 8 (4), pp. 403–426.

Spigel, L. (2010) 'Designing the Smart House: Posthuman Domesticity and Conspicuous Production', in Chris Berry, Soyoung Kim and Lyn Spigel (eds) *Electronic Elsewheres: Media Technology and the Experience of Social Space*, Minneapolis, MN: University of Minnesota Press, pp. 55–95.

Van Herck, K. (2005) '"Only Where Comfort Ends Does Humanity Begin": On the "Coldness" of Avant-garde Architecture in Weimar Period', in Hilde Heynen and Gülsüm Baydar (eds) *Negotiating Domesticity: Spatial Productions of Gender in Modern Architecture*, London: Routledge, pp. 123–144.

9

THE MEDIATISED HOME

Introduction

The aim of this book has been to trace key historical events and recent trends that characterise the complex relationship between householders, homes and media technologies. This final chapter draws together the threads of the analysis and raises some questions about future trends and directions for academic enquiry. The roles played by media in the home are situated within a wider process of mediatisation, with technologies no longer merely additional to the home. The previous chapters have pinpointed the multiple ways in which the symbolic boundaries around the home are destabilised by its transformation into a site of multimedia activity. The home is both a diverging and converging media setting formed by systems of globalisation, widespread internet access and mobile appliances. The intensified mediatisation of home as a feature of late modernity involves dramatic changes in types of connections with the outside world and new forms of household interactions through interactive, peer-to-peer, individualised modes of communication. Digital media and communication technologies now 'comprise' the home (Morley 2007).

The home has become a site of struggle over contemporary meanings and values associated with domesticity. 'Home' has not simply been conceived as a leisure haven brimming with media devices for us to 'retreat to' or a confined space to 'escape from' with the aid of portable and mobile media gadgets. Today's mediatised home harbours more complex and ambiguous meanings, particularly for certain social groups. For example, as we have seen in earlier chapters, for women with domestic and childcare responsibilities and home-workers, this setting is typically experienced as a site of work. And for parents, it is a site of parental monitoring of children's media practices, often involving continuous and fractious parent–child negotiations. For migrants and transnational families, media and communication technologies enable the negotiation of 'home' from a distance, continuous intimate contact and the experience of two cultures at once.

Today's mediatised home may seem more intimate and privatised yet, at the same time, digital systems of communication render the home more permeable, exposed to the agendas of the outside world. Social media such as webcams enable immersive and intimate modes of communication between family members, for example allowing them to share mealtimes at a distance. Yet, through these same technologies, including photo and video tours of home on property sale websites, householders regularly find digital doors to their homes opened for the outside world to peer into what is generally recognised as a profoundly intimate space. Personalised mobile media generate new domestic communication cultures expressed through new sites of interaction and media settings. Computer tablets and smartphones are new interactive modes of communication that form part of complex and finely tuned networked households and individuals, facilitating interaction with co-present household members while simultaneously engaging in conversations with personal public networks beyond the home. And as previous chapters demonstrate, home-centred digital communication systems enable new kinds of transnational intimacies beyond the home, even generating a new form of 'mobile domesticity' through mobile phone use. Although digital media systems can breach the boundaries around the home, they now play a fundamental role in reinforcing ideas of the home as an intimate sphere. The more that 'home' seems to be encroached on from 'outside' via digital connectivity, the more this space is defended and reclaimed as an intimate and private territory. These tendencies throw up major moral dilemmas about the ethics of perpetual observation.

This final chapter begins by examining key features of the mediatisation of home, identified in earlier chapters. The first section explores the contradictory discursive tendencies that shape and attempt to fix media imaginaries about the home as a domestic space. It highlights the struggles over traditional and modern meanings of the mediatised home, from a site of traditional family harmony to a postmodern site of mobility, agency and change. This section identifies four broad phases in the mediatisation of home involving distinctive domestic media imaginaries that underscore its contested and conditional nature. The second part of this chapter addresses the implications for children of the accelerated commercialisation of media. The third section highlights growing commercial media surveillance in the home as a disturbing contemporary manifestation of the permeable boundaries around the mediatised home.

Media imaginaries of domesticity

The processes of domesticating media and communication technologies addressed in previous chapters comprise both prerequisites and expressions of a mediatisation of home and everyday life. Mediatisation works and succeeds through domestication. Domestication therefore concerns the ways in which macro-social processes of mediatisation operate at micro-social levels (Hartman 2009: 234–235). For the process of mediatisation to work effectively at a macro-level, it must itself be domesticated. As Hartmann (2009: 234), puts it, domestication is a key strategy among householders for managing mediatisation. It is a 'coping mechanism'. The concept of media imaginaries employed in earlier chapters identifies the roles played by design, marketing, advertising and wider popular discourses in the creation of powerful public visions of a mediatised future. Following Hartmann, these media imaginaries can be conceived as discursive appropriations within utopian and dystopian debates about domestic media that feed into the domesticating processes involved in the mediatisation of the home and everyday life.

The historical span of events and processes detailed in the preceding chapters allows us to trace some of the main phases of the mediatisation of home that involve shifting domestic imaginaries. Four broad but overlapping chronological phases can be identified which underline the struggles over traditional and new meanings of the mediatised home. These phases have evolved from traditional to emergent, comprising 'traditional domestic imaginaries'; 'mobile domestic imaginaries'; 'home-working domestic imaginaries'; and 'cosmopolitan domestic imaginaries'. The first phase of 'traditional domestic imaginaries' comprises the early 1950s period when TV became a taken-for-granted feature of home life. During this phase, the widespread acceptance and success of broadcast media technology in the home depended on the transmission of traditional domestic ideals and family values through design, marketing, state policies and popular culture, as Chapter 2 confirms. Yet while traditional domestic imaginaries functioned to exclude alternative ideas of media engagement and unconventional families, TV's presence in the home during this phase sparked public anxieties that housewives would be distracted from their domestic duties and thereby destabilise family values (Andrews 2012; Spigel 1992, 2001). The advent of TV in the early 1950s is associated with and underpinned not only by new kinds of mediated home-based leisure but also by traditional domestic imaginaries expressed through TV programming and wider popular culture. Importantly, this traditional domestic imaginary is a dominant or ideal version of home which continues to be conveyed via the media, popular culture and public policy today to promote belonging and intimacy in a heterosexual nuclear family context (Gorman-Murray 2008; Blunt and Dowling 2006: 100–101). This imaginary competes with the following phases of the mediatisation of home.

Corresponding with the arrival of portable TV in the 1960s, a second phase of mediatisation emerged, characterised by 'mobile domestic imaginaries' to express modernity and scientific progress. Triggered by fantasies of escape and adventure beyond the home, this phase contested traditional domestic imaginaries. The rise of mobile media was accompanied by emergent media imaginaries of a mobile domesticity and more fluid spatial representations of the relationship between home and the outside world. This was epitomised by technologies such as portable TV and then the mobile phone. This phase has been identified and documented by Spigel (2001). A perceived erosion of traditional family values associated with more mobile lifestyles generated fears of domestic decline yet provoked a celebration of and desire for travel away from home. Home was reconfigured as a site of technological and scientific progress.

'Home-working domestic imaginaries' characterise the third phase of mediatisation from the 1980s. This phase is exemplified by the entrance of work-related information technologies such as the personal computer (PC) into the home. As described in Chapter 3, this stage signified the weakening of the ideological boundaries between paid work outside the home and domestic leisure. It involved telecommuting, telework and flexible work arrangements to facilitate more flexible working arrangements and gain a sense of control over paid work to create a work–life balance. Householders have struggled to cultivate the home as an entertainment hub and context for supporting children's media literary and wider education. Yet the home has also come to be strongly identified as a work hub as a response to managing work demands. However, for women as partners and mothers, the idea of a media-rich home as 'leisure' has always been contentious, given that domestic work and childcare are conducted in the same space. Home-working turned out to be something that women were most likely to take up, from an early stage, as a way to balance housework and childcare with work commitments. The reconfiguration of home into a place of paid work as well as domestic work made it difficult for women to establish clear boundaries between work and leisure in the home. Information and communication technologies (ICTs) were domesticated by their absorption into existing values and routines associated with home, often led by the juggling of work and domestic duties by women, not only in dual-parent households but also in single-parent households. Women have tended to manage the erosion of these traditional boundaries by increasing their home-centred workload and decreasing their leisure and family time (Shumate and Fulk 2004). Notwithstanding the challenges experienced and sacrifices made by women in sustaining their family commitments, a crisis of domesticity was prompted by public and popular perceptions that women were neglecting domestic duties, distracted by employment.

The fourth phase of mediatisation is characterised by a 'cosmopolitan domestic imaginary'. This stage articulates albeit hesitant aspirations for a mobile and digitally connected postmodern home. Associated with the advent of today's digital, mobile and integrative media technologies, this phase contests certain aspects of dominant traditional domestic values. By combining the conveniences and technological fantasies from earlier phases of domestic mediatisation, cosmopolitan media imaginaries echo the aspirations towards mobility expressed in the second phase but involve a new kind of media mobility. This phase features global connectivity from the home as well as an accelerated penetration of home by the outside world of work. Underpinned by notions of the 'smart home', cosmopolitan domesticity is epitomised by the digitally automated 'connected home' addressed in Chapter 8. It involves a masculine work aesthetic that celebrates a particular kind of creative professional work. Cosmopolitan domesticity is characterised by communicative accessibility, openness and yet also corporate surveillance. Creating the potential for continuous interactivity with the outside world through multiple smart and mobile devices, this digitalised 'home' is imagined as a flexible, permeable setting, one through which domestic tasks could even be obscured and dismissed via smart and connected homes. At both an aesthetic and practical level, the home increasingly resembles a work station, triggered by the preceding home-working phase. It even celebrates work as a new aesthetic through an exploration of masculine domestic identities involving technological convergence, networked mobility, flexible working arrangements, multiple leisure pursuits and digital home automation. Prompting the expression of new gendered domestic identities, men are conceived as the architects of this domestic space (Gorman-Murray 2008). Yet, at the same time as articulating the home as an efficient leisure and work hub, the cosmopolitan home has been 'opened out', exposed to corporate surveillance for marketing purposes. This issue is returned to below.

Each of these four phases draws attention to the disputed nature of mediated domestic space. While the home has traditionally been imagined as a feminine site, emergent and alternative domestic media imaginaries conceive of the home as a fluid, technologically connected and changeable space often linked to masculine identities. The living room becomes a highly contested and conditional space, exemplified by the disputes associated with the entrance of technologies such as radio and video gaming into the home. As Chapter 5 shows, the video game console's integration into the domestic routines of the home involved gendered as well as generational contestations of the domestic realm in the structuring of a moral economy in the home. The association of masculinity with digital and automated technology is also exemplified by the changing gendered identities involved in early tablet computer advertising imagery and visions of the connected home, involving mobile and convergent media. Simultaneously, the masculine domestication of home signifies the transformation of home from a place of housework and domestic 'duties' to a place of leisure and creative cosmopolitan business work, intimating a 'mobile' and active masculine domesticity. As Chapter 8 shows, the spatial aesthetics of 'homes of tomorrow', smart homes and contemporary digitally automated connected homes invoke new identities, associated with masculine control and agency, expressing a masculinisation of domestic space.

Mobile and digital media and communication technologies have, then, played a central role in uncoupling domesticity from the spatial specificity of 'home'. Increasingly treated as a place of work and networking, the home is a site of struggle over meanings of home as 'leisure' or 'work'. While dystopian scenarios identify a crisis of feminised domesticity, new visions of the mediatised home have conjured up utopian principles of a smart, clean, digitally automated home with an emphasis on leisure and digital agency and association of domesticity with masculine identities. As manifestations of the tension surrounding reconfigurations of home-based routines – involving leisure, domestic duties, teleworking and smart masculinised domestic identities – media imaginaries of home attempt to make sense of the changing nature of the household associated with the domestic appropriation of media technology.

Today's mediated conceptions of domesticity simultaneously evoke and contest earlier idealisations of domesticity. While traditional domestic imaginaries venerate housework as a confirmation of family values, emergent domestic media imaginaries transform the domestic space into an aesthetic that endorses neoliberal ideals about agency and self-regulation (Gregg 2011; Rose 1999). Ironically, visions of a utopian digitally controlled future home propelled by ideals of masculine agency, trigger nostalgic idealisations of domesticity as a lost feminine realm, exemplified by the current explosion of TV programmes on cooking, house buying and histories of past domesticity (see Andrews 2012). Despite their aesthetic and technological appeal, evidence suggests that new domestic imaginaries tend to leave gendered power relations intact.

The commercialisation of domestic media technologies

A major feature of the mediatisation of the home is the deregulation of media products and services leading to the increased commercialisation and privatisation of media access and use. Media transformations within and beyond the home are exploited by powerful commercial interests. This section looks at the implications of this trend by citing examples of issues concerning privacy regulation that affect the use of media in the home. In his analysis of convergence culture, Henry Jenkins (2014) confirms that 'the Web 2.0 business model seeks to capture, commodify and control the public's desire for meaningful participation' (2014: 267). In rethinking his earlier work on convergence culture, Jenkins admits that the idealistic motives that galvanised young entrepreneurs into Web 2.0 technology quickly led to changed relationships between producers and audiences after corporate ownership and venture capital were involved (Jenkins 2014). However, as early as 2006, Jenkins observed:

> Here's the paradox: to be desired by the networks is to have your tastes commodified. Those groups that have no recognized economic value get ignored. That said, commodification is also a form of exploitation. Those groups that are commodified find themselves targeted more aggressively by marketers and often feel they have lost control over their own culture, since it is mass produced and mass marketed.
>
> *(Jenkins 2006: 63)*

While the home has become the nerve centre of a 'public network culture' (Boyd 2010), future media innovations are likely to be propelled by the commercial imperatives of giant media corporations that dominate the invention and content of future domestic media technologies. This prospect is exemplified by earlier smart home technology, which was predicated on corporate synergies, branding and especially lifestyle marketing, as indicated in Chapter 8. The commercialisation of mediatised home life has become a major force of social change (Beck 1992). Corporate activity and wider commercial interests have gained extensive powers over consumer behaviour in diverse ways, including the marketing of media products and services. Media conglomerates are now carrying out extensive research using algorithms to harvest information about consumer tastes, gain advertising revenue and expand consumer culture. Engagement with the internet is now almost impossible outside a commercial structure. Householders are locked into a commercial organisation of their daily habits and routines. As such, market values and social values become intertwined as part of a marketisation of 'the hearth'. What are the implications of this encroaching commercialisation of the mediatised home?

The economic recession is compelling low-income households to withdraw into the home for their leisure. In addition, the commercialisation of media involves a privatisation of regulation. With regard to children's engagement with media, the responsibility for regulating children's media uses has shifted from the state to parents, teachers and children. As Clark (2013: 224–225) explains, the issue is much broader than a question of content made available to children on TV screens, gaming devices and mobile downloads. It creates a media system that relies on the principles of escalating consumption, and as Clark puts it: 'The overwhelming and unchecked power of corporate interests to dictate the terms of society' (Clark 2013: 224). However, she also points out that sociologists in the US have tended to view media through the lens of 'effects on individuals', concentrating on what individual parents should do rather than drawing connections between this corporate invasion and the need for media reform. Academic research confirms that the market targeting of children is ubiquitous – on the internet, in school, textbooks and in the playground (Schor and Ruskin 2005; Schor and Ford 2007). Techniques have branched out from product placement to wider and more subtle advertising through TV programmes and films. These marketing techniques create messages about media products, food and toys that not only influence what children want to buy but also shape their identities. They have invoked 'commercialised children' (Schor 2005; Schor and Ruskin 2005; Schor and Ford 2007).

The work by Schor and colleagues represents a perspective supported by academics, parents and educational bodies who argue that marketing to children needs more governmental guidance rather than industry self-regulation. However, as Clark points out, this type of research on the rise of the 'commercialised child' follows older models of mass communication research by employing an individualistic framework that recommends further studies of the effects of advertising on children and more policies that regulate broadcasted material. Although these are major issues, this approach fails to address the roots of the problem: media ownership, regulation and how parents can deal with the commercialised media environment. As Clark states, 'If media industries were regulated and held accountable for their role in fostering the public good we might have a different media landscape' (Clark 2013: 225). Rather than asking 'how the internet is or is not making children more narcissistic or isolated', Clark suggests that, instead, we should enquire into how media policies can be created to counter the trend towards an unregulated media commercialisation. As she points out, the report on UK media and families by Sonia Livingstone and Ranjana Das (2010) is an excellent example of an approach that begins by addressing public concerns and then goes on to reframe the debate. Clark confirms the need for family policy and media policies to be linked rather than dealt with in isolation.

Privacy and domestic media surveillance

The issues highlighted by privacy regulation concern the ways that individuals and householders manage current entertainment and informational boundaries. In today's digital setting, the home has become one of the most scrutinised and regulated of social spaces. However, through deregulation and accelerated commercialisation of media innovation, this surveillance has extended from the state to commercial interests. User-generated data is being shared across many domains, breaching traditional forms of privacy in relation to the emergent concepts of the 'connected home', mentioned in Chapter 8. Automation of surveillance involves the disappearing distinctions between those watching and those being watched (Adams and Jansson 2012; see Andrejevic 2007). In this section, I address the issue of domestic surveillance in the context of media commercialisation.

The contemporary family household now conducts a form of self-regulation away from the intrusion of state and market relations in what Nicolas Rose (1999) refers to as a 'strategy of family privacy'. However, in the digital era, multinational media corporations have taken over that role in the interests of capitalism. In the early twenty-first century, media convergence has brought with it a raft of new ways in which to digitally watch and listen to householders 'in the privacy of the home'. This raises new issues about privacy regulation and how households manage informational boundaries. Automated surveillance allows governments and commercial organisations to data mine globally. Little attention has yet been paid to the ethical issues involved in the continuous surveillance of home life now made possible by technologies such as smart TVs, gaming consoles and computer tablets. TV convergence is reconfiguring market dynamics and relationships. Smart TV sets connect to the internet to enable the downloading of programmes and films from services such as Netflix or BBC iPlayer. Experts now recognise that, as the internet can be used to bring information to the domestic TV, it can also be used to take information from that TV. Smart TVs have the facility to monitor users' viewing habits, collect the information and pass on the data to advertisers.

In the UK, the consumer association charity *Which?* conducted a study of smart TV in 2014.[1] It drew attention to the fact that consumers who agree to their smart TV's Terms and Conditions are often unaware that they are permitting the manufacturer to observe the ways in which the TV set is used. This includes an industry surveillance of the programmes watched and websites visited by householders who watch smart TV. The manufacturers argue that this feature facilitates the delivery of more personalised programme recommendations to viewers. However, the data gathered on households and families can be used to provide targeted advertising on owners' smart TV's homescreens. This is regarded by many as an invasion of privacy. *Which?* relates the experience of an IT consultant, Jason Huntley, who discovered that his LG smart TV was tracking all information about him and his family (Laughlin 2014). Huntley was disturbed to find that his children's names had been sent unencrypted over the internet to LG's servers. This information was obtained from a family video that he had made at Christmas and then watched on TV. When Huntley related his experience on his Doctor Beet Blog,[2] it reached headline news and led to an ongoing investigation by the Information Commissioner.

Huntley agreed to work with the *Which?* Consumer Association to investigate the kind of information the big brand smart TVs were tracking about householders. Using widely available techniques to monitor the streams of data from 2013 and 2014 models on each of the LG, Samsung, Sony, Panasonic and Toshiba brands, the investigation discovered that all the brands were tracking viewing habits to a certain degree. But most data is encrypted and therefore hidden from hackers. Nevertheless, they found that a Samsung TV beamed the location and postcode of the TV set unencrypted when the set was first switched on. Samsung's response was that location data is required to switch on the set. It was also discovered that LG has temporarily stopped this kind of tracking but that it has not ruled out resuming the practice. With regard to advertising, Toshiba, LG and Panasonic all deliver advertisements to smart TV homescreens. Owners of sets can prevent these advertisements from being compiled on households' TV habits, but they cannot block them completely. LG and Toshiba informed *Which?* that posting advertisements on smart TVs is 'standard industry practice' but *Which* found that Sony does not deliver advertisements. *Which?* examined the consequences of an owner declining the smart TV's Terms and Conditions. At the time of writing, it is impossible to use any apps or the web browser on Panasonic TVs if the Terms and Conditions are rejected. And if the apps are also blocked on the LG set and on Samsung and Toshiba TVs, the smart TV services are blocked. In contrast, Sony provides upfront options at the set-up stage to block the tracking and the only service lost is the content recommendations.

This kind of information tracking for the purposes of targeting advertisements to users is not equivalent to the free downloading of a smartphone app. The smart TV is an expensive commodity costing from £279 for cheaper models right up to around £20,000 on 3D models (at 2015 prices), and therefore likely to inhabit the living room for several years to come. The *Which?* Consumer Association have asked smart TV manufacturers to undertake the following: first, to keep smart TV tracking to a minimum and encrypt data on users that gets transmitted over the internet; second, to be transparent about the tracking process and its rationale; third, to allow consumers to opt out and retain the smart TV features that they have paid for; and finally to provide consumers a choice about whether to take adverts on their smart TV homescreens. *Which?* point to Amazon as an example of a commercial enterprise that offers a discount on their Kindle Fire tablets if the consumer agreed to have adverts on the tablet's screensaver. Content filters and advert-blocking extensions against search engines can be applied to PC, laptop and tablet computers, allowing the prevention of page elements such as adverts to be displayed. Yet these filters and blocks cannot be administered to a smart TV.

For some households, voice recognition is a welcome feature. However, at the time of writing, it was found that the smart TV produced by South Korean multinational conglomerate Samsung is programmed not only to understand certain commands such as 'turn on' but can also record all conversations in the room. In February 2015, US consumer rights group Electronic Privacy Information Center (EPIC) claimed that the terms in Samsung's privacy policy indicated the ways in which voice commands can be transmitted to a third-party service as part of its Smart TV's Voice Recognition feature.[3] Privacy advocates have argued that because the voice command feature of Samsung's Smart TV enables the TV to collect users' private conversations, this contravenes federal privacy law. In reply, Samsung has explained that such transmission can only occur when the user pushes a designated button. Samsung's Smart TV privacy policy initially contained the warning: 'Please be aware that if your spoken words include personal or other sensitive information, that information will be among the data captured and transmitted to a third party through your use of Voice Recognition.'[4] Samsung then clarified their privacy policy to better explain what occurs.[5]

In response to concerns, Samsung has stated that its Smart TVs are not eavesdropping on its users but the company have been unable to convince the EPIC who then filed a complaint with the Federal Trade Commission (FTC) suggesting that 'Samsung routinely intercepts and record the private communications of consumers in their homes' (Geuss 2015). An additional concern about the company's privacy policy involved the identity of the third party to whom the captured information is transmitted when the user activates the TV's voice recognition. Samsung responded by stating that they do not retain voice data or sell it to third parties. However, a third party was identified as Nuance, a US-based multinational computer software technology corporation that provides speech and imaging applications. Samsung stated that all the recorded data passed on to Nuance are encrypted but this has been contested by a computer researcher, leading the EPIC to file a further complaint.

The form of surveillance exemplified by smart TV technology is not restricted to this kind of domestic media equipment. It has also been revealed that Microsoft's voice-activated Xbox games console has the capacity to listen to all conversations in the room. Microsoft argues that they are only interested in voice commands to the Xbox, which may also capture ambient background noise. If users give Microsoft permission, commands are recorded whether the users are online or offline. Microsoft stores this data and, under its privacy policy, states that it can share it with 'affiliates and vendors'.[6] Yet, on Christmas Day 2014, Xbox's Live Platform servers were brought down by hackers, demonstrating that assertions of the security of data are highly questionable. Likewise, as mentioned, Amazon Fire TV entails voice recognition. It comprises a box that can be connected to HDTV to access games, music, films and TV programmes on video on-demand streaming devices and services such as Netflix, Amazon Instant video and HBO Go. Amazon Fire's terms of use confirm that that any voice recordings 'may be stored on servers outside the country in which you live'.[7] Moreover, certain smart TV sets not only have 'ears' but also 'eyes' in the form of a camera used for face recognition intended to permit only certain people to watch the set. Again, in its privacy policy, Samsung state that images of viewers' faces are not transmitted over the internet.

Unsurprisingly, these examples of surveillance have prompted public alarm and extensive media debate about how far these giant multimedia corporations can be trusted. These issues and ensuing debates about Big Data lead to important questions about the extent to which householders are being spied on. Their domestic habits and lives are used as sources of data by multinational corporations keen to find ever more sophisticated ways to persuade us to spend more money. For instance, by reading emails on its Gmail account and individuals' internet use, Google collects data to deliver advertisements to users about goods and services mentioned in their personal email communication. Moreover, with increasing numbers of devices linked to the internet, through the 'Internet of Things', companies gain information that not only allows householders to switch on the heating at home remotely via their smartphones but also gain information about residents' personal habits such as when they go away on holiday. While companies sell increasingly personalised products to track our behaviour and sell us ever more personalised goods and services, the question is whether they can be trusted to keep all this personal data secure and whether we are to be informed of who it is sold to and how it is used. Wider questions are also raised about how these issues of surveillance will evolve in the future and how they relate to future household dynamics.

Thus, corporate and state digital surveillance has reached new heights whose future consequences are difficult to predict. The embedding of everyday, technology-enabled home life through commercial systems is a feature of the mediatisation of home and everyday life that generates contradictory challenges. On the one hand, new media present us with untold freedom. On the other hand, this can only be achieved through systematic and widespread commercial surveillance. Mediatisation involves gaining access to media products and services providing we freely give away our personal and household data. Pam Heath and Nancy Bell (2006) argue that the development of 'smart' services and devices respond to consumers' growing expectations that 'content and information will become increasingly personalised. People want their technology to be personally meaningful, expecting their home technology to be "all about me and my family"' (Heath and Bell 2006: 259). However, recent developments confirm that this feature of the process of mediatisation tends to generate further and deeper media dependencies. Even though we are given more freedom to interact, we do so at a high price.

Households have, then, become the consumer targets of the global, commercialised media conglomerates that form today's leisure and entertainment industry.

Within a global reach, media corporations spend millions of dollars to cultivate children, youth and adults as media markets through the promotion of commodities within a mediatised framework. This drive is shaped by the promotion of niche markets and personalised gadgetry through a culture of planned obsolescence at the level of innovative design and technology. The outcomes do not necessarily serve the interests of consumers. Contemporary households have been laid open to the intrusion of market relations. A former dominant strategy of family privacy has been overtaken by domestic commercial scrutiny.

The contemporary mediatisation of the home involves positive consequences of increased connectivity between household members and between home and the outside world and, at the same time, negative consequences concerning increased commercial surveillance. These negative features prompt us to think carefully about the impact of current trends involved in the mediatisation of home life. The complex topic of commercial media surveillance raises important ethical issues about trust and privacy. It requires close academic investigation to understand the implications of the trend towards a commodification of home life and to develop media policies designed to combat this trend. In addition, studies of the changing roles of media and communication in the home require a convergence of research within sociology, media and communication studies, family studies and cultural geography.

Notes

1 Andrew Laughlin (2014) 'Smart TV Spying: Are You Watching TV or Is It Watching You?' *Which?* consumer magazine, 20 August, blog available at: *http://blogs.which.co.uk/technology/tvs/smart-tv-spying-weve-investigated/*, accessed 7 December 2015.
2 Doctor Beet's Blog is available at: *http://doctorbeet.blogspot.co.uk/*, accessed 11 August 2015.
3 'Complaint, Request for Investigation, Injunction, and Other Relief', submitted by the Electronic Privacy Information centre, in the matter of Samsung Electronics, 24 February 2015, Federal Trade Commission Washington, DC 20580, available at: *https://epic.org/privacy/internet/ftc/Samsung/EPIC-FTC-Samsung.pdf*, accessed 11 August 2015.
4 Samsung Privacy Policy – Smart TV Supplement, available at: *http://www.samsung.com/sg/info/privacy/smarttv.html*, accessed 11 August 2015.
5 See 'Samsung Smart TVs Do Not Monitor Living Room Conversations', blog available at *http://global.samsungtomorrow.com/samsung-smart-tvs-do-not-monitor-living-room-conversations/*, accessed 11 August 2015.
6 Microsoft Privacy Statement July 2015, available at: *https://www.microsoft.com/en-us/privacystatement/*, accessed 11 August 2015.
7 Amazon Fire TV Terms of Use, updated 24 March 2015, available at: *http://www.amazon.co.uk/gp/help/customer/display.html?nodeId=201348260*, accessed 11 August 2015.

References

Adams, P.C. and Jansson, A. (2012) 'Communication Geography: A Bridge Between Disciplines' *Communication Theory* 22 (3), pp. 299–318.
Andrejevic, M. (2007) *I Spy: Surveillance and Power in the Interactive Age*, Lexington, KY: University of Kentucky Press.

Andrews, M. (2012) *Domesticating the Airwaves: Broadcasting, Domesticity and Femininity*, London: Continuum.

Beck, U. (1992) *Risk Society*, London: Sage.

Blunt, A. and Dowling, R. (2006) *Home*, London: Routledge.

Boyd, D. (2010) 'Social Network Sites as Networked Publics: Affordances, Dynamics, and Implications', in Zizi Papacharissi (ed.) *A Networked Self: Identity, Community, and Culture on Social Network Sites*, New York: Routledge, pp. 39–58.

Clark, L.S. (2013) *The Parent App: Understanding Families in the Digital Age*, Oxford: Oxford University Press.

Chambers, D. (2013) *Social Media and Personal Relationships*, Basingstoke: Palgrave Macmillan.

Geuss, M. (2015) 'Privacy Advocate Tells FTC that Samsung Smart TVs Are "Deceptive"', Law and Disorder/Civilization and Discontents, 26 February 2015, available at: *http://arstechnica.com/tech-policy/2015/02/privacy-advocate-tells-ftc-that-samsung-smart-tvs-are-deceptive/*, accessed 11 August 2015.

Gorman-Murray, A. (2008) 'Masculinity and the Home: A Critical Review and Conceptual Framework', *Australian Geographer* 9 (3), pp. 367–379.

Gregg, M. (2011) *Work's Intimacy*, Cambridge, Polity Press.

Hartmann, M. (2009) 'Everyday: Domestication of Mediatisation or Mediatized Domestication?' in Knut Lundby (ed.) *Mediatization: Concept, Changes, Consequences*, New York: Peter Lang Publishing, pp. 225–242.

Heath, P. and Bell, N. (2006) 'The Changing World of Home Technology: A Microsoft Case Study', *The Information Society: An International Journal* 22 (4), pp. 251–259.

Jansson, A. (2013) 'Mediatisation and Social Space: Reconstructing Mediatisation for the Transmedia Age', *Communication Theory* 23, pp. 279–296.

Jenkins, H. (2006) *Convergence Culture: Where Old and New Media Collide*, New York: New York University Press.

Jenkins, H. (2014) 'Rethinking "Rethinking Convergence/Culture"', *Cultural Studies* 28 (2), p. 268.

Laughlin, A. (2014) 'Smart TV Spying: Are You Watching TV or Is It Watching You?' *Which?* Consumer magazine, 20 August 2014, blog available at: *http://blogs.which.co.uk/technology/tvs/smart-tv-spying-weve-investigated/*.

Livingstone, L. and Das, R. (2010) 'POLIS Media and Family Report, POLIS, London School of Economics and Political Science, London, UK.

Morley, D. (2007) *Media, Modernity and Technology: The Geography of the New*, London: Routledge.

Peil, C. and Röser, J. (2014) 'The Meaning of Home in the Context of Digital Mediatisation, Mobilization and Mediatisation', in Andreas Hepp and Friedrich Krotz (eds) *Mediatised Worlds: Culture and Society in a Media Age*, Basingstoke: Palgrave Macmillan, pp. 233–252.

Rasmussen, T. (2014) *Personal Media and Everyday Life: A Networked Lifeworld*, Basingstoke: Palgrave Macmillan.

Rose, N. (1999) *Governing the Soul: The Shaping of the Private Self* (2nd edn), London: Routledge.

Schor, J. (2005) *Born to Buy: The Commercialized Child and the New Consumer Culture*, New York: Scribner.

Schor, S. and Ford (2007) 'From Tastes Great to Cool: Children's Food Marketing and the Rise of the Symbolic', *Journal of Law, Medicine and Ethics* 35 (1), pp. 10–21.

Schor, S. and Ruskin, G. (2005) 'Junk Food Nation: Who's to Blame for Childhood Obesity?' *The Nation*, 29 August, pp. 15–17.

Shumate, M. and Fulk, J. (2004) 'Boundaries and Role Conflict When Work and Family Are Collocated: A Communication Network and Symbolic Interaction Approach', *Human Relations* 57 (1), pp. 55–74.

Spigel, L. (1992) *Make Room for TV: Television and the Family Ideal in Postwar America*, Chicago, IL and London: University of Chicago Press.

Spigel, L. (2001) *Welcome to the Dreamhouse: Popular Media and Postwar Suburbs*, Durham, NC and London: Duke University Press.

Ward, K. (2006) 'The Bald Guy Just Ate an Orange: Domestication, Work and Home', in Thomas Berker, Maren Hartman, Yves Punie and Katie Ward (eds) *Domestication of Media and Technology*, Maidenhead: Open University Press, pp. 145–164.

INDEX

Coventry University College